Handbook of Short Story Writing

Edited by Frank A. Dickson and Sandra Smythe

Handbook of Short Story Writing

WRITER'S DIGEST, 9933 ALLIANCE RD., CINCINNATI, OHIO 45242

ACKNOWLEDGMENTS

Most of the articles included in this book were either published originally or reprinted in *Writer's Digest*. Some appeared in slightly different form. Except as noted, each is reprinted by permission of the author.

"Of Course You Can," by Muriel Anderson, © 1963 by F. and W. Publishing Corp.; "Five Ways To Stay Creative," by Jean Z. Owen, © 1963 by F. and W. Publishing Corp.; "Are Writers Made or Born?" © 1962 by F. and W. Publishing Corp.; "Are Writers Born?" by Harry Golden, © 1962 by F. and W. Publishing Corp.; "An Interview with Berry Morgan," by Carlton Cremeens, © 1968 by F. and W. Publishing Corp.; "How To Get Story Ideas," by Thomas H. Uzzell, © 1924 by *Writer's Digest;* "Brainstorming by Yourself," by Dennis Whitcomb, © 1969 by F. and W. Publishing Corp.; "Bringing Your Characters To Life," by Pearl Hogrefe is from *The Process of Creative Writing*, by Pearl Hogrefe, © 1963 by Pearl Hogrefe, reprinted by permission of Harper and Row, New York; "The New Mallarkey," by Peg Bracken, appeared originally in the *Atlantic Monthly* and is reprinted by permission of the author's agent, Robert Lesher, New York. © 1955 by the Atlantic Monthly Co.; "Empathy Creates Living Characters in Fiction," by Brian Cleeve, © 1965 by F. and W. Publishing Corp.; "The Value of a Wart," by Clayton Barbeau, © 1962 by F. and W. Publishing Corp.; "The Use of Dialogue," by Bonnie Golightly, © 1963 by F. and W. Publishing Corp.; "Collaborators Anonymous," by Robert Portune, © 1961 by F. and W. Publishing Corp.; "Keep It Brief and Blend It In," by Don James, © 1969 by F. and W. Publishing Corp.; "Writing with Description," by Ruth Engelken, © 1969 by F. and W. Publishing Corp.; "Making the Scene," by F. A. Rockwell, © 1969 by F. and W. Publishing Corp.; "Scene-test Your Story," by Fred Grove, © 1966 by F. and W. Publishing Corp.; "Plot: Its Place in Today's Fiction," by R. V. Cassill, is from *Writing Fiction*, by R. V. Cassill, © 1962 by Pocket Books, Inc., and is reprinted by permission of Pocket Books, Inc., New York; "Developing a Short Story from a Premise," by Dennis Whitcomb, © 1967 by F. and W. Publishing Corp.; "So Wrong To Tell the Truth," by John D. Fitzgerald, © 1960 by F. and W. Publishing Corp.; "Stories Without Plots," by Marilyn Granbeck, © 1970 by F. and W. Publishing Corp.; "Transitions," and "Dramatizing Conflict in the Short Story" are from *The Professional Story Writer and His Art*, © 1963 by Robert C. Meredith and John D. Fitzgerald, Thomas Y. Crowell Company, New York, and are reprinted by permission of the authors; "How to Choose the Right Viewpoint for Your Short Story," by Louise Boggess, © 1967 by F. and W. Publishing Corp.; "How to Use the Flashback in Fiction," by Susan Thaler, © 1967 by F. and W. Publishing Corp.; "What You Should Know about Using the Flashback in Fiction," by Mariana Prieto, © 1969 by F. and W. Publishing Corp.; "Five Suggestions for Writing Transitions," by Val Thiessen, © 1963 by F. and W. Publishing Corp.; "In the Beginning," by Jack Webb, © 1955 by Jack Webb, is reprinted by permission of the author and the author's agents, Scott Meredith Literary Agency, Inc., New York; "The Story's Middle," by Katherine Greer, © 1956 by F. and W. Publishing Corp.; "How Not to Fizzle the Finale," is from *Modern Fiction Techniques*, by F. A. Rockwell, *The Writer*, Boston, © 1962 by F. A. Rockwell, and is reprinted by permission of the author; "The Twist Ending," by Dennis Whitcomb, © 1968 by F. and W. Publishing Corp.; "Is Slant a Dirty Word?" by Charles Turner, © 1968 by F. and W. Publishing Corp., is reprinted by permission of Curtis Brown, Ltd., New York, the author's agents; "Checklist for Unsalable Stories," by Allan W. Eckert, © 1961 by F. and W. Publishing Corp.; "Forbidden Subjects," by Merrill Joan Gerber, © 1970 by F. and W. Publishing Corp.; "The Short Story from a Purely Personal View," by Hallie Burnett, © 1961 by F. and W. Publishing Corp.; "Slick Fiction and Quality Fiction," by Rust Hills, © 1959 by F. and W. Publishing Corp.; "A Writer Never Quits," by Fred Shaw, © 1956 by F. and W. Publishing Corp.; "From Boy to Writer in One Night," by John Howard Griffin, © 1957 by F. and W. Publishing Corp.

First printing, March, 1970
Second printing, August, 1971
Third printing, October, 1973

Library of Congress Catalogue Card Number: 73-100315
Standard Book Number: 911654-15-1
Writer's Digest, 9933 Alliance Road, Cincinnati, Ohio 45242
Copyright © 1970 by Writer's Digest. All rights reserved
Printed in the United States of America

67982

Contents

Characterization

Dialogue

Description

The Scene

Plotting

Conflict

Viewpoint

Flashback

Transition

The Story's Opening

The Story's Middle

The Story's Ending

Revision

The Writer As Reader

A Writer Never Quits

Marketing

Index

Joyce Carol Oates

Preface: The Nature of Short Fiction; or, The Nature of My Short Fiction

Why do you write?

It is sometimes another writer who asks this question of me, and therefore a serious, even doomed person, but most of the time it is a man twice my size who has found himself seated next to me at dinner and can't think anything else to say. *Why do you write?* he says, though I don't ask him *Why do you work so hard?* or *Why do you dream?* I don't even ask him *Why must you ask that question?* When I am being polite my mind goes blank, and at such times I am most feminine; I usually reply, *Because I enjoy writing.* It is a harmless answer, and perfectly correct; it satisfies the kind of bullies who are always bothering me (on the average of once a week this past year) with questions designed to (1) suggest the writer's general inability to cope with the real world (2) suggest the questioner's superiority because *he,* certainly, need not resort to fantasy in order to survive.

Why do you write?

A fascinating question. Though I never explain or defend myself in public, in private I am obsessed with the motives behind writing or behind any kind of artistic creation. I am obsessed with the deeps of the mind, of the imagination, particularly of the semi-conscious imagination, which throws up to us bizarre and lovely surprises daily and nightly. I am not so different from the skeptic who asks me sardonically why I write, for he too "writes," he creates, he dreams every night and perhaps during the day, and his dreams are legitimate artistic creations.

We write for the same reasons we dream—because we cannot not dream, because it is in the nature of the human imagination to dream.

Those of us who "write," who consciously arrange and re-arrange reality for the purposes of exploring its hidden meanings, are more serious dreamers, perhaps we are addicted to dreaming, but never because we fear or despise reality. As Flannery O'Connor said (in the excellent book of her posthumously-collected essays *Mystery and Manners*) writing is not an escape from reality, "it is a plunge into reality and it's very shocking to the system." She insists that the writer is a person who has hope in the world; people without hope do not write.

We write in order to give a more coherent, abbreviated form to the world, which is often confusing and terrifying and stupid as it unfolds about us. How to manage this blizzard of days, of moments, of years? The world has no meaning; I am sadly resigned to this fact. But the world has meanings, many individual and alarming and graspable meanings, and the adventure of being human consists in seeking out these meanings. We want to figure out as much of life as we can. We are not very different from scientists, our notorious enemies, who want also to figure things out, to make life more coherent, to set something in order and then go on to something else, erasing mysteries. We write in order to single out meanings from the great confusion of the time, or of our lives: we write because we are convinced that meaning exists and we want to fix it in place.

"Art hallucinates Ego mastery," says Freud, who was as concerned with the mysterious symbolic (and therefore artistic) dimension of the mind as anyone who ever lived. This sentence amazes me. Everything is in it, everything is there. Art "hallucinates" as a dream; it is a dream made conscious and brought into the daylight, occasionally published in hard-cover and no doubt over-priced. If it is a really marketable dream it will be sold to the movies, that marvelous modern art-form that simulates our dreams for us, moving flatly across a screen in the dark, exaggerating images, faces, gestures, wonderfully suited for the conveyance of all kinds of nightmares. If it is a not especially marketable dream it may never be published but, like most human attempts, it will lie in some out-of-the-way place, harmless and ignored but still valuable. No dream is without value. It is a "hallucination" and all hallucinations, like all visions, are of inestimable value.

"We must be true to our dreams," Kafka wrote.

When people "begin" writing (though the notion of "beginning" to write is odd to me, like "beginning" to breathe) they are buoyed up by energy, the sense that they have something unique to say and that only they can say it. This energy, this mysterious conviction, is the basis of all art. But, in entering a craft that appears from the outside to be so formalized, so professional, perhaps even in 1969 so decadent, they are soon terrorized by the fear of not being technically proficient. Therefore they attend writers' conferences. They take courses in Creative Writing. They buy books to instruct them in the "nature of fiction." And none of these activities are misleading, for a writer can use any information he can get, but the basis of the writer's art is not his skill but his willingness to write, his desire to write, in fact his inability *not* to write. I always instruct my students to write a great deal. Write a journal. Take notes. Write when you are feeling wretched, when your mind is about to break down . . . who knows what will float up to the surface? I am an unashamed believer in the magical powers of dreams; dreams enhance us. Even nightmares may be marketable—there is something to be said for the conscious, calculating exorcism of nightmares, if they give to us such works as those of Dostoyevsky, Celine, and Kafka. So the most important thing is to write, and to write nearly every day, in sickness and in health. In a while, in a few weeks or a few years, you can always make sense of that jumble of impressions . . . or perhaps it will suddenly reveal its sense to you. Theodore Roethke would jot down a striking line of "poetry" and carry it around with him for years before it made its way into a poem. Or perhaps the line generated a poem around it. What difference does it make? Energy is sacred; we write because we have an excess of energy, because we are more nervous or lively or curious about life than other people; why not make the best of it?

And so it is true that art "hallucinates." Because, of course, art is not "real." You don't find your way around any terrain by means of art, but by means of maps that are faithful to the surfaces of the world; you don't locate human beings by reading, but by looking in the telephone book. Art is not "real" and has no need to be real, artists scorn mundane reality, they are fond of making statements (I like to think they make them at dinner parties, refusing to be bullied as I am always bullied) like "So much the worse for reality!" Reality—real life—the newspapers and the newsmagazines and what goes on across the street —these are the materials of great art, but not art itself, though I am conscious of the semantic difficulties inherent in the word "art." Let us say that "art" points to a cultural, and not an aesthetic, phenomenon: that a wilted spider put inside a picture frame somehow, magically, becomes a work of "art," but that the same spider, untouched, unnoticed, is still a work of "nature" and will win no prizes. This is a definition of art that greatly angers traditionalists, but it pleases me because it suggests how Gestalt-like and shapeless life really is and how necessary we writers (and scientists, and map-makers, and historians) are to make it sane.

Why do you write? To seek out the meanings of life, which are hidden. This is a possible answer, a pleasing, optimistic answer, though perhaps Faustian. I always take my materials from ordinary life. I am greatly interested in the newspapers and in the Ann Landers' columns and in *True Confessions* and in the anecdotes told under the guise of "gossip." Amazing revelations! The world is filled with revelations, with tragedies—go at once to the newspaper and look at page five or page nineteen and let your eye become drawn to a headline, any headline; here is a story. I can't begin to count the stories I have written that are based on the barest newspaper accounts ... it is the very skeletal nature of the newspaper, I think, that attracts me to it, the need it inspires in me to give flesh to such neatly and thinly-told tales, to resurrect this event which has already become history and will never be understood unless it is re-lived, re-dramatized. From the fragment of someone's life that is represented in a newspaper story the writer is drawn to reconstruct the entire object. It is like finding a single piece of a jigsaw puzzle on the floor ... with a little effort you can reconstruct the whole, why not? Or perhaps you will imagine a better whole than the "real" one. Why not?

Therefore, art "dreams" or hallucinates, broods, upon what is given in reality. An overheard remark, a sudden stabbing emotion, a sense of dismay, a sense of anger, a story in *True Confessions* that reads exactly like a nightmare: these are our materials. I don't want to write anything that couldn't have been written, first, for *True Confessions*. I don't want to write anything that couldn't have been sung, in some form, as a ballad, that barest and most dramatic of art forms, a dream hardly made into art. Critical writing intrigues me just as intellectual men intrigue me, perhaps to folly, and I can't resist matching my wits with those of other writers, analyzing and exploring their works, trying to make sense of them—but the gravest and most sacred task is not criticism, but art, and art may be easier to achieve.

Art hallucinates Ego mastery. What is the Ego? It is my Ego that is writing this, it is your Ego, your self, that is reading this. You are like protoplasm within a certain confinement—your *self* is not fixed but fluid, changeable, mysterious. It is never quite the same self, and yet it is never another self. When you die no one will take your place. When I die my particular being, my personality, will vanish forever—it may be a good thing—but it is an irreparable fact. Our Egos desire control; we desire "mastery." Reality always eludes us because, like ourselves, it is fluid and mysterious and vaguely terrifying . . . it is always beyond our grasp, even those we love and who love us and whom we imagine we control, a little, are ultimately beyond our grasp, very noble in their independence, doomed to private lives and deaths. But we want, we want desperately this mastery. And, wanting it, we must therefore create it; we dream; we create a world (let us say a short story) which is populated by people we have made, whose thoughts we direct, and whose fates we make sure add up to some sense.

Freud tells us that we need to know, economically, about ourselves as writers—we write in order to pretend mastery of the world. Unlike the typical skeptic who dislikes art because it is "not real," I find this immensely pleasing. I think it is a noble task. To attempt "Ego mastery" of the world, or of some bitten-off chunk of the world, seems to me noble. There is a sacred air about the lightest, most delicate of short stories (let's say Eudora Welty's—or Chekhov's) just as there is a sacred air, though a more profound one, about those monstrous works of the nineteenth-century, novels like *Moby Dick* and *The Brothers Karamazov*, written by men who wanted to get everything down on paper, everything!—because the artist is a kind of priest, or a kind of magician, or even a kind of scientist, fascinated by the meanings that lie beneath the surface of the world. To explore these meanings is a noble task.

All art is meaningful. Its meaning may be in the violent, rather vicious *process* by which it is created—let us say the paintings of Pollock or de Kooning—or it may be in the more traditional texture of the work itself, spelled out, so that a student may underline *Live all you can; it's a mistake not to* (in James' *The Ambassadors*) and feel that he is getting the "meaning" of the work, without double-talk. The "meaning" of *Moby Dick* is located not just in the famous chapter on the White Whale, but in all the chapters—the tedious ones as well as the dramatic ones—the entire work adding up to its meaning, which is the exploration of reality by Melville.

And so, *Why do you write?* To answer this distinguished question once again: we write because we are ordained to a noble task, that of making clear mysteries, or pointing out mysteries where a numbing and inaccurate simplicity has held power. We write to be truthful to certain facts, certain emotions. We write to "explain" apparently crazy actions . . . why does an intelligent young man go beserk and kill, why does a happy woman ruin her life by running away with someone, why does a well-adjusted person commit suicide? I confess that I am old-fashioned, conventional. I look and behave in a conventional manner and the stimulus behind my writing is conventional, not weird. I am fascinated by weird structures and points of view, and if I could I would tell a story hanging upside-down, or in three columns at once, but really behind all my meek extravaganza is a simple desire to make sense . . . I want to know the *why* behind human emotions, even if I can only say again and again that human emotions are our deepest mystery and there is no understanding them. I am less interested in technical gimmicks that explore the flat surface of the page, emphasizing its unreality (the works of Beckett, for instance, which mock the very process of writing), though certainly cubist and abstract artists have made beautiful things out of the canvas as canvas instead of the canvas as mirror. But mere intellect to me, as a woman, is quickly tiring; if a story is only intelligent, might it not be better as an essay or a letter to the editor? I am preoccupied with verbs that go nowhere except to suggest the fluid nature of the world we inhabit.

If a story is well done there is no need to emphasize its meaning or its bewilderment before the fact of meaninglessness: the story *is* its meaning, that is all. Any story of Chekhov's is its meaning. It is an experience, an emotional event, usually of great beauty and occasionally of great ugliness, but it is pure in itself, needing no interpretation. "The Lady with the Pet Dog," a typical Chekhov story, tells of a hopeless love affair between a very experienced man and an inexperienced woman, the wife of a dull, well-to-do man. They meet, they fall in love, they continue to meet ... she weeps, he is helpless, they cannot marry because of their families, their social obligations, etc. That is all the story "means." Chekhov gives us a sense of their dilemma, an unforgettable sense of their anguish, and the story need have no meaning beyond that. Surely they are not being punished for adultery!—nor are they being punished for not being daring enough to run away together, for not being romantic enough. They are ordinary people trapped in an extraordinary situation; "The Lady with the Pet Dog" is a record of their emotional crises, and we respond to it because, reluctantly perhaps, we see ourselves in such traps, deceiving ourselves, hopeless in spite of our cunning and intelligence.

As to the nature of short fiction? There is no nature to it, but only natures. Different natures. Just as we all have different personalities, so the dreams of our personalities will be different. There are no rules to help us. There used to be a rule—"Don't be boring!"—but that has been by-passed; today writers like Beckett and Albee and Pinter are deliberately boring (though perhaps they succeed more than they know) and anything goes. Outrageous exaggeration. Outrageous understatement. Very short scenes, very long scenes ... cinematic flashes and impressions, long introspective passages in the manner of Thomas Mann: anything. There is no particular length, certainly, to the short story or to the novel. I believe that any short story can become a novel, and any novel can be converted back into a short story or into a poem. Reality is fluid and monstrous; let us package it in as many shapes as possible, put names on it, publish it in hard-cover. Let us make films of it. Let us declare that everything is sacred and therefore material for art—or, perhaps, nothing is sacred, nothing can be left alone.

The amateur writer wants to write of great things, serious themes.

Perhaps he has a social conscience! But there are no "great" things but only great treatments. All themes are serious, or foolish. There are no rules. We are free. Miracles are in the wings, in the ink of unopened typewriter ribbons, craving release. I tell my students to write of their true subjects. How will they know when they are writing of their true subjects? By the ease with which they write. By their reluctance to stop writing. By the headachy, even guilty, joyous sensation of having done something that must be done, having confessed emotions thought unconfessable, having said what had seemed should remain unsaid. If writing is difficult, stop writing. Begin again with another subject. The true subject writes itself, it cannot be silenced. Give shape to your dreams, your day-dreams, cultivate your day-dreams and their secret meanings will come out. If you feel that sitting blankly and staring out the window is sinful, then you will never write, and why write anyway? If you feel that sitting in a daze, staring at the sky or at the river, is somehow a sacred event, that your deepest self is pleased by it, then perhaps you are a writer or a poet and in time you will try to communicate your feelings.

Writers write, eventually; but first they feel.

A marvelous life.

Muriel Anderson

"Of Course You Can"

If you are anything like me you can't resist an article on writing tips. I've read them all, the ones about inspiration versus perspiration; 1,000 words a day, every day; keep your desk away from the window with the view; don't talk your story away, write it; and always keep on keeping on. But there's one piece of advice I've never happened to come across in any of these articles and I think its important. Emerson put it this way, "Our chief want in life is someone who will make us do what we can."

The beginning writer who has an empathic relative or can find himself such a friend, teacher or boss, has a head start. Many young writers are filled with self-doubt, and let's not kid ourselves, the road to the printed page is for most of us a real obstacle course. Even older, more experienced writers have days when they wonder what ever made them think they could write for a living.

I was fortunate to have had a father who was good at shouting *of course you can* at just the right moments. Later I found a writer friend who was always able to bring me out of a bog of self-doubt and still later a boss whose *of course you can* got me a byline in a publication I would never have dared submit to without this encouragement.

The first time I remember my dad shouting *of course you can* in reference to my writing was in my second year of high school. We had recently moved to the city from the small town in which I grew up. I loved that little town and I had written an article about it. I wanted more than anything to see that article in my home town paper. The paper was a weekly with a tight budget; they bought almost no freelance material and certainly (I was sure) not from a high school kid.

My father said the piece was great. That was all I needed. I submitted it under a pen name so the editor wouldn't know how young I was and my covering letter called it a contribution, removing budget problems. My article appeared in the next week's paper and I received a glowing letter from the editor thanking me for my splendid contribution.

A few years later I met a girl who had been published in several religious and education magazines. She was not much older than I. We had many wonderful long conversations about writing. She read some of my work, suggested some possible markets and when I hesitated she shouted *of course you can*. My very first children's arts and crafts article found a home because of this girl's encouragement.

When we grow older we become more philosophical about our self-doubts, we accept them for what they are, and realize we have to hurdle each one as it comes along. It's much the same as with actors who confess that even after years in the theatre they die a little every opening night. Their hearts pound away like tom-toms, their mouths are dry as a duststorm and their hands are clammy. Does this stop them? No, because they have been through it all before, many times, so they bravely step from behind the curtain into the floodlights. Many of them can look back, however, on a time when someone stood in the wings, smiled, said *of course you can,* and gave them a push.

For several years I was on the staff of an art gallery, writing about exhibitions, children's classes, special activities, anything and everything that came under the category of publicity. Prior to one of our most outstanding exhibitions, a prestige magazine wanted an article about the collection we had gathered from museums, libraries, galleries and private collections all across the country. I was not an art historian and felt the Director should write this article. The Director had other ideas. "It's you who wants to be a writer, not me. I'll help you with the research. You write it. *Of course you can.*" To this day I treasure that byline.

Few of us are so lucky as to have someone at our side to encourage us in our writing for more than short periods in life. Most of us have to propel ourselves through some mighty choppy waters before the rejection slips start thinning out and finally give way to "we are happy to advise you" letters. The wonderful thing is that if we have heard *of course you can* often enough in the beginning, from people who matter to us, we find that these words keep echoing in your heart all through the years.

I have heard these words echoing many times in my years as a free-lance writer. The interviews I've dared to request, the subjects I've dared to research and write about because of these words!

Not long ago I was asked by our local university to assist in writing a syllabus for one of their Peace Corps Training Projects. I hesitated a few moments, then somewhere in the far corner of my mind a wheel turned and I heard *of course you can*. Today, thousands of miles from my home, Peace Corps volunteers are carrying this syllabus with them, and I have the inner satisfaction of having helped just a little with a very big job, all because I heard those words again.

A few years ago, *Reader's Digest* ran an article of mine called "The Gentle Art of Caring" which was originally published by *Together*. How did they learn of that article? I wrote them. One evening I sat at my typewriter and stared for a long time at a blank sheet of paper, asking myself "Can you possibly have anything here that would interest Reader's Digest?" I thought of my father, and that old girl friend, and that wonderful Director at the art gallery and I began to hear those words again, *of course you can!*

If you are a young writer it would be my hope that you will find yourself a relative or friend, a teacher or boss who believes in you. There will be many times in the years ahead when you will not believe in yourself, and you will benefit greatly from their faith and their encouragement.

If you are not so young any more, it would be my hope that you will look around you. Somewhere, almost near enough for you to touch, is a young writer, still struggling, who needs *you*. Find him, and tell *him, of course you can!*

Jean Z. Owen

Five Ways To
Stay Creative

I doubt if there has ever been a writer who has not been obliged, at some time or other, to put his work aside because of the demands of living. Illness, duty, joy, sorrow, adjustment, worry, pressure, travel, visitors, holidays—each of these factors has a tendency to move in on one's writing and push it aside, perhaps for weeks or months, perhaps for years. Sometimes a writer can emerge from a fallow period ready to work with renewed zeal and vigor. Frequently, however, the striking of the clock during these interims is in reality the death knell for a fine talent.

Bess Streeter Aldrich tells, in one of her novels, of a pioneer woman who came as a bride to a homestead in the Midwest. She dreamed of becoming a writer but there was a home and the family to be cared for; there was land to be tilled and crops to be harvested. Carefully, the woman ironed the creases from every piece of wrapping paper that came into the house, saving it to use when she would have time to put into written form the beautiful stories that clamored within her. And finally that day arrived ... the children were married and gone, the farm was self-sustaining. But the woman found, when she sat down to write, that her inherent ability had atrophied from years of disuse. She could still "feel" the stories she'd like to write, but she was forced to fold her shining dream and put it away, along with the stacks of paper she knew would remain forever blank.

Unfortunately, this woman made the same tragic mistake that thousands of other potentially fine writers have made—she felt that because her creative drive was "unusually strong" it was, therefore, completely safe from the debilitating effects of time and idleness.

It's a wise writer who accepts the fact that his writing ability cannot remain viable if it is merely left alone. Your automobile may be equipped with the most powerful battery on the market but if you let the car stand idle for any length of time your starter won't have enough *oomph* to turn over the engine . . . not unless you have taken the precaution of hooking it to a charger. One's creative ability operates on a similar principle. As long as you are writing regularly your talent does a pretty good job of regenerating itself automatically. If you are forced to put your work aside you must fasten it to something more vitalizing than mere daydreams if you hope to keep it functioning.

Here's a five-point "charger" program to help you keep your inherent ability in top form ready to use when your fallow period is over:

1. *You can read omnivorously.*

Not for a writer—ever—is the luxury of choosing his reading material by the whim-and-fancy method. He must read widely enough to maintain a broad-spectrum knowledge of the general publishing trends. He must study intensively the markets he feels might offer a suitable outlet for his type of material. He must keep himself informed of changes in word-length requirements and shifts in editorial emphasis. This can be done even if his schedule is too crowded to permit much writing.

Two aspiring writers called on me during the past week. One of them, a housewife in her mid-thirties, told me she thought her stories—when she has time to write them—might have a good chance in "magazines like *Woman's Home Companion* or *Today's Woman.*" She was aghast when I pointed out to her the unhappy fact that it had been years since either of these magazines had been on the newsstands.

The other eager would-be writer is a young man whose dreams are focused on two of the larger slick magazines. As he talked to me he demonstrated a fine knowledge of the requirements, slants, and editorial policies of both periodicals. He also has a workable understanding of the needs of some of the lesser markets for possible placement of the material he writes while he masters the fine points of his craft.

No one needs a crystal ball to predict which of the two aspiring writers is the more likely to realize his dream.

2. *You can keep in touch with other writers.*

It's hard to find anything more stimulating to a writer than a good shop-talk session. Writers' clubs, conferences, criticism groups, study classes—each of these can help a person who is not actively writing feel that he has a toe, at least, in the literary puddle.

Invaluable as such stimulation can be, there is one danger to keep in mind: writers' groups can be so *temporarily* satisfying, sometimes, that they can sublimate one's need for written self-expression. Every professional writer I've ever known has pointed sadly to friends who possessed outstanding ability but who frittered away their creative years in scampering busily from writers' clubs to conferences to workshops, seeking advice, instruction, and encouragement on work they rarely got around to doing. Those who actually *did* get some words on paper usually tailored them to the specific tastes of their fellow members rather than the general reading public. Writers' club members have a tendency, occasionally, to "take in each other's literary wash" and then wonder why they fail to show a profit!

So pause and take stock periodically. Remember you can't make a career out of belonging to writers' groups and still have a career in writing. But *do* seek out other writers and meet with them from time to time. Writing can be a lonely, discouraging business and everyone engaged in it occasionally needs a few sympathetic cohorts to help build up the fires of his enthusiasm when the embers begin to burn low.

3. *You can make notes.*

Beginners should keep a notebook of ideas, plot-germs, scraps of dialogue and bits of characterization. And this is something any hopeful writer can do *now*, while he is waiting for things to ease up so that he can devote regular working hours to his writing.

But here, too, one must have a care! Notebooks, like club meetings, can be overdone. Never permit yourself to lose sight of the fact that a notebook is merely a means to an end, not the goal itself.

However, when kept within bounds, note-keeping is invaluable. It helps keep your creative mind agile, receptive, and deft, and, at the same time, you will be accumulating a rich storehouse of material to use later.

4. *You can take another look at your day's schedule.*

No matter how crowded your schedule may be or how certain you are that you don't have time to write, go over your day's activities again, trying to be as objective as if you were a trained efficiency expert. Without cheating your family or employer or whoever it is who currently claims the bulk of your time, you can almost certainly find a *few* minutes during the day to use as you please.

I know of one woman who, in addition to doing her own housework, is working at two jobs in order to support herself and her three children. But she didn't fold her creative hands and say *"I can't."* By scheming and planning, she was able to pare a minimum of fifteen minutes free time for herself every day. Only fifteen minutes—but she is writing and *selling!* She makes only small sales, to be sure, but until she is free to devote herself to the longer, more intricate pieces she aspires to write she is keeping her talent alive and growing—and being paid for it!

Another writer I know used coffee breaks and lunch hours to write a novel that sold first to a leading publisher and then to Hollywood. I can point to writers who get up an hour earlier or stay up an extra hour at night. I know men who write on commuter trains and mothers of small children who join baby sitting pools in order to earn a few precious moments of creative solitude.

But let's get back to *you* ... suppose, now, that we find you have only, say, half an hour of "writing time" each day. And suppose you happen to be one of those persons who must work up a good head of steam before you can put down a single sentence and it takes you at least a half hour to heat your mental boiler? In this case it seems logical to assume that you'll just have to wait a few years, until the pattern of your life changes. Meanwhile, you tell yourself, you might as well use your half-hour to do something worthwhile (wash the car or wax the kitchen floor) or to squander pleasantly (have a drink with the fellows from the office or join in the neighhorhood kaffee-klatsch).

But wait a minute, friend. This is precisely the sort of thinking that can be literary suicide. That half-hour can still be put to creative use. Even if you are fairly certain that you'll have nothing but a blank piece of paper and a backache from sitting rigid and unproductive in front of your typewriter for thirty minutes, *sit there anyway!* Today. Tomorrow. The next day. And the next. It will be maddening and frustrating, I know. (Oh, how well, *how well* I know!) But you will have a powerful force on your side, starting to work for you—the thing about Nature abhorring a vacuum. Eventually, *if you keep at it,* toward the end of one of your half-hours, you are going to get a sentence or two down on paper. In order to get the third sentence down before you lose it you will snitch another five minutes or so from the rest of your schedule. And then ten, fifteen . . .

I see you shaking your head, certain that this might be possible for *other* people but not for *you* with *your* routine. But it *will* work for you if you give it a try. You'll see. As the story or article or novel you are working on becomes important to you, it begins to make demands of its own, just as a new baby manages to get bathed, fed, diapered and rocked by a mother who couldn't see how she could *possibly* fit another child into a schedule already jammed full. It's accomplished by clipping unclippable corners and by discarding a few "vital" activities that suddenly become not quite so vital as they once seemed to be.

Sooner or later, every writer must come to terms with one immutable fact: for the entire span of one's creative life seldom, if ever, will there be an *easy* time to write. Granted, it may be an overwhelming, act-of-God obstacle that has you stymied right now—but even when this barrier no longer exists there will move in, to take its place, a dozen good, sound, logical reasons why you should postpone getting down to serious work. No one but the aspiring writer himself can decide which activities are *really* important and which ones are cluttering his life because he hasn't sufficient will power to kick them aside.

It would be delightful if a person could decide, once and for all, to be a writer. But you can't do it that way. You must make the decision again and again, many times every day, and it's the sum total of all these decisions that mean success or failure.

Too many writers are like a talented young friend of mine who decided, painfully, to stay home and write instead of going abroad with her family for the summer. She had enough love for writing and sufficient self-discipline to make this *big* sacrifice—but it proved to be valueless, for she couldn't summon enough will power to say "no" to all the small compensatory pleasures that beckoned in the weeks that followed. At summer's end she realized, sadly, that she had frittered away all her working time in late sleeping ("A writer needs to be rested in order to do good work")—in swimming and tennis and bowling ("A writer needs relaxation and physical exercise to stay in top form")—and in going to luncheons and picnics and bridge parties and coffee-with-the-neighbors ("A writer needs to mingle, keep his finger on the pulse of humanity, doesn't he?")

So go over your schedule again, with an eye to screening out the nonessentials. You probably still won't be able to salvage—for now—as much time as you would like to have but there is an amazing difference in a time sheet worked out by someone eager to write—and someone subconsciously bent on finding excuses *not* to!

5. *You can keep the pathway cleared.*

Traffic lights don't stay red forever. Neither do literary stop signals. Often when a writer least expects it he finds that suddenly, miraculously, the impediment has been removed and he can now count on several hours of writing-time every day.

What will happen when the circumstances of your life undergo a change and *you* get *your* Go-Ahead? Will you be able to give full concentration to your work in order to overcome the natural rustiness that invariably occurs during fallow periods? Or will you find yourself facing overwhelming obstacles of your own making?

Eight years ago, when I first met Laura M., I was impressed by her fine mind, empathic insight, and amazing deftness with written words. I had never encountered anyone who seemed more surely destined to become a successful writer—but, as she expressed it, she was "forced to pack her literary daydreams away in mothballs for the time being" while she coped with family responsibilities.

Meanwhile, not wanting to let her talent lie idle, she wrote long, chatty letters to relatives and friends. She whipped up plays for school programs and Cub Scouts and social groups. She achieved a reputation for writing interesting club papers and everyone called on her for some of her "charming light verses" for place cards, shower gifts, parties and class reunions.

"Laura, you're so *clever*," everyone told her repeatedly, "you ought to be ashamed of yourself for not *doing* something with your writing!"

About a year ago, when her youngest child reached school-age, she was finally free to activate her talent. But although the sun was shining, Laura couldn't seem to make much hay. Oh, she *tried*—but she found herself confronting several unexpected blocks. She discovered (as writers have always discovered!) that writing for the competitive market is far more difficult than dashing off letters to Uncle Henry and Cousin Gladys. She found it takes a different kind of self-discipline to work on a story that may or may not appear in print sometime than it does to turn out a skit that is scheduled to be presented to a sympathetic audience a week from next Tuesday. Her self-confidence, accustomed to frequent booster-shots of glowing praise, collapsed under the impact of impersonal rejection slips. The same friends who had repeatedly urged her to "*do* something" with her writing reacted unenthusiastically when she suggested that, since she was working on a short story, it would be nice if someone else did the place card verses and club paper this time. Their hurt, outraged disbelief—"But, Laura, you just *can't* let us down!"—made her feel so wretchedly guilty it was almost impossible for her to concentrate on her story.

Too late, Laura discovered that she had squandered her fallow years unwisely. With the clarity that always accompanies hindsight she realized that she could have found *other* ways of serving her community and that she should have kept her writing ability more rigidly focused on the development of marketable material.

"I kept telling myself I didn't have time to write," Laura said ruefully to me a few weeks ago, "but it never occured to me that at least a few of the hours I spent working overtime on local projects could just as well have been used for turning out stories and articles. Maybe it would have taken me months to finish each manuscript, but even if I had never made a sale I'd be a lot closer to my goal than I am now, for I wouldn't have so many obstacles standing in my way."

Wistful, sit-on-your-hands type of *wishing* won't do it. It takes a tremendous amount of determination and self-discipline to keep "polishing" a career you don't yet have time to pursue. But you can do it if you really want to become a professional writer.

Don't merely "wait out" your fallow period and don't let your emotional and mental "writing space" become cluttered with a lot of rubble. Use your fallow period wisely—and when it's over you'll find you are ready to move forward swiftly, with the zeal and freshness of a beginner coupled with the maturity of an experienced writer. Very likely you will find that you have more than compensated for the period you were forced to put your work aside and you haven't lost as much time as you feared you had.

Fallow periods are a necessary, valuable part of every writer's life. The way they are used—or misused—can make the difference, later on, between failure and the kind of success you dream of having.

William Peden

Are Writers Made or Born?

Are writers made or born? In one form or another, this question is one of the oldest on record. I have heard it raised in every writing class I have ever conducted, at every writers' conference I have ever attended, and in almost every conversation I have had with groups of aspiring young writers. I might attempt to suggest the answer by asking several others. (Is a successful athlete made or born? Is an outstanding brain surgeon made or born? Or a good nuclear physicist, or architect, or composer?); but that is a disagreeable habit, so I shall try to state my opinion more positively: There is no such thing as a Literary Accident. The history of written literature contains no more literary accidents than does, let us say, the history of track and field competition contain "accidental" four-minute miles or "accidental" fifteen-feet pole vaults or "accidental" seven-foot high-jumps.

The student who has just completed his sophomore survey of English and American Literature may at this point rise to his feet to demand, "Well, what about 'Kubla Khan'? Didn't this come to Coleridge in a dream or something? And how about Poe? Isn't it true that he was stoned when he wrote 'The Fall of the House of Usher'?"

The reply to such comments is that those cases are isolated exceptions, or misconceptions. Like the anecdote, concerning the alleged death of Mark Twain, they are either greatly exaggerated or greatly misunderstood. Of the many misapprehensions which seem to fascinate the uninformed public, one of the most prevalent is the belief that works of art and literature spring spontaneously and effortlessly into being, fully formed, like Venus emerging from the sea. This misconception has become a myth, fostered from time to time by occasional writers who are basically frauds, and kept alive by naive laymen and thousands of would-be writers who yearn hungrily for literary fame and wealth but do not possess the fortitude to work for their rewards. It is impossible to eradicate this concept of the writer-as-pure-genius who is thought to toss off, in moments of ecstasy and inspiration, a literary masterpiece which becomes a National Book Award winner or Book-of-the-Month Club selection and makes a million dollars or wins the author a trip to Hawaii or an appearance on the Ed Sullivan show. Like all myths, it is larger than life, more real than reality itself and seems to be permanent a part of our thinking as are the legends of the Abominable Snowman or the Monster of Loch Ness.

The unavoidable truth is that success in writing is much like success in any other field of highly demanding, specialized human endeavor. Essentially, I think, it is a matter of individual ability, aptitude, and talent, combined with dedication to one's goal, belief in oneself, and an insatiable desire to succeed. It requires a long apprenticeship during which one learns the fundamentals of his art or craft; hours, days, months, and often years of dreary, unrewarded effort, constant and scrupulous attention to details; false starts, trials and errors, backing and fillings; uncertainty and despair; and still more hard work, the long grind of setting-up exercises and practice sessions, as it were, before participation in the main event.

Some beginning writers, to be sure, develop their skills much more quickly than others, because they are endowed with superior aptitude or genius. Truman Capote, while still a beardless boy, achieved breathtaking technical effects that many an adult professional had sweated for years to attain. Despite such individual differences, however, literature is the only important field of human endeavor in which many people feel that they have a *right* to success merely because they desperately *want* to be successful. Only an extremely naive or immature human being expects to be a competent doctor or engineer or physicist without years of preparation and specialized study; yet many a young writer tends to become discouraged or outraged if he does not attain success in a fraction of the time that it takes a medical student to become a practicing physician or a good young baseball player to make the leap to the major leagues. Is it too much to ask, as Erskine Caldwell has observed in a recently published article about writers and writing, that "a writer . . . prepare himself with no less study, training, and diligence than a lawyer or physician devotes to his profession"?

This fact can not be repeated too emphatically: A writer must be able and willing to make the same sacrifices as the aspirant to success in any other specialized field, or he should transfer his abilities and energies elsewhere. He must log in his hundreds of hours of reading and writing, of observing and studying and attempting to perfect his art. Just as an amateur baseball or football player, in addition to time actually spent on the playing field, devotes untold hours to reading about, and observing, the performance of established professionals, the young writer must constantly be learning by careful, disciplined, and analytical study of major literary works. Art is very, very long, and time is fleeting and one of the best ways the amateur can attain professional status is by learning something every day of his life. In addition to what he will inevitably learn by trial and error, he has at his disposal, if he will only turn to them for help, the greatest teachers any student could dream of—the writers who have contributed to the literature in his own field. All the technical problems which will ever confront him have been solved by better writers than he can probably ever hope to be, all the inspiration and guidance and stimulus he will ever need are to be found in better published stories and novels and poems than he may ever write.

Once a writer has begun to master the technicalities of his craft—the thousand and one details which go into the creation of a good short story or novel or play or group of poems—he would do well to heed the admonitions of most of the successful professionals of his own day. Characteristic is James Michener, whose great success with *Tales of the South Pacific* and *Hawaii* has won him the respect of fellow writers and critics and the envy of amateurs whose mouths water at the thought of all those gate receipts. Speaking recently to a group of writing students at the University of Missouri, Mr. Michener commented on the labor which went into the production of *Hawaii*. Not until he had completed several years of painstaking and arduous research, Mr. Michener said, did he begin his actual writing; and, the task once underway, he worked from around seven-thirty in the morning till around one or one-thirty, for fifteen months, including Saturdays, Sundays, and holidays—whether the work was going well or badly, regardless of how he was feeling, or what other commitments arose.

With few exceptions, every successful professional I have ever known or heard of will corroborate Mr. Michener's emphasis on work, work, and more work. Whether an author works from midnight till three in the morning or from daybreak to high noon; whether he writes in a rundown rented room above a bowling alley or in an air-conditioned study or in a bathtub; whether he uses a three-cent pencil or a five-hundred-dollar electric typewriter, most professionals will insist that, of all the skilled professions, that of the writer is perhaps the least understood and the most demanding in terms of daily output of emotion and sheer physical energy—in addition to being one of the least rewarding financially.

On the other hand, hard work and great desire are often not enough. The individual must have talent to begin with, and in this sense and this sense only, it is true that writers are born rather than made. Few spectacles are sadder than that of the would-be author who is utterly devoid of talent but who cannot be convinced that his energies and abilities should be diverted into fields other than those of imaginative writing. I have known highly intelligent, perceptive people who yearned to be short story writers, novelists, poets, or dramatists, and who worked hard and devotedly, but were never able to achieve more than superficial competence. They simply lacked that indefinable quality which in the final analysis separates the men from the boys.

Yet they could not be persuaded to abandon their folly. I have seen such people damage and in some cases ruin their lives by persisting in a career for which they were completely unsuited. I have seen marriages ruined, homes wrecked, children neglected, physical and emotional health and well-being undermined, by misguided men and women who, on the brink of disaster, insisted that their "writing came first"—who were sure that they were misunderstood geniuses and that nothing would stand in their way. It is unfortunate that such compulsive effort is not enough to insure even a modicum of success but the unhappy fact remains that you can't make a literary silk purse out of a sow's ear.

Effort, discipline, sacrifice, and study will be of little avail unless the writer possesses individual aptitude, talent, genius—call it what you will. Without this, the writer's efforts will come to naught. Without it, he should think of his writing as a pleasant, undemanding hobby, like collecting autumn leaves or raising miniature seahorses; or he should abandon it completely and devote himself to something quite different.

Are writers made or born? In summary, it seems apparent that literary success is determined by two factors: the possession, to begin with, of native ability, and the *need* (willingness is too weak a word) to develop this native ability, through dedicated effort, to its fullest dimensions. All the latent genius in the world—the genius of a Keats or a Charlotte Bronte or a Thomas Wolfe—will be of little value to the individual or to his society unless the writer is determined to work and work hard.

Harry Golden

Are Writers Born?

Men are not born writers any more than they are born corporation presidents or curveball artists. If there is such a thing as a born writer then there must also be such a thing as a born bad writer and the metaphysical conditions attendant on this proposition are complex. It is much easier to see with Martial, the Latin poet, "He writes not whose poetry nobody reads."

If you can learn to tie your own shoelaces you can probably learn how to be a writer—with this difference: You have to tie your own shoelaces or you can't get into kindergarten! No one *has* to be a writer. What makes a man into a writer? Work. What kind of work? For the most part, reading other writers; particularly, reading good writers, reading writers who had something to say.

Nor do I insist here that every artist is explainable in specific human and psychological terms. I am at a loss to explain Shakespeare, at a loss to explain Mozart, nor can I explain exactly what the handle is that makes *Leaves of Grass* the best American poetry ever. But I do know this about most writers: They cannot be writers unless they are readers. For it is by reading that writers are able to relate to the past and it is only from a relation to the past that we achieve a sense of the present, and a sense of what is going to happen next.

Ernest Hemingway did something of a disservice to young writers when he had himself photographed with a bottle of gin and a fishing pole and when he talked of how he cheered at the bull fights and of the adventures he had in Spain, in Cuba, in France and in Africa. Hemingway was a great writer, perhaps one of the greatest of this century, and it would have been just as nice to have had as many photographs of him reading as fishing or hunting. For he did more reading than he did fishing; he did more reading than he did drinking. He read every day of his life in a soundproof room for at least three hours. Pictures of him reading would certainly have done young writers as much good as those pictures of him triumphant over a fallen water buffalo. Ernest Hemingway read everything of consequence as fast as it came off the presses.

There are no primitive writers. There are only writers who read. Without books, there are no devices for writers, just as, left to his own devices, no child would even bother with shoelaces.

Where you find library upon library and book upon book there also will you find writers upon writers. That does not necessarily mean that you find genius upon genius, but it is only in atomic-bomb laboratories that geniuses congregate anyway.

I have been accused often of romanticizing the Lower East Side of New York City. It was here that the mass of Jewish immigrants settled when they came to America and it was here that I spent my boyhood. It may well have been that I made the Lower East Side too cozy, too charming a place for those who remember its poverty, its wretchedness, the unheated tenements, and the exploitation of the sweatshops; but these evils exist everywhere, in every time and in every place. What was unique on the Lower East Side was its intellectual vitality, and this I did not romanticize.

From 1880 to 1920 the Lower East Side of New York was mostly composed of immigrant Jews who had fled the pogroms in Russia and the political and economic disabilities imposed upon them in other countries of Eastern Europe. When these Jews got off the boat at Ellis Island their first thought was "When will I be an American?" They looked at the native-born walking the streets, and their sole idea was, "When will I be like him? When will I understand?" The way to be like him and to understand him was through school and study and—the English language.

All over the East Side there were signs reading "Lecture tonight." In the settlement houses, along with basketball, the immigrant boys stopped at the libraries and read, and their fathers, who peddled the pushcarts or who carried pails of coal up five and six flights of stairs, carrying their first papers tucked in their back pockets, also read in order to become Americans.

Because of this intense preoccupation with learning, coffee houses were filled with playwrights who produced two and sometimes three plays a month—none of them perhaps destined for posterity, but probably all of them as good as, if not better than, most of our modern plays which are also not destined for posterity. The newspapers were filled with translations of Shaw and Ibsen and Chekhov and with poems written by printers and garment workers, anarchists and socialists.

Now the sons and the grandsons of these immigrants are all out in the suburbs and if they read at all, their attention is concentrated on the local brokerage letter which promises the market will continue its upward swing if there is no interruption in the economy.

It is quite true that the Lower East Side did not produce a major figure in world literature. That is neither here nor there. It could have. Out of 100 million people in the rest of the nation, only three or four writers have made their mark. We Americans have always been a little fatuous about writers. We expect them either to be rich or famous. A writer does not ask his insurance-salesman friend to make the million-dollar-a-month club year after year. If he asks him anything, the writer asks his friend to read. But the insurance salesman who has a writer for a friend wants that writer to be a great writer and a rich writer and a national celebrity. This is because the insurance salesman believes that if a man is going to indulge in a trade as risky and as hazardous as professional writing, he must be a born writer. But writing has never been an aristocracy (which is, I suspect, the only thing one is born to). Writers are not born with pedigrees like dogs or the people who populate The Four Hundred. All they inherit is the tradition. They must make of it what they will.

Carlton Cremeens

An Interview with Berry Morgan

When Berry Morgan of Port Gibson, Mississippi, published her first novel, *Pursuit,* in 1966 at the age of forty-seven, the critical reaction must have been as diverse as that following the publication of any of Faulkner's early books. Walker Percy, a National Book Award winner and a novelist of enviable stature, endorsed her book and said a major new creative talent had been discovered. Some of the critics agreed. Others didn't know what to make of it and frankly said so, while others, unable to understand their own perplexity, simply dismissed the book.

In this country, a writer whose first work appears after the age of forty is considered a late starter which, according to the thinking of some, is quite often synonymous with an early finisher. But—not for Berry Morgan, if the old maxims of hard work, stern discipline, dedication to craft and faith have anything to do with success in writing. She says they do. And practices what she believes. Since *Pursuit,* she has written and published a number of short stories in the *New Yorker.* She is hard at work on two more novels in her scheduled series, runs a large plantation home for her husband and four children and keeps a set of books for her husband's business enterprises.

When we met, I asked the usual question: "How do you find the time?"

"It's simply a matter of organization," she said, with one of the softest, most gentle voices I've ever heard. "I get up at four o'clock every morning and write until three in the afternoon. Then, I do my other work. You can imagine how carefully I have to budget my time. But, I *do* have one advantage. I love to work. Work is my hobby. And I particularly like to write. There's only one thing I like as much as writing and that's farming. I like any kind of farming, dirt farming."

I told her of my interest in the plantation in Mississippi and how I had hoped the interview could be conducted there. She laughed, saying it was not the plantation in her novel, but that I had open invitation to visit there any time I wished. It was necessary, she said, to maintain a second house in New Orleans because of her husband's business affairs.

"And does your writing go as well here in New Orleans," I asked, "as it does at your plantation home?"

"Oh, yes," she said. "It doesn't matter where I write, as long as I can write. I've adjusted to both places."

She glanced at the fire in the fireplace, its leaping shadows. It was cool for New Orleans, but pleasant there in the room.

"I was thinking," she said, "about a time recently when I couldn't write. It was last summer. I had some worn out discs and a fusion of two vertebrae in my neck, and at first I didn't pay too much attention to this other trouble. I had done heavy work all my life. Farm work. But then, I started getting numb, and I thought it might be some kind of pressure on the brain. So, I came down here to New Orleans and went through neurology and all that. They discovered that my trouble was a very severe arthritis in the spine and there was great pressure on the nerve roots. And the only thing I could do, the only way I could get well, they said, was to go to bed and do nothing. Well, my husband bought me a brand new thing to dictate into, but I couldn't dictate because I had been used to writing with my fingers. It was a terrible experience. I couldn't write a thing, and I was almost hysterical."

Thinking such a strong compulsion to write must have developed at a very early age, I asked her when it all began.

"It's difficult to say just when it began. I started telling myself stories when I couldn't have been over three or four years old—just to amuse myself—to get out of reality. That may have been the beginning. Perhaps the little routine of telling myself stories made a very subtle transition into the desire to write something down on paper. I don't remember. It seems to me now I've always wanted to write. As a matter of fact, there was a time when I wanted to write so much that I actually would lie about having written something. Which reminds me, I think most writers are instinctive liars, pathological liars, because all his life, what a writer *thinks* has to be so much more important than what is *true,* there is really a transmutation there. In other words, he may frequently tell someone he has written something when he has only thought about it. He keeps thinking about it wanting to do it so much that he will lie about it."

Having discovered her sense of humor early in the interview, I though my next point would be safe.

"When did you stop lying," I asked, "and get down to the actual business of writing?"

"When I was in my thirties, about fifteen years ago," she laughed, "I wrote a mystery story, and it was the first thing I ever finished. It was long, I guess about fifty or sixty thousand words. I sent it to Hiram Haydn, a very fine novelist who, I believe, was then with Atheneum. I'm not sure. Anyway, he wrote back and said the piece was professionally written. He said he couldn't use it right then but suggested that I send it around to other places. I don't know why, but I just didn't. I knew there was something wrong with my work, but I couldn't figure out what it was.

"Well, after the mystery story, more years went by. And I kept thinking about writing. But certain things prevented it. I kept busy with my children and other obligations. Then, finally, when I was forty-three I decided it was now or never. I said, "Well, girl, you're either going to make it or you're not. You can't start much older than this, so you had better get going.' I *did* start and I stayed with it. After a time, I was like a person possessed. I wrote *reams.* Perhaps a million words. I just kept writing. I had turned on the tap, and I didn't care what I wrote."

I interrupted her. The words *structure* and *form* were bothering me, and I told her so. Somewhere along the way she must have run head-on into the business of structuring all that material?

"Oh, yes," she said. "After writing and writing, I started writing things over. And out of this came some short stories. I sent them out and got some encouragement, but no acceptances. I sent a feeler to Houghton-Mifflin, mentioning the volume of writing I had done, and I received a letter from them saying they would be interested in seeing some of it. Of course, I was thrilled out of my wits. I got the best I could together and sent it off. Well, three or four months went by, and I didn't hear a word. Doubt replaced thrill. I thought they didn't like my work, and I understood, because I didn't like it either. But, finally, a letter came, saying they had read everything and would like to see more. No commitments. I tried reading between the lines, but the letter simply said they would like to see more. So, I prepared some more stuff and sent it to them. Another three or four months passed, and I had almost lost hope when the next letter came, saying they *did* like my work and that perhaps we could publish a book. Well, I don't think I can ever express the joy I felt on that particular day.

"But wait, that's not all. At about the same time, they called me on the telephone and said I had won the Houghton-Mifflin Fellowship Award. That amounted to five thousand dollars and a whole lot of encouragement."

Throughout the interview, I had been aware of her eyes, large and brown, smiling one moment—compassionate, sad—the next. Now, they were glistening.

"And this was the beginning of your novel, *Pursuit?*"

"Yes," she said, "this was the beginning of *Pursuit*—the beginning of everything. I wrote *Pursuit* four times before it was published, but not once, during all that time, did I permit myself to lose faith, to become discouraged. A publisher had expressed confidence in me and had backed that confidence with good money.

"*Pursuit* is the first in a series of novels called *Certain Shadows*. No one likes that title except me, because there is nothing very certain about a shadow. But the project includes a lot of novels. It includes *The Mystic Adventures of Roxy Stoner* and *Fornica Creek,* to name two."

I was interested in her short story writing. I had read some of her stories, liked them, and wanted to know if any had been sold before her novel.

"No. As I mentioned, I had been sending several out. I worked on one short story of about two thousand words for at least five months. I kept rewriting it, and I kept sending it back until finally they took it. I was so thrilled that, out of happiness, I sat down and wrote another short story, right off. I sent it to the same magazine, and they liked it much better than the first one. Now, I've fallen in love with short story writing."

I asked her how she approached the writing of a short story.

"I begin with feeling, with emotion. This has to precede everything else. It's almost necessary to use emotion as the raw material. I try to get the emotion, the feeling, on paper. Without it, I have nothing."

"Then what happens?"

"I back off," she said. "I use my head. I back off and look at it. It has become somebody else's work, you see? And as I start rewriting it, I very tenderly and cautiously try to give it structure. It has to make sense. Out of all this raw material, this raw emotion, has to come something believable, real and honest. You have to believe it, and you have to ask yourself if others will believe it. I like to think of it as precision, fitting all the pieces together, and I have great fun with precision.

"Now, there's another thing I enjoy very much. I not only want to get a sentence right, but I want to try all the different ways I can get it right. I call this the orchestration stage, because you find yourself changing words just for the technique. It's great fun. It's getting the sound of it. The sound is all important. If the sound is right, if the count is right it's a great feeling. You have to find your way to this point, and you'll know it when you do, because it's then you begin to feel natural. You make a rough draft, and the next time you come around you get a little closer, and the next time a little closer, until finally, you achieve that balance of orchestration—the correct sound." She paused for a moment, looking thoughtful, then smiled. "But," she said, "there is no such thing as perfect, is there? Maybe that's why it's so much fun."

I asked her if she had any opinions on why people enjoyed reading interviews with writers.

"Because," she said, "for struggling writers—and I think all writers are struggling writers—an interview is a link with someone who shares their anguish, their frustrations and even their joys. Could anyone but another writer do that? Don't look for it in your friends. If you go to enough people, it will be like a circle, and if you go to three hundred and sixty people, each one will knock you out by degrees. You really have to go it alone. That's why it's such a lonely business, and that, of course, is another reason why the interview is important. Someone is communicating with you who shares that terrible loneliness.

"Now, I don't think I have to say much about the rewards for all this punishment. If you are a writer, you're hooked. You had to be rather mad to start it. And if you like it, as I do, nothing else is going to serve you. If you are a writer, you'll set aside a certain amount of time each day and write, and nothing will stop you. That's the way I do it, and in spite of all the suffering, I love it."

Thomas H. Uzzell

How to Get Story Ideas

At the very outset of your writing efforts you will most certainly "run short of ideas." Even professional writers who earn a living with their typewriters frequently encounter this difficulty. More literary careers come to an end at this moment than at any other time. "Here I am a writer—with nothing to write!" says the hapless writer to himself; the irony, or the humor, of the situation is too much for him and he gives up in disgust.

Perhaps he should give up. If it is literally true that, with all the willingness in the world to perform, no recognizable thoughts about his life and environment pass through his mind, then he is indeed barking up the wrong tree; he can never succeed at the craft of fiction. But it is obviously impossible that he should have no thoughts whatever about life. The truth is simpler and more disagreeable: good story ideas fail him mainly because he refuses to do the *work* necessary to turn them up! He wants not ideas, but moral muscle. The problem is not to get great or astonishingly original ideas, but rather how to get a steady stream of ideas good enough to work with. Ideas of matured wisdom come only from matured, experienced people; but if the writer waited until he was matured and experienced he might, in middle age, have ideas, but no art to express them. In your student days, your craft, your habit of expression, is everything.

Getting story ideas is a matter of method and energy, especially energy. From discussing the problem with many young writers with empty literary larders, I have learned that their trouble arises from certain fundamental misconceptions of their task. Here are three of these misconceptions, all very important:

1. *They wait for inspirations:* The young writer, being also a lover of good literature, often has the notion that writing is a sort of sacerdotal function, a divine art, in pursuing which great ideas descend upon the chosen like radio waves broadcast from heaven. Actual writing requires effort; to get words on paper, one must put words on paper—there's no escaping that; but ideas—how can work help you there? You have ideas or you haven't and that's all there is to it!

But that is *not* all there is to it. Getting story ideas is a department of your work that needs organization and system and energetic enthusiastic attention just as does the writing of manuscripts or selling them. If you wait for an inspiration, you're as likely to forget a good idea as to remember one. The way to get story ideas is to do something about it; put down in notebooks, journals, or scrap paper, thoughts, observations, records of all kinds; get the habit; keep it up. Don't censor your stuff too severely at first; let it come. Later you can go over it, take the best and throw the rest away. Most great writers kept notebooks continuously during their productive years; you can not afford to do less.

2. *They don't believe in themselves.* With the young student, the chief impulse to write comes from his love of reading. The great works of literary art stir him profoundly, arouse in him burning desires of emulation and launch him forth without his quite knowing it, on a deliberate, rash enterprise of writing equally well and that rather soon, too! Worthy ambition! The trouble with it is, however, that a young writer's first scribblings in comparison with these majestic performances just about floor him; the contrast is too great. His own ideas—how utterly trite, banal, childish! Too often he abandons his own ideas and tries themes like those of the great masters. Again, they are too much for him; and he comes to grief.

The young writer seldom remembers that these masterpieces which he adores are *never typical of the work of their performers.* They are the careful selection from the output of an entire lifetime. How unfair to yourself, then, to shrink from the bold expression of your own thoughts because they are not so exalted and passion-hued as those to be found in the few greatest writings of the greatest masters? You must have your beginnings, just as the masters did. Give yourself time. Don't try to imitate anyone else's style. Believe in yourself. The first output is nothing; the habit everything.

3. *They are not really interested in life.* Ask nine out of ten beginning students of writing what they want to write about, and their answers will have little to do with a deep, abiding interest in human beings and their doings. Even as you read this, you may be saying to yourself "Oh, yes, I'm interested in people; I am sure of that," and yet in the sense in which you must be interested to succeed at writing you may not be at all.

The distinction lies here: You like to be with people; you have many friends; you are a discriminating gossiper; you like to read about "characters;" but this isn't enough. You can be and do all these things and yet not be genuinely interested in an analytical, probing, literary sense at all. You may be so dynamic yourself that you have no patience with people who are not dynamic and aggressive. You may be a stern idealist, religious or moral, and the vices of people distress and appall you. If you think only of their goodness or badness, you will not be really interested in a genuine literary sense. A writer's task is more to portray than to judge. Literature is a record of human frailties; you must be sympathetically interested in these frailties and your curiosity must endure till you have gone to the bottom of them.

In order that you may apply the general ideas given above in a practical way, please consider the following suggestions which have been used successfully by many beginning writers:

Getting started: If you find yourself ready to "get" story ideas and absolutely unable to write a single word, do not be shocked or panic-stricken. Your trouble is not that you do not have ideas, but that you *do not have the habit of setting them down.* The very first thing is to cure yourself of "typewriter panic." Write *anything.* Begin by cultivating a habit of writing, of setting words on paper; the quality of the copy is sure to improve as you persist. At first write for quantity only. When you have trained yourself to set down with fair rapidity, say one thousand words on the interesting events of the day, you may conclude that you have broken yourself in and are ready to begin to try to improve the quality of these notes, cull them and start storing away your best ideas with definite system.

Notebooks and files: Every well-equipped writer carries some kind of pocket notebook for jotting down brief memoranda at any time of the day or night, and has in his study some means of sorting and storing away longer sketches, studies, and plots. For the first purpose a small loose-leaf notebook, pocket size, is adequate. For the second, the ideal equipment is an office file, though a stack of large manila envelopes will answer the purpose. Remember, that one of the best ways to master a given subject is to collect, *organize* and file away material bearing upon that subject. So do not despise this seemingly mechanical part of your task.

Your reading: You should read much, voraciously, especially in your student days. This should be done not so much to learn *how* the other fellow does it with the object of imitating him, as to *increase your fund of information about life* and the world we live in. Beware of "stylists" who appeal mainly to the sensual ear! Cling to those who interest you most by reason of the mental stimulation, the intellectual inspiration they bring you. All books which deepen your eager interest in and understanding of the life about you deserve your attention.

The "Romantic Complex:" This term I apply to beginning writers who simply can not be made to believe that their own lives and environment are interesting. They cling to the delusion that real romance, real adventure flourishes best among strange and distant peoples, remote climes, or longpast periods of time. But this does not change the fact that *the amount of literary material in any region is exactly proportionate to the number of people who dwell therein.*

Writing up yourself: Fiction writing is the most intimate of all arts and any follower of it who hopes to charm the popular ear by keeping his uniquely precious and sacred emotions locked forever in his jealous bosom had better try something else. Be certain that your best writing will be that which is most *you.* What are your dreams, your ambitions? Write them up. What were the main turning points in your life? What factors were involved? What happened? What is the significance of each experience? Try to imagine stories around these crises, putting other people in them if you wish, but keeping the same issues, the same emotions.

Your home a laboratory: Most students can profit by a concentrated study of the human-interest problems being worked out in their own homes. Your home surroundings may be tranquil and their events, so far as you can see, quite commonplace, but the chances are that the issues being faced among your relatives and friends suggest very definite story ideas which may by imaginative manipulation be made highly dramatic.

For example, a younger brother or sister is under your observation. Watch him with your imagination at work and what do you see? What does he do? What are the problems that absorb him? Who is his hero? How is he working out his worship of that hero in his own activities? Suppose he were to learn in some way that his hero had done some peculiarly ignoble thing? What effect might it have on him? What is he planning to be? What is there in him that will make him succeed in that career? Has he any qualities that he will have to fight in order to succeed?

Besides your intensive study of individuals close around you, you will do well to get in touch with some special phase of life; become intimate with a particular social problem, preferably one you will be able to study at first-hand. Study this problem, seeking especially to discover the emotional quality of every phase of it. Have patience with this work. If you choose the problem of education or divorce, or city politics or the younger generation or business morals, decide whether you will center your attention on the comic aspect, the grim tragedy, or the high adventure of your topic. Don't imagine that you can master it by any mystic process of "thinking it over." Write!

Writing reveals life secrets: In all your observations, reason back from the facts to their larger significance. Remember that the big human problems don't jump out and bark to let you know that they are there. The most important thing to bear in mind is that you can not begin to understand a human situation in its larger aspects until you have attempted to express it. You can accomplish little by mulling over your vague thoughts about people. Don't be a "writer who does not write." You must record in full detail the character's behavior on innumerable occasions. Presently you will begin to see relations between these various details which you missed in your first formless thought about the person. The writing brings out the significance.

Learn from great writers: With many writers, characters do not begin to perform until words about them are put on paper. Turgenev wrote long, rambling character studies before he began a line of his story proper. Chekhov wrote beginnings and threw them away. Nearly every beginner postpones too long the hour of beginning. He hopes for the beautifully finished plot, the perfect work, the high aspiration. The greatest writers, I repeat, cannot afford to do this; the beginner must not do it. In these moments when it seems your mind literally will not formulate ideas good enough for a plot, you cannot do better than to write what you *do* know. Put away what you have written. The day of inspiration will come.

I have tried to set forth, in the above article, not the whole truth about getting ideas, but those truths which come from the study of the processes of successful writers and which beginning writers find hardest to understand. They seem to be methods that get results. If you, the reader, are skeptical, I hope that, before condemning, you will make an experiment with them. I will vouch for the result.

Dennis Whitcomb

Brainstorming by Yourself

I'm convinced that many good story ideas touch our lives daily and are completely unnoticed. F. Scott Fitzgerald said "A writer wastes nothing." It sounds fine, but of course it isn't true. If we could ever harness all the potential story material that flows through our lives, I think a week's worth would keep us at our typewriters for the next two years for five days a week. I'd venture to say that even an Erle Stanley Gardner who manages to put out fifteen to twenty novels a year doesn't use all the story material that goes through his brain. I'm not just referring to things that might have happened to us, personally; I include every channel of thought and inspiration: incidents told to us by other people, newspaper stories, magazine articles, editorials, proverbs that provoke thought, history we happen to read. Each of these may carry the makings of a thrilling story *if we are consciously searching for it.* In its raw form it may not be a story but it can give us something to build on; clay to be molded, to be added to or subtracted from, shaped into the dramatic structure commonly known as a plot which has poignancy or illustrates a truth, makes a wry comment about human nature, or in some way stirs the mind of a reader. After all, what is our work but taking a bit of reality and arranging it in such a way that it is no longer a set of random happenings, but instead, a meaningful whole experience which we offer as a gift to anyone who will take the time to look?

The biggest and best help I've ever found is Georges Polti's *Thirty-Six Dramatic Situations* (published by *The Writer*), from which I have made what I call "plot cards." These cards are an endless source of story ideas and often do a lot of the plotting of sequences when you get used to them. Here then is a method of brainstorming that can be done by yourself.

I got the book from the library and began jotting down each separate classification of plot on a large index card. As you may know, the thirty-six categories are extremely broad. A person could limit himself to writing in any one of them and still never run out of material in a lifetime. A few random samplings from the book include:

> Desire to escape, or see another escape a disaster or misfortune.
> Desire to see all obstacles to love removed.
> The enforced making of a daring effort.

I changed the wording on my cards to such headings as "Escape," "Obstacles to Love" and, "Daring Enterprise." Under these headings I began to list some of the most probable variations I could think of, so that in reading them over they would serve to remind me of all the different types of stories I might care to write. Often the cards will suggest a scene or two in the mind that will spark a whole plot outline. Most important, they offer a place to begin hunting and get your mind geared immediately to workable dramatic situations rather than allowing you to waste time thinking about unexciting notions or pondering about whether it's hot enough to turn the sprinklers on the lawn that afternoon. I've spent five minutes before realizing I've done nothing but contemplate a crooked dart board across the room, debating whether to straighten it or not. The cards settle me down to business. I may decide to take fifteen or twenty minutes thinking about each card, or I may flip through them quickly to see all the far-out possibilities open to me. For example, one card may read:

Revolt

> Standing up for a principle and making a crusade of it, then discovering one's self wrong.
> Attempting to get another to stand up for his rights even though he (or she) would rather not.
> One person getting others to support him in a just revolt against a tyrant.
> An attempt to get others to support an unjust revolt against authority.
> The defense of a seemingly hopeless cause out of principle.
> The attempt of a person or group to place the blame for revolt against authority on an innocent person and that person's subsequent attempts to protect himself or take revenge for his unjust treatment.

There are, of course, many other patterns to revolt stories. As I see, read or think of new ones, I will add them to the card.

Let's suppose I have just read an article about a man who went on a crime spree across the country. I became intrigued with his character or the idea of telling a story about a person who has defied the establishment so flagrantly. How shall I etch my lead character? I have many choices, depending on what he represents to the story. He could be a loveable con man, a rash fool, a madman, an idealistic revolutionary, whatever is most effective in making a point. Going through the "Revolt" card I see some of the forms my rebel could take.

Falling Prey to Cruelty or Misfortune

The innocent taken advantage of by those whose rightful duty it is to protect. Criminals or slaves mistreated or exploited by unprincipled masters.

A favorite or intimate friend; a lover, finds himself (herself) taken for granted or forgotten due to some distraction, or some circumstance which leaves the friend or lover tainted.

A person loses the favor of a powerful protector and must find a way to fight an enemy who has caused him to lose that protection.

One falls under disfavor by his superior or by some strong power.

One attempts to officiate justly though hampered by the orders or pressures of those higher up.

A man or woman used as a scapegoat by another or by a group.

One who is treated cruelly or unjustly (or the relative of the victim) seeks to obtain revenge and/or to clear a good name.

It wasn't long before I found it would be helpful to make out two separate stacks of cards; the first for working in dramatic plots, the second for comedy. I suppose I could have used the same set for both types of stories but it saves time to have two sets. When I'm looking for a notion for the development of a comedy, I can immediately count out such things as murderous adultery, natural catastrophes, the slaying of an unrecognized kinsman and unnatural love affairs. They're all pretty heavy for comedy. Besides that, comedy looks at the world in a slightly different way and the cards should reflect that point of view if they are to make good suggestions. Thus, the "Hatred of a Kinsman" card, slanted for comedy will be "Rivalry of Relatives." Compare the difference in the two:

Hatred of a Kinsman

A mother or father torn between two sons who despise one another (or two sisters; brother and sister, etc.).

One brother's (sister's) secret hatred for another.
Hatred among relatives over who is to inherit family wealth and/or position.
Hatred of the member of a family for another who has betrayed a trust.
Hatred of a father for his son or a mother for her daughter.
Hatred of two relatives who are bound by their mutual love of a child (or a mother or a father).
Hatred of in-laws bound by their love of their mutual relative(s).

Rivalry of Relatives

Two brothers at odds over the same girl.
Two sisters at odds over the same boy.
Sibling rivalry to accomplish the same thing or to win a contest.
Husband and wife in competition for the same goal.
A dare or bet (or other challenge) between members of the same family.
Rivalry of in-laws as to what is best for a member of the family.
Resentment between a wife and mother-in-law.
Resentment between husband and father-in-law.
Rivalry between husband and wife about whose family is superior.
The meddling of in-laws between husband and wife.
Resentment among relatives as to who is to receive a family honor (being best man, bridesmaid, godparents, etc.).

I think it is interesting and helpful to watch television or read stories with the cards nearby. When the story is over, see if you can find it within the cards and consider how it was developed from its skeletal outline. You'll soon find it has strengthened your own ability to develop situations from the one-liners on the cards. If you don't find the particular variation of story you have just read or seen, then you have found one to add to those you have already listed.

I once found a short historic account of a supposedly haunted gold mine and wrote a story with the suggestions of a card that said, "Strange or mystical occurrences are found to be caused by schemers who will gain by frightening others with supposed ghosts or some magic power." The heading for the card was "The solving of a riddle." I wrote a story entitled, "The Man Who Wouldn't Stay Buried." It tells of the killing of a prospector by two men. When his nephew shows up to claim his mine, the two killers try to plan a way to get rid of him. They're afraid another "accident" would throw suspicion on them, so they try to scare the young man out by masquerading as the ghost of his uncle.

This business of changing mental straw into gold is as elusive as quicksilver. There is nothing so slippery as an undeveloped story idea and this system is the best way I know to clear away the mist and get a firm grip on an interesting thought. I've tried many times to trace the steps in the development of a story but it's useless. Each one materializes in a different way. I, for one, refuse to be the slave of inspiration. I have nothing against it, I just don't feel it's necessary to wait for it to strike like a bolt out of the blue. Besides, like lightning, it may never strike twice—at least not for some time. There is a certain amount of technique that can be applied in the bringing together of characters, situations and the catalysts that forge fascinating tales. Play your cards right and watch the lightning flash almost at will. The name of the game is "Brainstorming . . . by Yourself."

Pearl Hogrefe

Bringing Your Characters To Life

When you write well about people, your characters will be individual people, not stereotypes. Acquiring this skill is difficult. You may be hampered because you know too much (and must select carefully) about a real person, or you do not know enough, or because there are so many methods of characterizing.

First, you may consider direct explanation; that is, the writer explains his own views of a character, the views of others about him, or the character's views of himself. In theory this method is likely to be dull, especially in the hands of an amateur. But when used by a sharp observer with maturity of style, it becomes effective; it is useful in long fiction when a writer is introducing a character; and, used briefly, it is effective in short narrative. Sinclair Lewis sometimes used well single sentences of explaining:

> Mr. Tozer was thin and undistinguished and sun-worn as his wife, and like her he peered, he kept silence and fretted. (Sinclair Lewis, *Arrowsmith,* [Harcourt, Brace, 1925])

Later, in a brief narrative about a character, you may need to use an occasional sentence of explanation; the test, again, is your ability to use the explaining smoothly, so that it seems a natural part of the narrative.

Second, among the methods of characterizing, you may describe a character, using specific and active details and selecting only those that show individuality. Third, you may use the surroundings of a person to show us what he is like—the habitual surroundings which he creates himself—or his reaction to an alien environment. Fourth, you may use the thoughts of a character, either the stream-of-consciousness flux or preferably the controlled thoughts about specific things. Fifth, you may show us how your character reacts to other people. Sixth, you may let him talk. Seventh, you may use his actions, including little mannerisms which are habitual, either his specific movements in a one-time, one-place situation or his pattern of action in a whole story. If any general conclusion is sound, talk and action are the most effective methods of developing a character, but when you examine good narrative you are likely to find several of these methods skillfully combined.

If writing about people seems difficult, you are probably asking yourself questions like these: How can I know people well enough to write about them? How can I be fair? In writing (and also in real life) you may need to decide on a basic trait, or a quality that is fundamental, constant, and significant. If you were picking a personnel man, you might decide that shrewdness about judging people is basic; if you are considering marriage, you may believe that an enduring loyalty is basic. In preparing to write, you may think that a fondness for perfume is constant but neither fundamental nor significant. If you are an aesthetic person, not an average one, you may think that indifference to beauty is fundamental. To most of us, indifference to human suffering seems more important. Also to most of us generosity, stinginess, kindness, cruelty, honesty or dishonesty in some form, courage or cowardice seems significant. As all creative writing is an expression of individual values, your selection of a basic trait is your honest individual choice. Sometimes you may choose a trait so important that it will lead your character to success or ruin; sometimes, merely the little foible that amuses you where others see an unreal perfection. You have nothing worth telling about people except your own discoveries; each discovery comes from your own growth and is a stage on the way to an ultimate truth you will never reach. But it is not a scientific conclusion.

Why do you need to emphasize a basic trait? You might answer the question by asking yourself another: Why do you need to aim at a bull's-eye, instead of the side of a barn, when you are developing skill in shooting? You narrow your target to gain skill. But when you write about a person you need not be so rigid that he is stiff, like a dry skeleton; at your pleasure he may say other little things which do not contradict his basic trait. If you need a basic trait for your own guidance you also need it for your reader. To tell him all would probably do nothing but confuse him. Your composition would thus lack the essential one-ness which comes from selection and arrangement, a oneness which is intensified by repetition and subtle implication. For instance, if your character is insolent, do not tell us or show us once only; let him swagger and speak with contempt through your whole unit. Repeat and repeat, with variations and by implication.

Whenever you write about people in narrative, your ability to make your major character seem like flesh and blood is the real test of your skill. You would like to present not a puppet, an automaton, a generalized abstraction, a flat, one-dimensional figure, but a rounded, individual, three-dimensional figure. When you are reading narrative written by other people, you sometimes find yourself responding to a character: you see him enter a room, hear his voice or his breathing, strain your muscles with his; you hope and fear for him if you sympathize, and if you do not sympathize you hope and fear for others; you understand his motives and his mind. You have the feel of his experience as you read. That is, a character seems alive for you as a reader when you realize him with your *senses,* react to him with your *emotions,* follow him with your *mind.* Can you bring your characters to life for your readers?

Perhaps no one can tell you fully how to breathe life into your characters. Certainly there is no magic formula, or more characters in literature would give the illusion of flesh and blood. Knowing your character is your best approach. Here are two working hypotheses. First, your chances for bringing to life your own character grow as you understand him with your *mind,* your *senses,* and your *emotions.* Second, you can do something to know your character by *your conscious effort.* Then you can hope to fuse your details into a created experience that will give him the spark of life.

Professional writers take great pains to know their major characters. A man who had his fourth novel under way was asked by a group of students about his methods. "Oh, *no!* No outlines." As he spoke he was pulling from his brief case a sketch of his village with its chief trees and houses, a summary of his central idea, plot scenarios, the wording of his closing paragraphs, and biographical sketches of his characters. For his main character he had a synopsis covering ancestry, past life, environmental influences, occupations, future aims, physical appearance, emotional drives, and a basic trait. He had built his main characters from years of unconscious incubation, using the problems of his own family and the people in the community where he spent his childhood. He was using conscious incubation also, trying to "get inside the skin" of his chief character. Since experienced writers take so much trouble before they write a narrative, perhaps you may need to try knowing your characters before you begin to write.

How can you know a character? You can begin by watching people. Some of these questions may help you:

What is the person's face really like? What is individual about his eyes, mouth, nose? Does his expression change easily? (Observe him in different situations—when he talks to a girl he likes, to a man he likes, to a man he distrusts, when he feels inadequate, when he is happy, anxious to please, ready to drive a bargain, asleep, adjusted to a formal social affair.) What is his hair like, in color, in texture, in arrangement? How does he manage his hands and feet? What gestures does he use? How does he walk—does he stride, wobble, saunter, sneak, lurch, march? Are his muscular movements free and spontaneous? Do they reveal his urges and aversions? What mannerisms does he have? Does he narrow his eyes when he thinks? Does he snap his fingers when he is perplexed? How does he shake hands? Does his bodily position or his expression change when he is with inferiors, superiors, when he is asked to use his mind or his hands, when he is caught off guard? Can you realize his inner feeling when his face takes on a certain expression? Could you describe him, selecting the physical details to make him seem an *individual?*

How does your character speak? Does he drawl? Does he clip off his words? Is he precise or slovenly in his enunciation? Is his voice high or low, thin or rich and resonant, easy or strained? What are his pet expressions, bywords, expletives? Is his language informal or bookish? Is it idiomatic and picturesque, or flat, conventional? When you close your eyes and listen to his talk, do you hear an individual speech rhythm? When he is absent, after you have observed him carefully, can you hear his voice in your imagination? Can you make other people hear his voice?

How does he laugh? Does he express honest amusement, or is he covering up other feelings? If you heard this type of laugh from an unseen stranger, what would you think of him?

As you study any character, you will observe more shrewdly when you notice that physical details have their constant and their changing elements. For example, your character's eyes are always blue, but they may look a lighter blue when he is happy and a steel blue when he is angry. His voice, too, is always the same in some ways, yet it changes in other ways to reveal his moods. Then your character is one person when he is static and another when he is active—or perhaps he is a dozen different persons as he takes part in different activities. He will probably interest you and us more when he is active. Then be sure to observe him in at least one activity.

As you observe physical details, using your senses, you are also learning to understand your character with your mind. What do you know about his inclinations, tastes, interests, favorite sports, reading habits, ambitions? If his ambitions are strong, are they controlled by scruples? Is his vanity strong? What are his fixed ideas? His prejudices? His dominant motives? What does he desire most or value most? What does he think about when he is most himself? What thoughts does he have which he would be unwilling to tell his best friend? Would he tell any of these thoughts to a stranger? How does he treat equals, superiors, children, servants? (Although you probably cannot know all these things about one actual person, the questions may help you sort out what you do know. But when you create a character, from the dust of your experience, you can know these things and more.) What is his basic trait? Why does he have this trait?

As you use your senses and your mind, learn your own emotional attitude to your character. Do you reverence, admire, love him? Do you envy or pity him? Do you feel dislike, aversion, disgust? Does he make you angry? Is your feeling so complex that you have trouble analyzing it? How do your own muscles behave when your character approaches?

Try to realize what emotions your character is feeling and then suffer or enjoy with him if you can. If your sympathies are narrow, begin with characters like yourself. Then enlarge your powers; for example, imagine yourself "inside the skin" of a small boy with a fishing pole, three small fish, and an interest in snakes. Can you hear the faint squish of dust under his bare feet, feel the fishing pole growing heavy on his shoulder? Can you identify yourself with a boy watching a fire truck—hear the truck, feel his tense muscles, see the firemen as they adjust their bodies to speed, and also feel a longing to ride on that fire truck? Can you at least sympathize with the characters you choose to write about?

Sometimes "to know all is to forgive all"; sometimes your sense of values, as you understand a character keeps you from sympathy and even gives you a positive aversion. If you find yourself neutral or lukewarm after you have observed your character, do not waste time writing about him. If your interest was genuine to begin with, your attempt to grasp him with your mind and your senses has probably clarified and strengthened your attitude.

Peg Bracken

The New Mallarkey

One of the writer's big problems, as he creates his beautiful, brave, lovable characters, is making them beautiful enough and brave enough, and still keeping them lovable.

The fact is, times have changed. Today's sophisticated reader will no longer buy yesterday's heroine, who walked in virtue, her eyes blue as the sky over Naples, with cheeks that shamed the rose. He is equally unconvinced by yesterday's hero, that big handsome broad-shouldered curly-haired package of incorruptibility.

A thing called Reader Identification has set in. The reader knows, deep down, that *he* is not as beautiful or lovable as that, and furthermore he doubts whether anyone is.

The twin horns of the writer's dilemma are distressingly clear. The writer must, to put it bluntly, lay off the mallarkey. But he knows, too, that his feminine readers will refuse just as flatly to identify themselves with a thick-waisted heroine or one who has a front tooth out; nor will his masculine readers stay long with a potbellied hero.

It is encouraging to be able to report that writers have solved the problem—not with the faint praise which damns, but with the faint damn which praises. For example:

> Brad looked at Pam. She was too thin, her checkbones too high, her eyes too wide apart.

Now, there is Reader Identification with a hey-nonnie. Every woman wants to be too thin. And love those high cheekbones, those wide-set eyes! But here she finds them brusquely dismissed as faults.

Well, the reader has faults, too. She knows how it is. And while she privately imagines the heroine to be about as beautiful as any girl can be, she derives a certain feminine comfort from hearing that not everyone thinks so. The reader immediately joins the heroine's team. She becomes her Secret Pal.

It is not easy, this matter of presenting virtues as faults; the writer must remember at all times that Pam's legs may be too long, but not so her nose. Her eyes may be too large, but never, under any circumstances, her knuckles. "Pam's too-generous mobile mouth" is always acceptable to the reader, but "Pam's big flopping mouth" would be rejected instantly. No, it isn't easy, and the writer encounters the same problem when he describes the house or the room Pam lives in. Yet, here again, the same approach will ease the way to Reader Identification:

> It wasn't a smart room. Obviously no interior decorator had had a hand in assembling this casual collection of odd pieces; no decorator would have condoned the faded chintzes and the clutter of books. Even the kindly firelight burnishing the rocker and the old copper kettle couldn't quite hide the shabbiness of the rug. Yet Brad liked the room, felt at home there . . . .

Note the shrewd use of the "yet" instead of a "therefore." Observe its magic effect in making the reader feel superior to the writer, as well as at home in the room. "Why, that's my kind of place!" the reader thinks. "What does this silly writer want, a store window? My stuff doesn't match either. And as for books, well, I always say a room just isn't a room without books . . . ." So the reader is more than ever ready to share Pam's problems and eventual joys.

The aspiring glossy fiction writer should know that his heroes will respond just as nicely to the faint damn as will his heroines and his settings. When a man reads that

> Brad's face was casually put together, the nose jutting, the lines deep—a face marked by the hard living of forty-one years

he feels better about his own face, which was designed a bit haphazardly, too. Also, the suggestion of manly dissipation enables him to write off his own extra rounds at the nineteenth hole. At the same time, he senses that none of these things is going to handicap Brad in the slightest. Brad is obviously a nice combination of valor and virility. He will go far, and the reader will follow him all the way.

It is true that there are pitfalls with heroes, as with heroines, and the alert writer will keep them in mind. For instance, a tight-lipped hero who grins an occasional crooked grin will be readily accepted by the reader, even though these traits, in real life, are usually an indication of bad bridgework. But the reader will quickly shy away from Brad should he have foot trouble. Foot trouble, for some reason, belongs to men named Harold Buebke, not Brad Reynolds; and heroes are never named Harold Buebke.

It is all a matter of knowing how and what to insult without insulting. It is for this reason that the writer so often seems preoccupied with the hero's hair. Brad can have hair like old rope, and often does. Or he can have mussed-up hair, although the better adjective is "unruly," or he can even have hair that's growing thin on top—no matter, it will lower him not one whit in the reader's estimation; moreover, it will provide a comfortable bond of Reader Identification.

No discussion of the praise-while-damning method would be complete without mention of the flashback to adolescence—a technique which has been often and profitably used by writers who know their business. One of its many merits is that it permits the heroine to be an absolute dilly from the first moment she appears.

> Brad looked at Pam Harrison, slim, poised, perfect. There had been a little Pam Harrison once, years ago, before the war had torn and twisted so many things . . . . Pam Harrison, the little kid next door.
> "Pam, are you the same girl that—" Brad stopped, feeling like a fool. This girl, this copper-haired beauty with the exquisite legs, the warm ivory skin, the marvelous laughing mouth—she could never have been that skinny brat with the freckles, that kid with the braces on her teeth.
> "You mean, was I the kid you used to chase home from school with snowballs?" Pam wrinkled her nose, charmingly. "Yes, Wasn't I *awful?*"
> Brad grinned.
> "I was pretty awful myself," he said ruefully. "Remember how . . ."

Now, this isn't as easy as it looks. It's quite all right for the child Pam to be remembered with braces on her teeth, a skinny freckled gamin. But the reader will never make contact with Pam if she used to be doughfaced and overweight. Once in a long time a writer will fatten up a young heroine and get away with it, but the trick lies in the use of the word "pudgy," which has a rollicking cherubic quality that's rather fun.

However, once these problems have been met and mastered, the writer finds himself in a nice position, and can get on with his story; he has given his principals a reasonably repulsive adolescence, and the reader shouldn't quibble over their distinct charm as adults. After all, fair's fair.

This takes care of all the description the writer has to worry about, with one exception. If it is ever necessary to describe someone asleep in bed—and it is surprising how often this is necessary—there is only one way to do it:

> Lying there asleep in the rumpled bedclothes, he looked defenseless.

A querulous critic might object. Unless he is Lucky Luciano lying there asleep with his gat under his pillow and his finger on the trigger, how in the world else can he look? But that is mere carping, and it need not be considered here.

Brian Cleeve

Empathy Creates Living Characters in Fiction

We've all read books, and some very good books, in which the characters didn't live at all; in which they were just cardboard cut-outs,
mouthpieces for the author. (If what he had to say was interesting or
instructive enough, the flatness of the characters didn't matter too
much.) And there are plenty of mediocre books in which one or two
characters spring alive and redeem the whole thing.

Now it seems to me that this "springing alive" is a kind of small
miracle which hasn't a lot to do with other literary virtues—clean style,
an ability to invent and manage complex plot designs. It doesn't really
depend even on imagination except in a special sense. What it does
depend on to my mind is sympathy. Or rather, empathy—that special
kind of imagination which lets you put yourself in someone else's shoes.
(Any greater degree of imagination than that is unnecessary, and might
even be a hindrance. Because, for example, you might start imagining
what *you* would do in their shoes, and not what *they* would do.) Real
empathy requires subordination of self, a making blank of your own
mind to let another personality take over for the time being. Actors,
who are not always notably intelligent, have to do this all the time. And
a writer who wants to make a character live must *act* that character in
his mind. He must make his mind blank, he must receive the character
into the vacuum, he must *be* the character, he must listen to it, and not
tell it what to do or be.

This, of course, is fine metaphysical advice for anyone who already
knows and believes in the method. But not much practical help to anyone who doesn't.

Let's take a concrete example. For some reason you want to incorporate a bookkeeper in your new story. For plot purposes he needs to be frustrated, malicious to the point of murder, and so nondescript as to be unnoticed as he goes around. And yet you don't want him to be unsympathetic. You want readers to understand why he is as he is and feel compassion for him.

None of this is possible unless you understand him yourself. How do you understand him? Well, how do you understand your friends, your wife, yourself? By knowing as much about them as possible. The more you know, normally, the better you understand. Perfect knowledge would lead to perfect understanding. And to compassion, if compassion were needed.

Apply this to your bookkeeper. Why is he frustrated? Suppose he wanted to be a violinist, but his talent stopped short of his ambition. The ambition remains, curdled into poison. The desire for beauty remains, made hideous by inability to create it. Music is torture to the man because he can't make it as he wants to make it. And five days a week, eight hours a day, he tots figures: a job that a girl could do, a machine could do.

Given this nucleus, the man can begin to live in *your* mind before he has any externals at all, before you bother about his appearance, his daily circumstances, anything.

Empty your mind and see how such a man *would* look. That kind of inner misery would stamp itself on any face, carve lines round the mouth, do things to the eyes, show a kind of black flame under the skin, a stifled savagery of hatred.

Would he marry? Not really. If he let himself be trapped into marriage he'd take his life-hatred out on his wretched wife; bully her in thin and frightful mental ways, suddenly go on his knees to her, treat her like his mother, beg her to give him what it's impossible for her to give, a new mind, genius, happiness.

What does his boss think of him? What is his boss like? What does his boss' secretary look like, how does he think of her? Does he go home by subway, hating it? By car, biting his fingernails at the other drivers? How does he dress? What does he eat? What does he take for his indigestion? It feels like a snake eating his heart. Sometimes he stops in the street and holds his hands to it and thinks he's dying.

There are thousands of questions and answers like this that you need to know and feel. You don't have to ask them one by one. You can visualize a hundred of them in one mental flashlight photograph. Until suddenly you know this man like your brother. You can see him leaning against the dirty wall outside a subway station, half paralyzed for a few seconds by the pain in his stomach, masking it with the evening paper, clenching his teeth, his eyes shut behind the paper, thinking "Oh God, how long can this go on, and no one care?" His hair is a shade too long, a bit ragged over the collar. His shoes are a bit cracked across the uppers. He has a white silk handkerchief that costs more than his shirt and he wipes his face with it and clenches his teeth on it. And a girl goes past him, in cheap perfume, her dress too tight over her buttocks, a kind of insolent stupidity dripping out of her eyelashes. She looks at him behind his ineffective mask of evening paper and silk handkerchief, assesses him, writes him off. And for one moment of agonized humiliation she represents for him the whole stupid, arrogant world, God and man and life, that made him and has rejected him, and he feels that if he could possess her, if he could break her down, make her weep in front of him, crawl to his feet and kiss them, it would give him at least a little ease, a little revenge. He starts to follow her.

Now if you reread the preceding two hundred-odd words, you'll see it's a sketch for the opening of a story, using our bookkeeper as chief character. And in that sketch I've used comparatively little of the background material I started to assemble. Maybe five percent of it. But the other ninety-five percent affected what I put down, was present in it, just as the whole nature of a tree is present in and governs the appearance of the single plank that you may cut from the heart of it.

And as the story would develop, if I ever came to write it, everything the character did and the way he did it would spring from this reservoir of knowledge that I had about him. When he buys his subway ticket he takes his small change out of a greasy, worn leather purse. He has to. That's the way the man I now know like a brother *would* keep his money. That's how he *does* keep his money. For me, in my mind, he's already a living man with a will of his own. I know *why* he uses a purse.

But I don't need to put that down on paper. I just need to tell you that he does use one. And if I'm a competent enough writer, and have done my background work properly, you'll get two sensations from this small detail. A slight sense of surprise, almost of shock. And then a feeling of rightness. That, of course, such a man as I am describing *must* do this. And at this point, this longed-for point in a writer's working life, the character not only lives for his creator, he lives for the reader. He walks off the page and into the reader's mind.

And this is achieved not by an accumulation of detail on the page, which could read like a catalogue and stay as dead, but by the atmosphere of solidity conveyed by two or three strategically placed details which are organically connected under the surface, out of sight. Just as a sailor, looking at two or three smallish icecaps shoving up from a green sea, suddenly realizes that they are moving in concert, that they are joined beneath the surface by one tremendous mass of hidden ice, and gets from the realization of feeling of power and menace more dreadful than if he could see the whole iceberg floating above the dark oilskin of the water.

Because what is suggested is more powerful than what is shown. Providing that it is true, and that it carries instant conviction that it is true.

Now, I am not suggesting for one moment that I have made my bookkeeper live for you. But if anyone wanted to make him live, I suggest that this, or something very like it, is the method he'd have to use.

Clayton C. Barbeau

The Value of a Wart

"Watch for warts." This is the advice I find myself giving again and again to the aspiring writers with whom I come in contact.

Chaucer anticipated my advice by a few hundred years. In the Prologue to the *Canterbury Tales,* he introduces us to a whole array of pilgrims, devoting only a few descriptive lines to each one. Yet, within those few lines, he slices away this person from all the others making that immortal journey. "And at the point of his nose," Chaucer says of the Miller, "a wart he had, and thereon stood a soft tuft of hairs, red as the bristles in a sow's ear." That wart, with its growth of hairs, and the reference to a sow's ear might seem incidental to some, but actually that descriptive line does the job of making the Miller a character from every other person traveling with him. No one else has such a wart. More than this, we are able immediately to deduce much about the Miller's character. Even if Chaucer had told us no more about him, we'd know that he was no lady killer, that he wasn't going to mince his words and that he quite probably wouldn't spin any pious fairy tales for us when his turn to entertain us came along.

Not to be interested in warts is a fundamental oversight in one who is journeying along the path to publication. It is almost as fundamental a drawback as not being interested in people, because the two really go together. If we're interested in people, then we'll be keen on their warts. And, as all the world knows, you've got to be interested in people if you're going to write effectively about them.

People are fascinating not as the masses—there is much truth in the contention that the mob is a beast—but when taken singly. No matter what individual we're confronted with, he's unique. There is not, never has been, and never will be, another person exactly like this one. The problem confronting the writer is that he must, within the economy of his story, pinpoint that specific difference between this man and every other.

We could do worse, as writers, than to study the way in which truly great writers delineate character. Most of them do what Chaucer has done: They pay attention to specific details. A miller is a miller, but the Miller in the *Canterbury Tales* is an unforgettable character with a hair-sprouting wart on the very tip of his nose.

Any scholar will tell you that Chaucer deliberately set about to give us a cross-section of the English people of his day—from the pious to the impious, from the Nun to the Wife of Bath. But his book doesn't endure for this reason. The *Canterbury Tales* are remembered and revered because the people in it *live*. They may be representative of types, but not one is a stereotype. Each of them is an individual, and the description of each is, at once, vivid and eminently personal. And each of Chaucer's characters is unique because Chaucer paid attention to those details which set each apart from the other: In short, Chaucer knew the value of a wart.

Because he was so interested in their specific differences, the people Chaucer presents to us are vitally alive. G.K. Chesterton remarked long ago that "The Wife of Bath's Tale is not so good as the Wife of Bath; The Reeve's Tale is not so vivid as the Reeve; we are not so much interested in the Summoner's story as in the Summoner; and care less about Griselda than about the Clerk of Oxford. The Miller does not prove his own rather brutal energy by telling a broad and rather brutal story half so well as the poet conveys it in those curt and strong lines about his breaking a door by butting it with his red-bristled head. And the whole conception and cult of Chivalry is no better set forth, in all the seventy pages that unfold the Knight's Tale, than in the first few lines that describe the Knight." (G.K. Chesterton: *Chaucer* [Sheed & Ward, N.Y., 1965])

Let's look at some of the lines of character description that caused me recently to become a rather outspoken exponent of warts, Chaucerian and of other varieties. These three lines were imbedded in three different stories submitted to me during the Writer's Conference.

The colonel was an elderly man with gray hair and blue eyes.

A colonel with gray hair and blue eyes is just an elderly colonel. I've met my share of them and so have you. Some of them I didn't like and some of them I did. This descriptive line might have been all right had something more been given to us to go on, but it stood alone. Is it really necessary, at this point, to trot out what has now become my cliché and announce that this colonel needs a wart? The description above is too general to help anyone visualize the colonel, to make an estimate of him, to see him as a person. We need that added touch, that specific and telling item which will mark him off from every other gray-haired, blue-eyed colonel sitting in the parlor of the old soldier's home. Now if we had been told that *this* colonel was minus an earlobe, we'd have something to go on. Not everyone is minus an earlobe. Was it a piece of shrapnel that did the job or did some general do a rather thorough job of chewing him out? Whichever it is, we're intrigued by this particular man.

Rose was well-proportioned and her smile showed pretty, white teeth.

No warts on her, are there? "Well-proportioned" tell us nothing about Rose—to a midget she might seem huge—and her white teeth are standard fixtures on all the latest models. But what if we had also been informed that she had one earring hanging from her pierced right ear. Or, if you think that we're getting hung up on ears, what about a tiny heart tattooed on the back of her hand? Now, with something like that, the reader's imagination can run away. All warts don't have to be physical; they can be material, like the earring; decorative (in a sense), like the tattoo.

I looked at Charles. He was a rugged fellow, strong and quiet.

Charlie, I'm afraid we must admit, is nobody. He's one of a faceless, characterless mass of ten thousand rugged, strong, quiet fellows—until the author finds a wart on him. Now we've given examples of physical and material warts, so, for the sake of variety, let's ferret about for a mental wart. There must be something (indeed, there always is) we could mention about Charlie, some particular fact, which will lift him bodily out of that huge crowd of similar Charlies and put him up on his own unique pedestal. Perhaps *this* Charlie hates trains, has a deep and powerful grudge against locomotives of all types.

In each of the above cases, whether the wart we've found in the character is physical, a matter of taste, or a mental state—and there are many other possibilities too—we now have an outstanding clue to the character of this particular person, some specific note that underscores his individuality. Any writer worth his carbon paper must strive to do the same thing: to put before us the specific, concrete note which this character sounds and which no other character can sound.

The distinguishing specific fact might be nothing larger than a wart, an everyday wart with hairs on it, but it is essential to effective characterization. A writer should cultivate his eye for warts and, when he approaches the revision of a returned story, he might look at his characters. If they haven't any warts, he'd better give them some. It's the only way his characters will cease being stereotypes or puppets and become living persons.

James Hilton

Creating a Lovable Character

On account, I suppose, of Mr. Chips, I have sometimes been asked how one creates a lovable character in fiction. My first answer is that the worst possible way would be to take pen and paper or typewriter and say to oneself: "I am going to create a lovable character."

As a matter of fact, the process of artistic creation is mysterious, even to the creator; there is, as G.K. Chesterton once said, all the difference in the world between knowing how things are done and knowing how to do them. The artist knows how to do them; he does not as a rule care whether he knows how they are done or not. He leaves that to critics, commentators, glossarians, foot-noters, or his own biographer (if he is ever likely to have one)—but always with a wistful memory of Lord Balfour's remark in the British Parliament—"Gentlemen, I do not mind being contradicted, and I am unperturbed when I am attacked, but I confess I have slight misgivings when I hear myself being explained."

How many authors have had similar misgivings when enthusiastic admirers "explain" the significance of their characters, or when some well-meaning professor lectures learnedly on their writing methods! I once knew such a professor; he drew fascinating diagrams on a blackboard showing that So-and-So (I think it was Conrad) attacked his subject from the north-east corner; and the moral was that if we students only got ourselves in the right corner we might improve our literary output. The advice, however sound, was for me somewhat discredited by the fact that I did not want to write like Conrad anyway.

The only trick I know in writing is to have something to say, or some story to tell, and to say it or tell it as simply and as effectively as possible. The proverb in *Alice in Wonderland* cannot be bettered—"Take care of the sense and the sounds will take care of themselves." So far as "style" goes, I am a functionalist; if a sentence represents exactly the idea I wish to convey, I am satisfied with it. I dislike "style" that has a look or sound of having been stuck on afterwards, or "style" that employs unusual words with no intention but to startle the reader, send him to a dictionary, or give the snobbish feeling that because he cannot properly understand what he is reading he is therefore improving his mind enormously. And I am ready to use any words that seem useful, whether the purists object to them or not—"intrigue" as a verb, for instance, which conveys to me a definite and needed shade of meaning between "interest" and "absorb."

As for creating character, I think it is one of those things that are not to be learned and cannot easily be counterfeited. Anybody, of course, can construct a dummy with an assortment of attributes attached to him like labels, and some writers have so successfully convinced the public that this is character-creating that the very word "character" has come to have a secondary meaning nowaways—i.e. we say a man is a "character" when we mean he is a little bit eccentric. Every stage-actor knows how much easier it is to put over a juicy bit of character-acting than to portray an ordinary person who might be you or me; and most actors know also (to their own dismay) how readily the public is taken in by this sort of thing. A genuine creation should *have* character as well as *be* one; should have central heating, so to say, as well as exterior lighting. When Sir Walter Scott introduced any new personage into his novels he usually began with the hair and finished with the heels, making a complete inventory of dress and featues all the way down; the result was that you felt you might possibly recognize the fellow if you were ever to meet him and he happened to be wearing the same clothes. But when Dostoyevsky or Dickens gives you a character, you feel that you know him with your eyes shut. It is the difference between—"He had light blue eyes, lank hair, slightly stooping shoulders, and wore shabby tweeds"—and (I think Morley wrote this in one of his novels)—"Everything of him was *rather*, except his eyes, and they were *quite*." Please don't take this sentence as any sort of model; it is merely an example of how a good writer blows you a petal of meaning instead of felling a whole forest for you—hoping you'll be just as satisfied, edified, and instructed.

So far, you may have noticed, I have been evading the question I began with—how a lovable character can be created. Frankly, I don't know. If you have a story to tell and tell it simply and without fuss, some of the characters may be lovable and others not so; you can hardly create them to specification. But sometimes, after you have finished with them they ring a bell in your heart and afterwards in the hearts of your readers.

People love lovability; we all do; it is still human nature to admire goodness. Our admiration, at its core, is sharp as a nerve; let them once touch that nerve, and stories have a good chance of being popular. But if there were any formula for touching it, believe me the world of fiction would be swamped with "lovable characters." The truth is, the nerve is as secret as it is sensitive; try to create lovability to order and you will probably produce a mess of mawkishness that nobody will enjoy. The only recommendation I can give is that a writer should create the characters he has in mind and let them be lovable if they will.

Bonnie Golightly

The Use of Dialogue

When I was a mean young thing, writing term papers and short stories at twenty-five cents each for indolent and/or untalented classmates in eighth-grade English, I found the Houdini trick for throwing off the most iron-clad of dialogue shackles—i.e., how to get around the frustrations of: "Hello, how are you?" "Fine. How are you?" which seem to me to open all but the most inspired conversations of human life. It was easy, I concluded. Simply bypass these encrusted hollow amenities and get on with what there is to say.

Giddy with success, I then proceeded to the next pitfall and fell in. There was nothing I liked better during the next few years of my writing life than to painstakingly insert dialect within the simple, eternal he-said she-said frame, spelling the English as she is spoke with such phonetic fidelity that a special dictionary (twice the size of the created work) would have been necessary for translation. A Bobbs-Merrill editor gently pointed out this base and home truth to me when rejecting my second (and still unpublished) novel, the first to make the rounds. The cast of characters in this complicated composition were all Southern and from all classes—which is to say Upper and Lower, the feudalistic arrangement that existed in the South until after World War II. I enjoyed dialecting my lower class people more; their accent was pungent, hard to reproduce, and at variance with the usual, accepted pronunciations, being more faithful to archaic English. Then, too, their grammar was picturesquely atrocious, and the voice tones were not embellished with the little affectations and sophistications that trilled and rippled through the speech of the upper classes. Consequently, I eagerly tackled the challenge—only no challenge happened to be offered. It was Me vs. I, and while I still feel that I mastered the problem of faithful rendition of yokel and local accents, the sad fact is that next to nobody cared. It was a novel I was writing, after all, not a Ph.D. dissertation on Elizabethan and modern-day phonetics in the South. I remember my indignation when I learned from the editor's letter that she considered the pronunciation of "on" to be exactly the same, whether I put it down as "awn" in the mouth of one character, or as "ahn" in another.

But after the stinging stopped, and my scholarly pride had returned to size, I had to admit that her criticism was justifiable, however inaccurate. Those fine decibels I heard between the three sounds simply did not matter.

What is said is more important than how it sounds, and if meaning is obscured by phonetic stage direction, then the outcome is failure. Further proof: many published novels and many post-South years later, I am unable to wade through that rejected novel's passages of dialogue, and I am grateful to that long-ago editor for her indulgence.

All this is not to say that dialect in dialogue writing is strictly prohibited, but it is a little like garlic in haute cuisine; Peter De Vries once wrote that there is no such thing as a touch of garlic—ideally it should be rubbed on the cook. And the same thing goes for dialect: it is more becoming in the author's mouth than it may be on his manuscript page—and sometimes less embarrassing. Ernest Hemingway, who was supposedly America's crack-shot dialogue marksman, must have found egg on his typewriter after reading what critics Robert Graves and Alan Hodge have to say about a passage of dialogue in pseudo-dialect in his *For Whom The Bell Tolls.* The following is a part quote from their excellent *The Reader Over Your Shoulder—A Handbook for Writers of English Prose—*(Macmillan).

> [She] . . . said calmly, "Then just shut up about what we are to do afterwards, will you, Ingles? . . . Take thy little cropped headed whore and go back to the Republic but do not shut the door on others who . . loved the Republic when thou wert wiping thy mother's milk off thy chin." . . . "I am a whore if thee wishes, Pilar," Maria said. "I suppose I am in all case if you say so. But calm thyself. What passes with thee?"

About this short passage the *Handbook* authors have a number of things to say, most of which center around Hemingway's attempt to make the English sound like Spanish. (Even movie scenarists realized the fatal imbroglio which usually resulted from using this vehicle and more or less gave it up years and years ago.) Then Graves and Hodge rebuke Hemingway for his ungrammatical use of the English familiar tense, and go on to say that if this is supposed to represent a translation, the passage is overrun with mismated styles.

Graves and Hodge comment that by mixing Pilgrim Father English ("thou wert") with Pennsylvania-Quaker English ("if thee wishes") and present-day colloquial English, Hemingway ". . . suggests, falsely, that peasants in Spain make the same sort of mistake in speaking their native dialects."

These chastisements prove that even the master may be falling over his own feet just when he thinks he is tripping his lightest fantastic. *For Whom The Bell Tolls* was an act of love for the Spanish peasants, yet in his very desire to present them not only faithfully, but with purity, Hemingway so distorted them and his own work that the book is almost unreadable in the sections where he attempts to mirror their dialect.

I would have been consoled to read about Hemingway's dialectal mistake at the time I made my own, but it would not have helped me.

After I had scrambled out of my deep sandtrap with a score of far too many thousand word strokes over par, I began to give the whole subject of "How to Write Dialogue" a microscopic scrutiny. When it worked, why did it; when it didn't, why not?

It is the absolute duty of writer and editor alike to be as alert as possible to all changes and nuances of speech patterns, written and spoken, all accepting, of everything from "beat" talk to new assaults on Fowler's *Modern English Usage.* His knowledge of idiom, slang, and formal English should be encyclopedic, a constant tool, as necessary as his Webster's Unabridged, and as reliable even if it is impossible to be as extensive. And the only way to hone this tool is by constant "hearing"—a combination of sharp listening and sharp reading. (And keeping a notebook of phrases is a good idea for any writer.)

A writer of fiction is more or less a word juggler; he must keep many elements of action, plot and background going at the same time. But dialogue is his most useful prop, and the author's skill in its use often determines his talent, success and professionality. The words in quotes transfer, if they are any good, into being the reader's own words. Consequently, the wise writer will know when to be sparing and when to be lavish. Too much dialogue, no matter how informed, coruscating and interesting, can easily overpower that audience in the armchair—just as the most brilliant raconteur who never gives the other person a chance can become a monumental bore.

Clarity in dialogue is also a must: muddy dialogue is as fatal to a good piece of fiction as soiled hands are to a surgeon at the operating table. If it wanders around aimlessly, stuck in thickets of such writerly self-indulgences as fancy descriptions of the speaker's left eyebrow as he cynically says, "Oh, yeah?" or the listener's animal-like grimace, all is better off lost.

Clarity extends, too, to the matter of making certain that each character has his own tone, his own stamp, his own brand of speech pattern —if all voices are only an extension of the author's own idiom, be it brilliant, breezy, or just plain balmy, there is no character, just author. To test for whether or not this is taking place, eliminate the he-saids/ she-saids between speeches. Can the reader determine which character is speaking?

The whole matter of he-said-she-said could alone fill a handbook on dialogue writing. Are these interpolations necessary at all? If so, when? And how? And should the accompanying descriptions of how she or he said it be extensive, and what should they consist of? This is a subject that each dialogue writer has very definite opinions about, if he has been a writer for any length of time, with definite habits formed. But like all opinions and habits, some are right, some are wrong. One of the rights is, again, clarity and/or simplicity, without being too sparing. He-said and she-said often work alone without any addition of, for instance, "he said jokingly." Good dialogue can almost always stand on its own two quotation marks, and frequently does. After the writer sets the dialogue in motion between two characters, identities established, it then resembles the action in a ping-pong match between experts volleying the ball back and forth over the net to each other, again and again, before it is allowed to touch down on the court once more for a special stroke of some kind.

Hemingway had a brilliant flair for the table-tennis method of dialogue writing, and is often credited with the invention of this literary sport, but he had his own agile contemporaries, and he has certainly had more than agile followers. J.D. Salinger, Shirley Ann Grau, and John Updike can write yards of dialogue between a pair of characters, before needing to touch down to the he-said-she-said, or its equivalent —just to name three among many who actively use this effective, economical device in today's fiction.

Then there are others who have found that the semi-abandoned mine of the unadorned he-said-she-said can be reopened and made to produce with striking results. Muriel Spark, the Scottish-English novelist and short-story writer, seldom adds anything to "said" except the necessary pronoun. She is a writer of extreme wit, seriousness and discernment, and every work she puts to the page is pinioned there alive. She artfully employs both methods of dialogue writing, with rapid, perfectly-aimed skill, like an ambidextrous tennis player who changes from left hand to right, using both with equal ease, knowing exactly where and how to place the ball on the court. Like the early novels of Evelyn Waugh, Anthony Powell and Angus Wilson, hers are composed of roughly one part dialogue and one part description.

But to give dialogue a special stance or pose is often desirable, and a qualifier can add great significance. However, if this descriptive stage-direction of the actor's action or thought is to be added, it must always be looked at with a beady critical eye, before it is allowed to stand. If the author feels that it in any way detracts from previous action, misleads, opens him to ridicule or slows down the impact of what is said, it must go—no matter how tempting, or how fine the writing. The good writer never sacrifices his craft for his art unless by so doing he establishes new standards for everybody: dramatis personae, readers, and self.

One of the best cautionary measures for a dialoguist is to know his grammar—particularly must he be familiar with the difference between adjectives and adverbs, and their uses. One of the worst errors commonly found in dialogue is the following fallacious usage: "I know it," he *laughed*. "Don't tell me," she *sighed*. "They bore me," he *sneered*. "Said," may be implied, but only the sloppy non-grammarian is willing to let an action verb go it all alone, thus making him a candidate for the derision showcases of *The New Yorker.*

Similarly, the cavalier dialoguist quite often fancies himself as a word coiner, though often the word coined is a simple misuse of an existing one which is suitable for use as is: *"That will be enough!" he cried lungingly,* and other related follies, are fatuous rather than inventive.

And other *ignes fatui* abound to lure the dialoguist: one of the deepest pits into which he may fall is that of the supererogatory explanation of what the character has just said: *"You think you're the cat's nightgown," she remarked wittily.* Usually following this is a boner-compounding phrase such as, *And everybody laughed and laughed.* Assuming for the moment that the remark in quotes was intrinsically clever, being told this by the author is insulting to the reader's ability to recognize humor, and makes him put the witticism to special test. If "wittily" is followed by the author's report that his invented audience laughed and laughed, the reader will undoubtedly balk at this sly method of persuasion, and decide himself not to laugh at all, whether it was funny or not. And meantime, regardless of how agreeable, lenient and suggestible the reader may be, his interest has been clogged, if not indeed frozen, and therefore damaged. Almost any reader resents such editorial bossiness and, if he continues to read the story at all, is mistrustful of the author and finds the work less convincing than it should be.

Since this dangerous pot-hole is easily avoided, only the amateur should by all rights be found squirming at its bottom. The best way to get around almost any tricky dialogue technique is to play it down if it is important to play it at all. Obviously, a humorous work of fiction must have a character or characters who speak as well as act in a humorous manner. Taking the foregoing example of a piece of dialogue which is meant, by the author, to be funny (and seems so to him), a more successful rendition might go like this: *"You think you're the cat's nightgown," she remarked, and was pleased to see the grins on at least three of their faces.* The reader may not add a fourth grin to the group (I, for instance, don't) but he won't feel coerced, and can go on reading without stopping to consider whether or not he should have laughed.

Another rock on the rocky road of dialogue is the matter of spacing. Almost all dialogue, especially when presented in long stretches unbroken by any lengthy description or editorial direction other than he-said she-said, depends greatly on the effective insertions of he-saids and she-saids. And it is much more than simply putting these speech credits in the proper places. The reader's attention is jarred if not marred by coming across the he-said placed in an awkward spot, one which breaks the rhythmic flow and possibly the thought. A good ear guards against this, of course, but lacking that, a writer should read copiously and study any good dialoguist's style he comes across. An example of bad and good dialogue breaking might go like this:

> Melvin spoke up. "There is no question in my mind. Ellie is dead."

A more effective presentation would be:

> "There is no question in my mind," Melvin broke in. "Ellie is dead."

Admittedly, there is an almost invisible line of difference between the two, but in the body of a work, reserving the surprise element could make all the difference between reading suspense and conviction and casual acceptance by the reader of the news offered. Further, the very character of Melvin himself is changed by the two different versions. The first might indicate a hitherto timid soul, or a silent, pompous one, finally moved by reasons of his own for stating an unsolicited opinion. And the second Melvin could well be an impetuous man, given to conversation interrupting, and a person of very definite opinions.

Dialogue, the precious bearer of information, plot, and characterization, is, perhaps, most sorely constrained by its limited bridges: the he-saids and she-saids. Since good writing forbids such easy outs as "he laughed," "he shrugged," many a lip has been masticated to the Blue Cross claiming point by authors in search of exactly the right version of "said." Here each is on his own. *Roget's Thesaurus* is practically the only friend. Some writers thriftily compile lists of "said" variants for quick reference when the heat is on, and others simply say to hell with it, and put down said, answered, replied, and let it go. Still others leave the space blank until a more auspicious time comes for reflection and choice—the second draft, say. But this should be the least of any dialogue writer's worries. The important thing is that old journalistic rule about who, what, where, when, etc.

Establishing the order of presentation of such can be studied to advantage in play and movie scripts. My experience in novelizing movie scripts revealed a lot of short cuts—and showed me where to axe out a lot of dead wood that I would never have suspected of even malingering if I had come across such dialogue in a novel or a short story, hiding its decay behind a lot of adroit he-saids and diverting descriptive material.

So to those who find the field quaking under their feet, I would strongly suggest this is the only remedy; the only way to learn that rules were made to be broken: Know the rules first, then godspeed!

Robert Portune

Collaborators Anonymous

"It seems to me," the Unpublished Author said, "that the most difficult task of all is making the reader see what I see."

"Visualization," the Published Author murmured, nodding.

"I beg your pardon."

"Visualization," the P.A. repeated. "That is, the technique one employs to write a scene of a short story or novel in such a manner that the
reader sees what the author sees." The P.A. lit his pipe and settled
himself more comfortably at his desk. "Perhaps, in all honesty, I
should say we make the reader see *more* than we see."

"More?"

"Much more." The P.A. nodded again, smiling at the other's surprise. "This technique of visualization is a joint effort, a collaboration
between writer and reader."

"Are you suggesting that your readers do some of the work on your
novels?"

"A great deal of work." The P.A. made a sweeping gesture with his
hand. "Could you describe this room?"

"I think I could."

"Suppose you begin."

"Well—" The eyes of the U.A. shifted. "I'll start with the bookcase—"

"Shelves of white pine," the P.A. interrupted: "Dimensions, one by
twelve by seventy-two, walnut stained, supported on metal brackets
which are attached to the wall by three-inch—"

The U.A. laughed. "Do you want all that detail?"

"It's in the scene you're observing," the P.A. said dryly. "There isn't
a blank spot within your field of vision. Every book on the shelves has

size, color, a certain composition, a title. There are about three hundred books there, you know. Perhaps you would care to list all the titles."

The U.A. hesitated, and then he shook his head. "If I described every detail, the passage would be too long," he admitted.

"And quite dull," the P.A. agreed. "You might mention a couple of titles, however, to suggest my personality."

The U.A. inspected a row of books, frowning. "The subjects are too varied," he objected.

"Be selective," the P.A. said flatly. He pointed with his pipe. "There's Plutarch—and down there is Tacitus. Select those and you make me a classical scholar. Selectivity is the secret. Here—" He clamped the pipe in his teeth and concentrated for a moment.

On the dark walnut shelves (he said) dusty volumes were crowded with no regard for size or color. Tacitus—Plutarch—all the ancients crammed together in the shadows—

"I don't see any other ancients," the U.A. said.

"Neither do I. But the reader, coming across a passage like this, would instantly collaborate with me. The reader, bless him, would fill out that dusty collection with titles from his own experience. The imagination of the reader seizes on the few details selected by the writer and fills out the scene with his own memories. Otherwise we should be forced to enumerate the flyspecks on the wall or describe the individual tufts of wool in the carpet." The P.A. stretched his arm and drew Plutarch from the bookcase. He said, "Do you recall the anecdote about the sign on the fish market that said FRESH FISH FOR SALE?" He flipped the pages of the book.

"Do you mean the one about the owner erasing the words FOR SALE because everybody knew the fish were for sale?"

"Yes. And then he erased FRESH because everybody knew he wouldn't sell stale fish." The P.A. held his place in the book with a forefinger. "Eventually the sign was blank." The U.A. laughed "Are you suggesting a novel with blank pages?"

"We won't go that far. But I'm suggesting that very few elements of a scene must be put into words, provided those selected are truly important." He opened the book.

> As soon as it was light, [he read] he marched his infantry out of the city and posted them upon a rising ground, from whence he saw his fleet make up to the enemy. There he stood in expectation of the event; but as soon as the fleets came near to one another, his men saluted Caesar's with their oars; and on their responding, the whole body of the ships forming into a single fleet, rowed up direct to the city.

He closed the book with a bang, so that the U.A., who had been listening intently, gave a start.

"Out of that entire scene, Plutarch selected only these bare elements to describe the fall of Mark Antony. How much did you see?"

"Everything," the U.A. exclaimed. "The two lines of galleys approaching each other, their rows of oars dipping into the water—that hillside crowded with Antony's troops—all of them waiting for the clash of ships—"

"How many ships?"

"Oh, hundreds. Jammed with warriors. And then that moment when they saluted each other—swords and shields lifted—oars rising from the water—"

"You're collaborating," the P.A. pointed out. "You're transforming a few well-chosen words into a complete picture, filling in the gaps, painting in the colors, adding the sounds. Every reader does this. And every writer has first visualized his scene and then very carefully erased all of it but the elements that will provoke the reader to collaborate." He returned the book to its place. "The important technique, of course, is the selection. How do you pick out the provocative elements from the mass of detail in every scene?"

"How do *you* do it?" the U.A. asked bluntly.

The P.A. smiled. "First let me explain how I discovered the technique for myself. At the time I was working on my first novel I used to ask my wife to read each day's work. One evening, after I had spent the greater part of my working day struggling with a scene in which one of my characters climbed a flight of stairs, I gave the page to my wife. When she finished reading it, I asked her to describe the scene in her own words. Her description contained so much more detail than mine that I was led to the conclusions we've been discussing." The P.A. pulled the novel from its place between the bookends on his desk. "This is the passage."

> He was breathing heavily when he reached the top of the narrow stairway that led to his office. He was out of condition, winded by a simple walk down Columbus Street, his lungs straining, his thighs aching. He was grateful that George Potter wasn't at hand to see him clutching the shaky bannister for support, catching his breath. George wouldn't understand physical weakness. He would take it as a sign of weakening spirit.
>
> Karl closed his eyes, picturing himself as paunchless, firm-fleshed, with tendons like wire cable. He pictured this dynamic figure bounding up the steep stairway, teeth flashing in an easy smile. If I were ten years younger, he thought with sudden regret. And then he opened his eyes, feeling guilty. He cast an anxious glance at the worn, dark paneling of the second floor landing, as though the wood might echo his lie.

The P.A. stopped reading. "Do you see the stairway?"

"Of course."

"Good. Now let's isolate the descriptive elements." He found them and read them aloud.

Top of the narrow stairway—shaky banister—steep stairway—worn, dark paneling of the second floor landing—wood. He closed the book and pushed it aside.

"I thought there was more than that," the U.A. said.

"Collaboration again. I could have described the type of wood in the banister, or the cracked steps—any number of things, including the dust between the railing posts. My wife saw all of these things anyway."

The U.A. nodded. "I'm beginning to understand what you're telling me," he said. "You say that was your first experience. Perhaps you'll give me an example of what you've done with the technique since then."

"One more passage," the P.A. agreed, taking up his latest novel. "Here are some visual elements I selected for my reader-collaborators to help them picture a cafe."

> Fred could see him near the door [he read], seated at a table, his face hidden in the darkness. Sunlight slanted through the drawn venetian blinds and was scat-

tered by the chair and table legs into a dusty pattern that almost touched the old man's feet. Somehow the presence of the solitary figure added to the empty, unused appearance of the cafe. It was as if the room had never known loud voices, and rough shoving bodies, and the crash of Mr. Silverman's cash register, and the clatter of Dakota behind the long bare mahogany bar. Despite the blast of noise from the radio, there was a cool serenity to the scene, an air of unhurried peace that was almost churchlike. For a moment Fred experienced a sense of wonder. In the whole city, on this golden September afternoon, there seemed but one refuge from trouble and confusion, this shadowy saloon with its worn linoleum and scarred tables and stacked chairs, a white cloth draped across its altar of bottles, a streak of errant sunlight falling across the raised piano as on a pulpit. Like the church of los' souls, he thought: Old Blind Majuh's an' mine.

"I see it," the U.A. told him before he could ask his question.

"You're collaborating again, I'm certain."

"Not very much. I mean, there's a lot of detail there."

"No more than a fraction of the actual scene," the P.A. insisted. "No windows, no doors, no shape of table or chair, almost no color— yet I imagine you visualized these details."

"Yes."

"And placed the cafe in a city, perhaps?"

"Well, of course—"

"And peopled the city, and moved automobiles along its streets and supplied a thousand and one details that no book is long enough to include?"

"In a way, I suppose I did," the U.A. admitted. Suddenly he grinned. "You know, I'm anxious to look into some of the books in my own library—if only to see how much detail is left out of them."

"That's the secret," the P.A. assured him. "Once you realize that your reader is the best collaborator you have, that his supply of memories and experiences will put the finishing touches on your sketch, then you'll begin to develop the technique of choosing the elements of a scene that suit your purpose best."

"There's just one thing," the U.A. said doubtfully. "I mean, will the reader see what I see? I mean, what I really see?"

"More," the P.A. said, as he had said in the beginning. "More than you can possibly imagine. And that," the Published Author told him wholeheartedly, "is what makes the book reviews so interesting."

Don James

Keep It Brief and Blend It In

Description still may be essential to most fiction and nonfiction, but for some time the word has been out to keep it brief and blend it in.

A study of magazines and books published over the last half century indicates that it has been a good many years since many readers have been very interested in long passages of description, heavily larded with adjectives and adverbs, and dedicated to the art of colorful prose. Busy readers in today's world of competitive communication usually look for "the action." They want the story—not lovely prose.

The trend has been to blend description with the action, both in fiction and nonfiction, but this process of blending frequently seems to cause beginning writers considerable trouble.

When do I describe the setting? The characters? The period? Do I describe the setting of the scene first or begin the story? How much should I describe?

There are no set rules. At times all of us must play it by ear. But there are a few accepted practices that make good sense.

Background, action, and characters frequently can be described quickly and effectively in an opening paragraph.

An excellent example is the opening paragraph from the best seller, *Valley of the Dolls,* by Jacqueline Susann, [Bernard Geis Associates, 1966]:

> The temperature hit ninety degrees the day she arrived. New York was steaming—an angry concrete animal caught unawares in an unseasonable hot spell. But she didn't mind the heat or the littered midway called Times Square. She thought New York was the most exciting city in the world.

In less than fifty words the author skillfully sets the scene in New York, during a heat wave, describes Times Square, and introduces a girl who believes that she has just arrived in the most exciting city in the world.

Let's look at another example.

> The little Daimler buzzed out of its garage between the rhododendrons and rolled across the raked pebbles in front of the house. The next Linda saw of it, Jeremy had turned up the gravel path past the tennis court and was heading for the gap in the rosy brick wall which squared the kitchen garden.

This opening paragraph of *Orchestra & Beginners,* a novel by Frederic Raphael [Viking, 1968] performs multiple tasks. In a continuing flow of movement the author describes a setting, creates a milieu, and introduces two characters in fifty five words. Note how description is blended in.

A quick research of newsstands and bookracks will supply writers with dozens of similar examples. The technique is the accepted and not the exceptional. Blend description into the action.

Beginning writers frequently ask, "When do I describe the characters?" Again there is no rule. In fiction there appears to be a satisfactory trend to describe a character as soon as the character is introduced.

Morris L. West sets his first scene in *The Tower of Babel,* [William Morrow and Co., Inc., 1968] through the eyes of a character:

> The watcher on the hilltop settled himself against the gnarled bole of an olive tree, tested his radio, opened his map case on his knees, focused his field glasses and began a slow meticulous survey from the southern tip of the Lake of Tiberias to the spur of Sha'ar Hagolan, where the Yarmuk River turned southwestward to join the Jordan. It was eleven o'clock in the morning. The sky was clear, the air crisp and dry after the first small rains of autumn.
>
> He studied the eastern ridges first . . . .

The author goes on for almost two full pages of description and action through the eyes of the watcher. With the first two words the reader is into the action of the story and the description—background—is blended into the story through the eyes of the watcher.

Leon Uris sets a scene through a character's viewpoint in the first chapter of *Topaz,* [McGraw-Hill Company, 1967]:

> The day was balmy. That certain magic of Copenhagen and the Tivoli Gardens had Michael Nordstrom all but tranquilized. From his table on the terrace of the

Wivex Restaurant he could see the onion dome of the Nimb, saturated with a million light bulbs, and just across the path came a drift of laughter from the outdoor pantomime theater. The walks of the Tivoli were bordered with meticulous set-in flowers which gave a riot of color.

A character might walk to a window, and through description of what he sees the mood of the character may be suggested, or pertinent facts about the setting described.

In two paragraphs, shortly after the beginning of *Airport*, [Doubleday, 1968] Arthur Hailey describes a key character, dresses the stage, and presents some of the problems with a succinct use of description.

Mel, airport general manager—lean, rangy, and a powerhouse of disciplined energy—was standing by the Snow Control Desk high in the control tower. He peered out into the darkness. Normally, from this glass-walled room, the entire airport complex—runways, taxi strips, terminals, traffic of the ground and air—was visible like neatly aligned building blocks and models, even at night their shapes and movements well defined by lights. Only one loftier view existed—that of Air Traffic Control which occupied the two floors above.

But tonight only a faint blur of a few nearer lights penetrated the almost-opaque curtain of wind-driven snow that was piling up new drifts—at the same time that plows were clearing the old. Maintenance crews were nearing exhaustion.

Because we know that Mel is conscious of these things, the descriptions help to define his problems and are part of the action. Hailey is expert in using the technique.

If you must write long descriptive paragraphs, your best bet today may be in the Gothics. Such passages frequently are a great help in creating a mood of suspense, an ominous background, an exotic setting, or unusual circumstances. They should be blended into the story, however, and not stand alone as the author's tribute to purple prose.

When description is necessary, write it well. Use words that describe. "The 'wino' *slouched* away from us." "The horse *pranced* toward us." "The gale *threatened* . . ."

Avoid the passive voice. Instead of: "There was a great quantity of fallen timber on the mountain slope" try "Fallen timber covered the mountain slope." Instead of: "We were forced down by inclement weather" try "A storm forced us down."

Remember that good description observes *all* the senses. Not only do we see the forest setting, but we can *hear* the wind through tree tops, *smell* the frying bacon, *feel* the warm morning sun, *taste* the hot coffee.

Write with nouns and verbs. Shun adjectives and adverbs unless they strengthen your piece. Occasionally they do. Usually you get better emphasis, description, and writing when you rely upon nouns and verbs that do the job for you.

Beginning writers frequently become addicted to adverbs: he said *angrily,* she said *consolingly,* he replied *grudgingly.* Let the dialogue speak for itself. Let the man's words be angry. Let the woman's words console.

An over-abundance of adjectives in any description weakens the material. Adjectives should be used with greatest care. Beware the trite. Learn to use a good figure of speech occasionally.

Check back through the examples above and discover the impressive absence of adverbs. While you're doing it, notice how sparingly adjectives are used.

Avoid qualifiers such as: "He was a *really* honest man." "It was a *truly* beautiful sunset." "It was a *rather* warm day." "The *honest* truth was that . . ."

Occasionally we can give inanimate things personification: "The mountain lifted angry crags to the sky" or "The tree spread its branches over the group."

Also remember that it's a shrinking world. Sometimes a short, identifying description is all we need to set a scene in New York, Italy, San Francisco, or London. Almost everyone has become acquainted with almost everywhere through television, motion pictures, photographs.

Readers want to know the setting in relation to the story and the characters. In other words, we're back where we started. Description may be essential, but the word is out: keep it brief and *blend it in.*

It goes better that way!

Ruth Engelken

Writing with Description

The more I study the trade of the journalist, the more I agree with the writer who said: "There are no dull subjects, only dull writers." The old saw states the same truth a different way: "It ain't what you say, it's the way 'at you say it." Certainly every topic under the sun has appeared in print and will, undoubtedly, continue to do so because every subject is marketable *somewhere;* but whether or not the manuscript ultimately sells *anywhere* depends upon the author's skill with words. While styles in writing just as styles in clothing change with time, the age-old literary giants and the present-day best-selling authors have one thing in common: both have mastered the art of vivid prose.

There are no magic formulas to ensure a neophyte writer the ability to create flesh-and-blood characters or physical descriptions real enough to jump off the page, but there are aids for sharpening visual acuity and, hence, descriptive ability. In his piece "The Summing Up," Somerset Maugham hammers on the head of truth when he says:

> Many writers seem not to observe at all, but to create their characters in stock sizes from images in their own fancy. They are like draughtsmen who draw their figures from recollections of the antique and have never attempted to draw from the living model. I have always worked from the living model.

When assessing his own literary career, Maugham expressed thanks for the fact that he had had medical training. As a young doctor, he not only saw bare bodies which revealed varying bone structures, but he also saw naked emotions stripped to the veneer of respectability. These experiences with raw life made an indelible impression upon the young medic who stored them in the reservoir of his subconscious to be surfaced when needed. He developed early what I believe every serious writer must develop: the ability to see the ordinary extraordinarily well.

When you look at a face, what do you see? If you see in general two eyes with brows, a nose and a mouth, you need your vision sharpened. You need to learn to see as a doctor or, better still, as an artist. (Maugham, incidentally, was both.) You need to see sizes, colors, shapes, and relationships. Maugham took seriously the writing bromide: "Describe the character when you first introduce him." He was able through his meticulous descriptions to create memorable characters. Who can forget his Mildred in *Of Human Bondage?*

> She was tall and thin, with narrow hips and the chest of a boy . . . . She had the small regular features, the blue eyes, and the broad low brow, which the Victorian painters, Lord Leighton, Alma Tadema, and a hundred others, induced the world they lived in to accept as a type of Greek beauty. She seemed to have a great deal of hair: it was arranged with peculiar elaboration and done over the forehead in what she called an Alexandra fringe. She was very anaemic. Her thin lips were pale, and her skin was delicate, of a faint green colour, without a touch of red even in the cheeks. She had very good teeth. She took great pains to prevent her work from spoiling her hands, and they were small, thin, and white. She went about her duties with a bored look.

Or, who can forget his missionary in "Rain"?

> He was a silent, rather sullen man, and you felt that his affability was a duty that he imposed upon himself Christianly; he was by nature reserved and even morose. His appearance was singular. He was very tall and thin, with long limbs loosely jointed; hollow cheeks and curiously high cheek-bones; he had so cadaverous an air that it surprised you to notice how full and sensual were his lips. He wore his hair very long. His dark eyes, set deep in their sockets, were large and tragic; and his hands with their big, long fingers, were finely shaped; they gave him a look of great strength. But the most striking thing about him was the feeling he gave you of suppressed fire. It was impressive and vaguely troubling. He was not a man with whom any intimacy was possible.

Or, who, for that matter, can forget the cameo description of Sadie Thompson, the prostitute, in "Rain"?

> She was twenty-seven perhaps, plump, and in a coarse fashion pretty. She wore a white dress and a large white hat. Her fat calves in white cotton stockings bulged over the tops of long white boots in glace kid. She gave Macphail an ingratiating smile.

Again and again when Maugham first brings a character on scene, he lets us *see* this character. He confessed that studying and analyzing people was almost an obsession.

> Sometimes he found himself looking at them to see what animal they resembled
> . . . and he saw in them all the sheep or the horse or the fox or the goat.

Obviously, Mrs. Davidson, the missionary's wife in "Rain," reminded him of a sheep.

> She was dressed in black and wore round her neck a gold chain, from which dangled a small cross. She was a little woman, with brown, dull hair very elaborately arranged, and she had prominent blue eyes behind invisible pince-nez. Her face was long, like a sheep's, but she gave no impression of foolishness, rather of extreme alertness; she had the quick movements of a bird. The most remarkable thing about her was her voice, high, metallic, and without inflection; it fell on the ear with a hard monotony, irritating to the nerves like the pitiless clamour of the pneumatic drill.

Miss Wilkinson, the spinster governess in *Of Human Bondage,* reminded Maugham of a bird of prey.

> She had large black eyes and her nose was slightly aquiline; in profile she had somewhat the look of a bird of prey, but full face she was prepossessing. She smiled a great deal, but her mouth was large and when she smiled she tried to hide her teeth, which were big and rather yellow. But what embarrassed Philip most was that she was heavily powdered.

While Maugham is perceptive in his descriptive powers, he is by no means unique. All first-class writers have labored to perfect a similar ability. They have learned to take a character's outstanding features and translate them into words. A caricaturist translates these same features into exaggerated squiggles and lines. Like the writer, the caricaturist lifts the extraordinary from the ordinary. Any beginning writer who develops this critical eye gives himself a writing plus. Can the eye be trained to analyze? I think so.

Before you write many different stories, chances are you are going to find yourself hung up on the same labels; all eyes are "brown with amber flects" or all "features are sharply chiseled." One student in a writing class last year gave every main character "cobalt eyes." His fondness for a color has literary precedent: Flaubert wrote largely in blues, and George Moore, the Irish novelist, had a passion for gray.

To keep from stereotyping your own descriptions, broaden your terminologies. What can you say about an eye beside the fact that it is blue, gray, green, hazel, brown, violet or chameloon? You might consider the eye's shape—round, almond, slanted (oriental), elongated, slatted, and so forth. How are the eyes placed—close-set, wide-set, or regularly spaced? Are they deep-set under beetle brows or do they protrude like a bug's? Most likely, neither is the case; but it pays to be aware of differing ocular structures. What about the size of the eyes? Are they large, small or medium with expanded, contracted, or average pupils? Their condition, too, demands attention. Are they healthy eyes —clear, sparkling, with white membrane surrounding the iris? Or are they "sick" eyes—rheumy, blood-shot, mattery, or with yellowed membrane? What about the area surrounding the eyes? Is it dark-ringed or puffy? Are the lids encrusted, or tinted, or outlined? What about the lashes and brows? Are the former long or short, thick or thin, curled or straight, dark or pale, false or non-existent? Are the latter straight or curved, craggly or plucked, penciled or plain, pointed a la Fu Manchu or winged a la Marlene Dietrich? Do they start over the tear duct or do they cover the bridge of the nose, punctuating the face with a long, hairy dash?

Willa Cather in *Paul's Case* took care to describe Paul's eyes:

> His eyes were remarkable for a certain hysterical brilliancy, and he continually used them in a conscious, theatrical sort of way, peculiarly offensive in a boy. The pupils were abnormally large, as though he were addicted to belladonna, but there was a glassy glitter about them which that drug does not produce.

Vladimir Nabokov in *Pnin,* likewise, paid special attention to Liza's eyes.

> Actually her eyes were of a light transparent blue with contrasting black lashes and bright pink canthus, and they slightly streched up templeward, where a set of feline little lines fanned out from each.

Beginning writers generally find the nose more difficult to describe than the eyes, the lashes and brows. I suspect that the problem stems from two sources: the novice's unfamiliarity with names for basic nasal shapes and the limited color range that can be applied to the nose.

Chaucer put a wart on the Miller's nose, Rostand elongated Cyrano's breathing apparatus to ridiculous proportions, and Dickens reddened the beak of Mr. Macawber; what terms remain to define a nose? Many. Let's look first at some basic shapes and perhaps some clue figures that will help you remember them. Broadly speaking, noses are aquiline (hooked like an eagle's—witches); Roman (having a prominent bridge —Dick Tracy); patrician (aristocratic looking); retroussé (turned up); bulbous (shaped like a bulb—W.C. Fields); ski-shaped ("bridgeless" with curved tip—Bob Hope); pug (short, broad, somewhat turned up like the dog's of the same name); flattened (like the prizefighter's); straight; broad; thin; fleshy; or broken. In addition to the shape, of course, the color ranges on the spectrum from off-whites through pinks, reds, and purples (and all the synonyms therefor). The nose's condition also supplies adjectives—pocked, blue-veined, swollen, runny, mottled.

Clever writers have displayed ingenuity in describing noses; James Joyce speaks of "the wings of the nose." Nabokov gives Pnin "a fat glossy nose" and later he has him "put on his heavy tortoise-shell reading glasses, from under the saddle of which his Russian potato nose smoothly bulged." Again, he gives to an old man "a tumefied purple nose resembling a huge raspberry."

The writer wishing to describe lips thinks first of a color and looks toward the red-purple segment of the color wheel—or at least he did until recently. Now, with the off-shades of lipstick so popular among the avant-garde set, he may find himself consulting the yellows or the palest greens and blues. Lips can be full or thin, the Cupid's-bow strongly defined (like Theda Bara's from the days of the *femmes fatales*) or non-existent (like Katharine Hepburn's and Bette Davis'), and the cut of the lips (or more accurately, the mouth) can be wide or narrow. A "generous" mouth connotes a loving, expansive person while a thin-lipped character suggests stinginess or meanness. Teeth could be a topic by themselves. They are sparkling or stained, even or crowded, tiny or buck, double-rowed or missing. The subjects are, moreover, sometimes under-jawed or over-jawed. Today when the writer speaks of his heroine as being gap-toothed he means that a large space exists between two teeth (usually the front incisors). In Chaucer's day the opening had an amorous connotation. When he gave his Wife of Bath a gap-toothed (or gat-toothed) mouth, his readers knew that he was presenting a lustful woman; and, indeed, her admission that she had five husbands would support their premise.

Descriptions of ears, hair, neck, arms, feet, stance, body build, tone of voice, and type of gesture have all been used as character clues by one writer or another. Certainly one of the reasons why beginning writers are urged to read widely is to learn how top professionals write pictorially. Studying the prose of accomplished writers reveals the fact that the most ordinary subject may be made extraordinarily interesting. I recall once being given a piece to read on snail culture and actually enjoying the assignment! The writer had applied the rule: the clearer the subject, the livelier the writing. Few novices could hold a reader's attention with a topic like tooth extraction, but Vladimir Nabokov could, and did, in *Pnin*.

> A warm flow of pain was gradually replacing the ice and wood of the anesthetic in his thawing, still half-dead, abominably martyred mouth. After that, during a few days he was in mourning for an intimate part of himself. It surprised him to realize how fond he had been of his teeth. His tongue, a fat sleek seal, used to flop and slide so happily among the familiar rocks, checking the contours of a battered but still secure kingdom, plunging from cave to cove, climbing this jag, nuzzling that notch, finding a shred of sweet seaweed in the same old cleft; but now not a landmark remained, and all there existed was a great dark wound, a terra incognita of gums which dread and disgust forbade one to investigate. And when the plates were thrust in, it was like a poor fossil skull being fitted with the grinning jaws of a perfect stranger.

No, there is no such thing as a dull subject.

F. A. Rockwell

Making The Scene

An expert has been defined as "someone who knows no more than you do, but who has it better organized and uses slides."

How true this is of the expertly-written published story versus the rejected one! The latter may include ideas and characters as good as those in the professional piece, but it usually does not have the plot-organization or the colorful pictorial quality that scenes give a story and slides give a lecture. Perhaps it wallows in rambling narrative, because its amateur author has forgot that just as one picture is worth a thousand words, one suspenseful, well-structured scene is better than an infinite number of words of exposition.

A story or novel that is an unfolding pictorial drama of crescendoing scenes thrills the reader by giving him the chance to see in-depth action. Then too, he has a sense of actual participation and the excitement of playing a marvelous game with your characters and with you, the author. If he wins the absorption and entertainment he wants, then you win the publishing success you want.

Today's editor buys (because the reader wants) fiction that is *iconographic,* which means representation by pictures or images rather than by narrative expounding of thoughts and ideas.

But haven't pictures always been the protoplasm of good writing? Mankind's first writing was in pictures drawn by those talented enough to record happenings, ideas and objects for their fellowmen and for posterity. Since these beginnings, every society's gifted members continue to record memorabilia in pictures, the symbols for objects and ideas, and words—which became the symbols for pictures. Our electronic Age of Circuitry seems to be revolving the circuit back to our picture-origins. But the great writers have always been persons with the ability to see life graphically and to choose the right words to transmit focused drama to their readers in scene-form.

Many prolific and popular writers play the scene-game, which has been P. G. Wodehouse's method of creating best-sellers for over sixty years. This is his only plot secret: to build a fascinating scene which becomes a magnet for a whole story. He says:

> I like to think of some scene, it doesn't matter how crazy, and work backward and forward from it until eventually it becomes quite plausible and fits neatly into the story. Like in *Something New*, which started with my thinking it would be funny if somebody touched a cold tongue in the dark—ox tongue, I mean, not human tongue—and thought it was a corpse . . . In my *Something New* that's what happens to Lord Emsworth's secretary, Baxter, about halfway through that opus, and it came out smooth as butter after I had got the events leading up to it.

Whether you work like Wodehouse and start with an exciting scene and build your whole story around it, or whether you map out your plot first and then break it down into scenes, each scene must contain:

1. Sharply delineated characters.

2. Clash or conflict that keeps building actively as *something happens.*

3. A time boundary. (The When.)

4. A place boundary. (The Where.)

5. An emotion boundary. (Its own specific mood in the story.)

It may help you to study dictionary definitions of *scene:*

> 1. One of the divisions of a drama; especially: a) A division of an act during which there is no change of place or lapse in continuity of time. b) A part of drama or narrative presenting a single situation, dialogue; an episode. 2. The place in which the action of a story, play, etc. is laid; hence, place of occurrence or action; 3. Something viewed as a whole or as a detached unit, as a sylvan scene, the American scene, (the hippie) scene . . .

Think of each scene as a microcosm in the macrocosm of your entire story. It has a beginning, middle, and end, with a strong reversal of the opening at the closing and with pluses and minuses in between.

The basic problem in Merrill Joan Gerber's "Invitation To The Dance" (October, 1966, *Redbook*) is lack of communication between life-hungry Elaine and her inhibited, stuffy, life-retreating professor-husband, Richard. When he loses the fellowship that would have taken them to Italy, they spend a day at Catalina, where she wants to stay over, dancing, participating in the gaiety and buying a flowered Hawaiian dress (which she hopes will be a maternity frock). He's aloof, wetblanketish, thinks the dresses overpriced and insists on going back to L.A. on the next boat. Look at the plus and minus action (psychological and physical) and reversal in this beautifully-constructed scene. Richard, frowning, and Elaine, disappointed, are waiting for the boat that will take them to L.A. when Mexican mariache musicians sing and play, drawing Elaine into their circle where she dances to their directions:

. . . She spun, she twirled, and the clapping bacame more impassioned. She stamped her feet with the crowd and her blood sang in her ears. She had no idea what the song was about, except that it was about love. And lovers. She knew that much Spanish.

She heard the coins falling about them and saw them flying through the air like falling stars. The song was endless, and each time she made as if to step out of the circle's center, the same smiling Mexican stepped in to turn her faster, till she was spinning like a top.

Above the din of it all she heard dimly the warning blast from the ship's funnel, and the crowd began to fall away and hurry down the pier. The people thinned out, but those who remained clapped louder, and she found herself thinking that she would never be able to stop.

She spun and laughed and clapped, and as she turned, her eyes sped past Richard, now standing almost alone with her and the musicians and the few island people, *himself* clapping loudly and laughing—Richard, out of himself, enjoying something—his muscles flexing under the thin shirt as his arms moved widely, without self-consciousness.

She had known it could be done! Her clapping seemed to be applause for the two of them—they both were enjoying something, and for once, instead of talking she had acted.

Dizzied and exhilarated—by the wine, by the music, by love—she slowed her spinning; the pier and the men rose and fell in waves before her eyes. Gasping, she came to a halt, and tripped and stumbled to where Richard caught her in his arms. The musicians stopped playing and, in a body, bowed and threw her kisses from their lips. A kiss formed in her mouth to send back, but instead she placed it on her husband's lips.

She was smiling so widely she could barely gasp, "We'll miss the boat!"

"Lets stay the night," Richard said, "We can buy you one of those dresses and go dancing."

Elaine, remembering the colored blooms on the Hawaiian dresses, said, "Let's just stay the night. I've already been dancing."

This scene is so typical of Merrill Joan Gerber's dynamic method of unfolding a story in well-constructed scenes, it's easy to understand why her stories are in demand.

When an entire story is told within one viewpoint, it's simple to achieve the in-depth emotional reaction of your protagonist to other characters and events. Extroverted Elaine strives for communication with her introverted husband and tries to make him want life, joy, excitement and a baby as she does. In each scene she tries different methods of approach, with no luck, until this outburst of her pent-up emotions kindles and liberates his.

Make complete scene outlines of professional stories and TV plays and you'll learn the scenic reversal rhythm yours must have. A scene that starts with a plus ends with a minus, etc. It's true always, no matter how new or old the story.

An ancient Armenian folktale, "The Scar" tells of a handsome young Prince shocked by an oracle that says he'll marry a cowherd's daughter whose body is swollen and covered with ulcers. He finds her, stabs her and leaves her for dead, but the stabbing drains the swelling, restores her beauty and, unknowingly, the Prince later marries her, only to discover the abdominal scar and the powers of Fate. Let's look at this folktale as a series of scenes:

Scene 1. From plus to minus: Happy young prince, returning from successful hunt is told by a fortuneteller that he'll marry the sick, swollen-bellied daughter of a cowherd. Shocked but superstitious.

Scene 2. From minus to plus: He goes to the described cowherd's poor shack, finds the unconscious girl exactly as in the oracle, stabs her with his poniard, leaves money for her family and leaves, relieved, thinking she is dead and he has beaten the prophecy. Happily, he has freed himself from Fate, the girl from her misery and her parents from their dire poverty.

Scene 3. From minus to plus: Her grieving parents think she's dead but soon realize she's asleep and on her way to recovery and beauty. The money the prince left makes them wealthy.

Scene 4. From plus to minus: The cowherd builds a magnificent villa which, along with his daughter's great beauty, attracts many suitors, including the prince, who loves, courts, and marries her. When he sees the abdominal scar and learns the truth he realizes that he has not outfoxed Fate, but actually been its instrument. Even though this has a "fairytale happy ending" his ego and self-confidence are taken down a notch or two!

Before you start to write *your* story, block it out into scenes, each of which presents a vivid time, place, mood, conflict, and reversed character-relationships. Be sure that *all* scenes contain these, in addition to which, the opening scene must ask an intriguing question with such powerful suspense that the reader is hooked into reading on.

Make your very first sentence arouse curiosity, like: "You wouldn't think that a New England spinster born over 100 years ago could have said it all. But she did." (Lynne Kaufman's "Wild Nights" in *Ladies' Home Journal*, October, 1967).

Usually the opening question applies more specifically to the story's main characters, as Ray Bradbury's "The Man In the Rorschach Suit" (*Playboy*, October, 1966), which asks why psychiatrist Dr. Immanuel Brokaw, who was "Gandhi-Moses-Christ-Buddha-Freud" to his many patients, deserted his practice and disappeared. Margaret Bonham's "Wish For An Afternoon" (*Good Housekeeping*, August, 1967) probes the emotions of a childless actress, Vera Foster, who is confronted by an adoring teenage fan who turns out to be the natural daughter she gave up thirteen years ago. Elizabeth Spencer's "A Bad Cold" (*New York*, May 27, 1967) asks why a father avoids looking at his children. Jonathan Craig's "The Man Must Die" (*Hitchcock*, March, 1967) arouses our curiosity with its first sentence:

> His hatred for the man in the newspaper photograph was so intense that for a moment the stern, strong-featured face seemed to blur, as if obscured by a pale, pink mist.

As does John Haskin Porter's opening for "Cruel Kiss" (*Cosmopolitian*, August, 1967):

> Now that she was in love, she was aware of only two great fears in her life. One was new, and one was old.

Consider also the opening of Isabel Langis Cusack's "What A Way To Go" (*McCall's*, October, 1967) and the beginning of Maeva Park's "Call To A Stranger" (*Redbook*, August, 1967):

> I waited, my thin, schoolgirl's hand irresolute on the dial. I could imagine the phone shrilling into the night in some unknown house, waking the occupants and arousing terror, perhaps, in some soul as timorous as I am.
>
> "It's so late, I don't think we should," I said feebly.
>
> "Oh, don't be such a worrywart, Melody!" Rae said, her gay laugh whirling through the quiet room. "Bet and I have done this lots of times."

And Hemingway's opening to "The Short, Happy Life of Francis Macomber":

> It was now lunchtime and they were all sitting under the double green fly of the dining tent pretending that nothing had happened.

In addition to suspense, who, where, when and why, the opening sets the flavor of the story's market. This opening from Mary E. Butt's "The Other Wedding" (*Chatelaine*, April, 1967), is feminine in tone:

> Aline, mother of the bride, bought herself back to the present with a jerk. It was shocking that her only daughter's wedding should be eclipsed by this nagging problem.

This one is masculine—a *Playboy* shocker opening (William F. Nolan's "The Pop-Op Caper", October 1967, *Playboy*):

> The room was full of naked blonds. An even dozen of them were sprawled across the blood-soaked Persian rug like so many big, beautiful, broken dolls—and the weasel-faced kid with the wild purple eyes was coming at me, fast, a smoking cannon in each crippled fist. I knew he was kill-crazy. Twelve natural blondes had died under his guns in the last five minutes, and I was next.
>
> The kid was grinning, his thin, scarred lips pulled back from pointy little teeth. God, he was ugly! My arms were useless; he'd already planted a slug in each of them, so I kicked out desperately at him. And missed. He raked the side of my face with one of his irons and I went down hard. Both cannons were aimed at my head.
>
> "Insane purple light danced in the kid's eyes. Then, still grinning, he fired—and my skull exploded into raw, red fire.
>
> At this point, I was either dead or dreaming. And I wasn't dead.

Each opening has a different flavor. "The Other Wedding" is as feminine in style and subject-matter as "The Pop-Op Caper" is masculine, but both have suspense and the sharp basic conflict that will continue throughout the story, to be satisfactorily solved in the final scene.

In two different, October 1967 short-shorts the protagonist is worried about growing older, and each finally experiences Revelation or a Moment of Truth which is shown through symbolism. The grouchy husband in Florence Engel Randall's "First Chill' (*Redbook*) fears that his virility and vigor will end as summer does with the equinox on September 23. (The poor man is obviously suffering from an affliction formerly ignored in womens' fiction: the male menopause.) As the first chill of autumn threatens to terminate summer sports, joys and warmth, he becomes more depressed. His wife is the cheerer-upper, providing the revelation in the final scene:

> I looked at my husband and said very quietly, "You didn't give us the real definition of equinox."
> He was puzzled. "It's the end of summer," he said. "Everyone knows that."
> "It's when the nights and the days become equal," I said. "It's the end of one season but the beginning of another."
> "Oh," he said. "Is that what it is?"
> He brushed my cheek with the back of his hand, and that night when it got very cold, he closed all the doors and the windows and whistled softly between his teeth as he turned up the heat.

In Ralph McInery's "When A Girl Is Twenty-Five" (October, 1967, *Good Housekeeping*), Jane is just as depressed on the birthday that makes her "a quarter of a century old and feeling it." She feels that along life's corridor, the doors that are open to younger girls are closed to her—especially since the man she loves (Matt) is apparently giving her the brush-off. While she still carries the torch for Matt, she keeps refusing invitations from Charlie. The final scene reverses this when, after a frosty phone conversation with the uncaring Matt, she agrees to go to dinner with the genuinely-caring Charlie:

> "Just give me a moment to comb my hair." In the bathroom she stared at her reflection in the mirror. If life is a corridor, there are many doors. The door to her own future, for instance, and she had been keeping it closed. Back in the living room she blew out the candles.
> "Did you make a wish?" Charlie asked.
> "Sort of."
> He held the door open for her and she found herself laughing with him as they went out together.

Every type of story has revelation in its final scene, usually a more realistic or deeper one in a quality than a slick or pulp story. In "Bobby", Joseph Whitehill (*Atlantic Monthly,* May, 1967) bachelor John Dimit is so sad about "the cooling and stilling of his sister, Francy's marriage," to a nice guy and their planned divorce that he takes their twelve-year-old son, Bobby, on a fishing weekend to get him out of the unhappy atmosphere. Throughout marvelous scenes depicting Bobby's brattiness and tyrannizing of John, his willful disobedience, egoism, unnerving curiosity and selfish bossiness, we have a cumulative insight into Bobby as well as the decreasingly patient uncle. The last two scenes show Bobby's deliberate intrusion on John's privacy, interrupting his intimacy with his sweetheart, Kathy Breen (a widow who's also dominated by her selfish children). The final scene begins with Bobby's self-pitying nausea caused by his monstrous overeating and crying about a sunburn (which is the result of disobeying Uncle John) plus other attention-claiming tricks. Note how all builds up to a quality-story-type of revelation:

> "Lord is she *still* here?" Bobby said.
> John was up and at the boy at once. Guiding him by his thin hot arm, John moved him to his bed and forced him down on it. "Here's the Noxzema. Use it yourself. And don't open the door again, hear?" Bobby screamed into his pillow and shook the bed with his trembling.
> John closed the connecting door loudly enough for the boy to hear it over his screaming, and met Kathy standing concerned at the foot of the bed. He kissed her hard, and she inhaled through her nose in surprise. Then he gave her a fresh highball and sat her on the bed beside him. "Hush a minute," he said. The boy's screaming and sobbing came plainly through the door. John took up the telephone and gave the operator a Tulsa number. While it rang many times, John rubbed Kathy between her shoulder blades. "Hello? Hello, Francy? John. You awake? Yes, I know it's late. Goddamnit . . . Listen, Francy. Listen. I know what's wrong with your marriage . . ."

The revelation in quality fiction is often the reverse of that of commercial stories. Whereas the women's slicks show a parents' quarrel calmed by their mutual love of a child and thus blaze forth the corny premise "A little child shall lead them" this revelation is more honest and timely in our Age of Permissiveness which produces monsters like Bobby: "A little child shall lead them into misery . . . or divorce." Here we also have the added revelation that subjective emotional involvement makes us unable to diagnose our troubles as well as someone on the outside who has the advantage of objectivity.

Explanation must also come in the final scene, tying up all the knots and loose ends. Always leave important points unexplained throughout the action to rivet reader-attention to the culmination where all is explained. Throughout Gerald Green's *Playboy* story, "The Dispatcher" (August, 1967) the military designation M.A.C.E. works magic and plays havoc, impressing an array of characters and affecting plot action until the final touch:

> "Colonel, did you ever hear of an outfit called M.A.C.E? Just after the war?"

"M.A.C.E.? Yes, I remember it. It was obsoleted a long time ago. We tried it out briefly. A pilot project, a really primitive one. We were just sort of fiddling around in those days."

"What did the letters stand for?"

"Military and Civilian Enterprises. Nothing mysterious about it."

"It was abandoned?"

"Naturally. We've got more sophisticated systems today. Data programming, circuitry. The whole operation is computerized. I must say, somebody in Washington is doing a marvelous job. M.A.C.E.! My goodness, I haven't thought about that old one-horse operation in years!"

In addition to revelation and explanation, you can pack into your culminating scene a surprise that is credible according to the characterization and story development, but really unexpected. There's a good one in "Room 312" by G. L. Tassone in *Playboy* (August 1967). Brutal, lascivious, stingy, fat, and sloppy Sam Webster owns a run-down hotel which is discovered to have a magic room, 312. Whoever occupies it disappears, leaving no trace. Sam exploits it, renting it to people who want to get rid of someone and eventually uses it to get rid of his own fat, middle-aged wife, Hilda. Later, he's amazed to see her dancing in a chorus at the Grove Theatre as she looked thirty years ago. She is slim, lovely, and dancing as she always wanted to do before her marriage. Sam, now certain that room 312 reincarnates a person into the youthful achiever of his lifelong ambitions, goes into the magic room expecting to become a vigorous, virile football player. Here's the surprise:

> . . . He turned the key in the lock and went into the dark room. He lay on the bed. He waited. Occasionally, he looked at the luminous dial on his watch. Football, coeds, crowds of screaming people were all busy in his head.
>
> Suddenly, there was a blinding light and the loud blare of music. He was upright and he could feel his arms and legs moving. Finally, he could make out faces through a white glare of light. His arms and legs were still moving violently. There were attractive young men and women all around him. They were all dancing. He looked down at his feet. His young, handsome legs were keeping time to the music. He saw it all clearly. They were dancers. They were all dancing. Sam Webster was dancing in the show at the Grove Theatre.

To be sure that your final scene has these triple features of revelation, explanation and surprise, plan and write it first, adding them as frosting to the five "must's of all scenes: sharp characterization, conflict, the where, the when, and emotional tone. Plan variety in the scenic content so that each moves the story forward without repeating what another scene has already accomplished. Since all scenes may share the story's fundamental conflict, you must move each scene in a different direction—if one ends in *plus,* the next ends with *minus.*

The conflicting entities may be opposing characters (hero versus villain or antipodal ideas.) In many ancient classics Good and Evil—or God and the Devil—vie for possession of the hero's soul. In one scene, one wins but that one loses in the next. Obviously, this creates a suspense teeter-totter that keeps the reader guessing which will eventually triumph.

This formula still holds. In fact, the old morality play trick of making opposing values of the characters, appeared in commercial fiction as recently as the August 1967, *Redbook* in Isaac Bashevis Singer's "A Match For A Princess". In this story Good Luck (Mazel) fights Bad Luck (Shlimazel) for possession of the hero's fate. You'll be wise to graft onto this basic pattern your own original characters, conflicts and timely problems like the generation gap, civil rights, international peace, a political subject for a political year or subjects slanted for a definite magazine or market. Clarify a strong, underlying conflict that forms different explosions in different scenes. Hugh B. Cave has published several stories treating a parent's inner conflict between suspecting his teenage child or trusting him.

In Joan Williams' "Paria" (McCall's, 1967) the two entities vying for Ruth Parker's soul are her need to drink, versus resistance to the temptation to drink. Ruth Parker feels rejected by her noncommunicative sixteen-year-old daughter, Cynthia, her openly disapproving husband, Dean, and the hostile ladies in her bridge club. Each scene in which she is frowned upon leads to her increased self-pity, which leads to more drinking. She feels that her little son, Peter, too young to understand or disapprove, is her only ally. A scene that starts with an emotional "plus"—her happy dancing with Peter—ends with a "minus"—husband Dean's breaking it up, bawling her out and banishing her.

> ... she was singing about loneliness to Peter when Dean arrived ... Peter was laughing. She was dancing with him about the dining room, holding him at eye level, as if he were her partner, moaning as a blues singer would, "Who cares for starlit skies—when your lovvv-er has gone," and together they made so much noise that they heard neither Dean's car nor his entrance into the house.

He suddenly stood in the dining room, and she thought he was sick. Pale, with shadows beneath his eyes, he crossed the room in two strides and set Peter down, demanding to know what she was doing with the child up at ten-thirty. Peter, already in pajamas, scuddled away, and she listened to his bedsprings as he jumped into bed. The suddenness of having him snatched away had thrown her against the wall. She remained there, dizzy and panting, but laughing so hard, still, that she staggered against the dining room table.

"Go to bed instantly," Dean said.

"Why should I go to bed?" she said proudly, and went from the room upstairs. "Just because you're a square," she said and, suddenly feeling like yelling, shouted: "A *square* who has one drink before dinner doesn't mean other people can't have two . . ."

Obviously, Ruth's self-pity and her feeling that she's right and that Dean is wrong, will lead her to increased drinking. Here's a scene that moves from "minus" to "plus". After a bridge-luncheon fizzled by her tippling, she drinks herself into a stupor and falls asleep.

. . . Cynthia tugged at the covers, saying, "Mother, where's Peter?"

She sat up, and in the dressing-table mirror saw a woman in a disarranged satin slip, with tousled hair and swollen eyes. What day, what time was it? She had overslept and would be late getting breakfast again.

"Mother, where is Peter?" Cynthia said.

"Isn't he in bed?" Have you waked him?"

Then Cynthia screamed, "It's almost seven at night! Is he at someone's house?"

Untangling the bracelet, she stood unsteadily. Cold swept along the floor and covered her bare feet. She thought of the hour she had gone to bed; it was then that Peter should have come home. There was nothing to say but the truth: "I don't know where he is"

Thinking of Peter in the snow, she realized he was still almost a baby. Why hadn't she realized before? The night was enormous and dark, cold and snowing.

Cynthia—her child, too—had tears running down her face. "Mother how could you not have watched Peter?" she said.

Dressed, she went downstairs, her shoes in one hand, holding the bannister with the other. In the hall, she had put on her shoes, thinking she would have to call the police, and in that moment saw what they would see, coming in. There was the table full of dirty dishes, the salad dissolved, a cat eating the cottage cheese. The kitchen smelled of liquor, and there stood the empty vodka bottle and the four drained glasses. In a house where children lived and a husband was soon due, no one had started dinner. It struck her enormously that she was responsible for Peter's life. If he had been killed, hurt, maimed, frozen, no one should ever forgive her. No excuse would ever do.

"What are you going to do?" Cynthia asked.

I'll have to call the police," she said, her hand on the phone. But at that instant, it rang, and a neighbor spoke, her voice distant, reserved, saying she had seen Peter out in the cold, without his boots, and had brought him inside, thinking surely Mrs. Parker would be home soon.

She motioned with a finger point for Cynthia to put on her coat and whispered where Peter was. Tears were in her eyes, and Cynthia holding her boots, hesitated, then hugged her in relief. "My daughter's coming right over," she said, her voice clearing of its final thickness. She apologized, but realized from the silence at the other end of the phone that she could not win back Mrs. Goodwin, who, from observation, had formed an opinion of Peter's mother. But those close to her could see her change, she thought.

In these preceding scenes, the author has pointed in antipodal directions, one toward increased alcoholism, the other toward reform. The crisis shock of Peter's neglect produced Ruth's regeneration, which is not realistic, considering the nature of the problem, so we need a final scene which adds a new idea: the alcoholic's recognition of her problem, her willingness to blame herself and not others for her misery, and her desire to seek help. By the time Dean comes home she has managed to clean up the mess, start cooking dinner and muster up the courage to tell him how her drinking loused up the bridge-luncheon and the whole day. For the first time in the story she admits guilt:

"I drank too much and went to sleep," hesitantly; but his eyes widened in perception. "And Peter got lost, but we found him. I don't want it to happen again."
"You want to stop drinking?"
"Yes, but I can't."
"How do you know that?"
"Because if you weren't here, I'd have a drink now."
Crossing the room, he put his arms about her; but love could not restrain her tomorrow, and she thought how awful that something else could be stronger.
Dean said they would find help, and she went on cooking while he washed his hands. In other rooms, she heard the children moving about, getting ready for supper. To make life exciting, she had escaped it altogether . . .

How many scenes should a story have? I wish there were a pat answer, like one scene for each 1,000 words, but there is no set number. It all depends on the story action required and the market (men's stories and pulps usually like more movement and more scenes than women's slicks or quality stories. But no matter the length or number of scenes, each must reverse action and character-relationships from the beginning to the end, and must contain the five ingredients: sharply defined characters, crescendoing conflict, a time boundary, a place boundary, and an emotional boundary.

Never write any fiction until you have first worked out a thorough blueprint of the scenes, and you'll blueprint your way to more steady selling success!

Fred Grove

Scene-Test Your Story

I've heard impatient beginning writers scoff at the dramatic scene as pedantic and artificial, when, instead, it is an indispensable and rewarding device which can be mastered with steady practice.

Advantages of the scene are numerous. It provides structure and continuity to your short story or novel. It takes care of chapter breaks, one of the frequent laments of the struggling young novelist. It advances character and plot, and the transition between scenes shows pas-. sage of time, for time must pass for characters to change believably.

The formula of the dramatic scene is a reliable way to test your story as you go along. Perhaps you begin to sense that nothing is happening. If you check your story against the scene, you'll probably find what is wrong. Maybe there's too much agreement and not enough active opposition. Maybe there is no purpose in the scene you *think* you are writing. Maybe your character is waiting for something to happen instead of attacking his problem. Maybe there is no menace or threat to him.

As a suggestion, place this formula near your typewriter and memorize it:

> 1. *Meeting*—of the two forces involved in the *conflict*. Remember the two forces or persons must clash. There must be emotion.
> 2. *Purpose*—make every scene have a purpose.
> 3. *Encounter*—containing these possible elements: attempts—to interrogate or seek information; to inform, or convey information; to overcome by argument or logic, to convince; to persuade; to influence, impress; to compel.
> 4. *Final Action*—win, lose or quit.
> 5. *Sequel or Aftermath*—(a. state of affairs; b. state of mind)—which leads into your next scene.

You have noticed that the first three elements in the *Encounter* present appeals to reason, the next two to emotion, and the last to force.

An example of a strong scene could involve the current movement to banish capital punishment. A young man is about to be executed for murder. Members of a state Pardon and Parole Board have recommended commuting his sentence to life in prison. The governor refuses to follow the board's recommendation.

So you can imagine this scene:

Meeting—between the chairman of the board and the governor in the state capitol.

Purpose—of the chairman is to convince the governor to change the prisoner's death sentence to life imprisonment. Why? Because the chairman feels the convict has been rehabilitated; because he feels it is morally wrong to take a person's life; because he believes capital punishment is ineffective as a deterrent to crime.

Encounter—as arguments sway back and forth. Furtherance and hindrance. The governor says the courts have decided the issue; that he has taken an oath to uphold the laws of his state. Tempers flare.

Final Action—again the governor rejects the board's recommendation.

Sequel—the board chairman leaves in anger, determined he will start urging members of the state legislature to repeal capital punishment. This points toward the next scene.

Thus, you see the *sequel's function is to demonstrate the character's response to what has just happened. It also activates his purpose for the next scene and forms the link or transition between the scenes.*

The late W. S. Campbell, who founded the professional writing program at the University of Oklahoma years ago and was an authority on the scene, described three kinds of scenes, each taking the form of a struggle to overcome or avert one of three things: an obstacle or barrier, an antagonist, or a disaster. For example, the off-duty policeman cannot arrest the criminal; the obstacle is the lack of a revolver. The wagon train cannot escape the Comanches; the barrier is the flooded river.

The second kind of scene, in which your character is up against a deadly human antagonist, is the one used most. Here human motives are involved. Conflict between persons is always effective.

In the third type of scene, your character is trying to avert some threatening disaster. An airman volunteers to help clear a Viet Nam air base of unexploded bombs. Or there is flood or fire or disaster to fortune or honor. Sometimes a man's efforts to prevent disaster are more interesting than his struggles to overcome an obstacle or an antagonist.

In your dramatic scenes you need: a contrast of characters; and you *must* place your characters at cross-purposes, which stirs the old warning that nothing is more dull than dialogue of agreement. Furthermore, it will increase reader interest if you select characters who, by the very nature of differing backgrounds and values, are unable to understand each other or agree at the outset. A good example of this is found in C. S. Forester's *The African Queen*—Rose Sayer, the missionary woman, and Charlie Allnutt, the gin-swigging cockney mechanic, and their struggles for survival in an African jungle.

Any attempt to carry out the purpose of a scene is a *furtherance,* and every effort to block that purpose is a *hindrance.* A good scene shows an alternating of each, a back-and-forth rhythm of advance and rebuff toward the purpose, in which one character is striving to accomplish something and the other is striving to prevent it. You see this vividly in crisp, face-to-face dialogue, or in a desperate physical struggle between two men, as first one gains the advantage, then the other.

Begin your short story or novel sometimes with a scene instead of a description. I used a scene to open a short story called "Be Brave, My Son" (published in *Boys' Life* and later chosen for a Braille edition of *Boys' Life* published by the Clovernook Printing House for the Blind). Horse, a slim Comanche youth, is aboard a train speeding him and other Plains Indians to prison in Florida. Time: the 1870's. The train is now east of the Mississippi River. Here is the beginning:

> In the smothering heat of the railroad coach, Horse breathed smoke and cinders. Beyond the window the white man's strange world was passing. He watched with faraway eyes, thinking of graceful brown hawks sailing across a bright sky and of blue-hazed mountains rising above sweeping folds of fragrant prairie.
> He turned. The guard was tramping down the aisle, scrutinizing each Indian and making marks in his black book.

Horse's *purpose* is to escape and somehow make his way home to the Southwest. He must use force to achieve his *purpose.* Not only must he free himself of the manacles around his wrists and manage to flee the train unobserved, but his resolve weakens when he thinks of leaving his friends, probably forever. (*hindrance.*) But Horse acts. He tears his slender hands free of the cuffs. (*furtherance.*)

> Then, almost against his will, he drew his blanket in front of his lowered head and plunged through the glass window.

A *hindrance* follows. He is stunned, unable to rise at once. Hearing boots pounding the roadbed, he pushes up and runs reeling into the darkness. (*final action.*) The *sequel* follows, pointing to the scene to follow:

> Not until he was panting within a thicket did he understand that he was actually free. (*state of mind.*) Later, when the lanterns disappeared, and the train chugged on, he turned his face to the west, following the trail of the iron road.

Sometimes you have only one of the elements of the *encounter;* and, obviously, only one of the three *final action* forms can occur in one scene. Also, *meeting* may precede *purpose.* But, above all, think in terms of purpose and conflict for a scene.

With purpose but without conflict you would have an *incident,* which is useful chiefly as a transition from one dramatic scene to another or as a means of characterization. This could come about when two friends meet on the street. One seeks information, which his friend supplies without opposition.

How do you go about creating a dramatic scene? My suggestion is that you practice thinking in scenes, of seeing your stories in segments of scenes. That you visualize a scene before you begin writing it. Then rough it out on paper.

Ask yourself questions. Is this plausible? List all possible purposes. What is the hero trying to do? Why is he in this strange predicament? Am I making it tough enough for him? Would a person act or react in this manner? Is his motivation strong enough? What is his state of mind? Is something important at stake? Imagine the expressive gestures, the characteristic gestures.

You can do this on a page of copy, more or less. Don't apply critical judgment until you've put down everything you can. Then start writing.

If you have a *meeting* or a *purpose, you have a beginning. Often the purpose will suggest the meeting. Many scenes fail for lack of a purpose simply because the writer hasn't given a character a goal to achieve. There is nothing worthwhile for the principals to struggle over.*

Other scenes fail because the beginner passed too swiftly through the steps, because he did not unfold the dramatic potential for which the reader was waiting, because he neglected to squeeze all the emotion from the situation. A long scene, such as in a novel, enables you to exercise all the elements in the encounter and develop characterization to the utmost.

Try the dramatic scene as a guide. If its structure is unfamiliar to you, it will take you places you haven't been before. It will give form and direction to your writing and plotting—provided, of course, you are willing to undergo the necessary honest self-discipline required to learn its possibilities.

R. V. Cassill

Plot: Its Place in Today's Fiction

A plot is one among several of the unities in fiction. Readers never see it in a pure state, for in a story it is trimmed, compromised, and adjusted to other elements for the sake of the unity of the whole.

However, in some stories, plot is flaunted on the surface while other ingredients are disposed of in brisk, offhand fashion. If such stories are usually low grade, we cannot make a rule that declares them all to be, for emphasis on plot should depend on the conception, on what the author has to say.

Sometimes the plot is so subordinated to other things that its function as an expressive or unifying device is evidently of small importance. It is then merely a hanger, on which more valuable goods are displayed. In some other cases—and this is often true of first-rate contemporary work—the plot is so elaborately interwoven with the other threads of fiction that its presence is only detectable under a determined scrutiny.

I can imagine, for instance, that a sensitive and responsive reader of Jean Stafford's "In the Zoo" might receive much of the impact of the story and much of its meaning without becoming quite aware that it *had* a plot. Such a reader might say, "It's just an account of two women recalling a painful stretch of their childhood. It's another of those *New Yorker* stories that depend for their effect on being so very well written and so candid in rendering miniature grief."

For such readers we may assume that the plot has done its work without being detected. And perhaps there is no higher tribute to the author's skill than to say she has so successfully hidden her principal expressive means.

The plot is obscured in this story because it does not open when the story opens. The first scene of the story is part of the end of the plot action. It is only in the flashback, beginning with a mention of the town of Adams, that our attention is subtly diverted back to the point in time where the plot may be said to begin.

It does violence to a beautifully integrated story to seize the inwoven thread of plot and pull it out to examine it in isolation. But that may be the briefest way to demonstrate that it is really there.

Roughly, the plot of "In the Zoo" is this: Two orphaned sisters come to a small town to live with a woman who runs a boardinghouse. The woman, Mrs. Placer, makes them miserable by her tyrannical and self-righteous supervision. *So,* they seek a partial escape by making friends with Mr. Murphy, a small-town caricature of Saint Francis, the patron saint of animals. *Because* he recognizes what they must suffer at Mrs. Placer's hands, he gives them a dog to ease their loneliness. *Because* any natural affection for man or beast seems to Mrs. Placer a criticism of her witchy puritanism, she destroys the relationship between the girls and their dog by corrupting the poor beast into her own image. *So* when Mr. Murphy learns that his charity has been frustrated by the witch, he goes with the children in the quixotic hope of setting things right once more.

Because Murphy has dared rebel against her sly (but powerful) tyranny, Mrs. Placer sets the corrupted dog to kill his monkey, Shannon.

This wanton slaying *motivates* the half-demented, good old man to poison the dog. *Because* the sly Mrs. Placer has tricked him into a realm of action where he is insecure and where his justifications are undemonstrable, Murphy is the chief victim of the rebellion against her. He has killed one of the animals he is bound to love because he could discover no other means of striking at the invulnerable Mrs. Placer.

Because the girls have been committed to witness his terrifying defeat, they in their turn make a final submission to the insuperable nastiness of their guardian. ("Flight was the only thing we could think of, but where could we go?") If Mr. Murphy was in the wrong—and obviously Mrs. Placer had put him in the wrong by forcing him into killing the dog—then the girls, whose most generous sentiments allied them with him, were in the wrong, too. (". . . Gran . . . held us trapped by our sense of guilt.")

So, because they are trapped by guilt, the girls are transformed into accomplices of the woman and the spirit of denial that has made them suffer so much. However much they may resent being accomplices and grieve that they have come to this, they must recognize what they are.

The action of the plot ends with this recognition.

There is the plot of Miss Stafford's story in its bare essence. It seems to me a powerful and terrible plot—in Aristotle's phrase, it inspires "pity and terror" even in the unadorned form I have given it.

Is it not a grim parable of all rebellion, a sort of pessimistic revision of the story of Don Quixote—since here the quixotic Mr. Murphy hardly accomplishes more than to deliver his followers to the evil enchantress? In Cervantes' novel there is more than a suggestion that, after all, the knight of the rueful countenance redeems his world by the indomitable spirit of his folly.

Whoever has seen the shape of modern war will find this plot a poignant reminder that in crusading to kill the tyrants of our century, soldiers of the good cause have been most notably successful in massacring the tyrant's victims.

Yes, this "hardly noticeable" plot turns out to be strong enough in all reality once we take the pains to isolate it.

But how and why did the author obscure it as she has? First of all, how?

1. By separating the opening of the story and the beginning of the plot action.

2. By allowing the plot action—which is firm and continuous in itself—to fade out of focus now and then. The reader is given a close, clear view of part of it. Other parts, and perhaps the most telling parts, come to the reader obliquely or only by the inferences to which he is compelled. In fact, the most important phase of the plot, the transformation of the children into accomplices in Mrs. Placer's evil, is not as directly told as the part about Mr. Murphy and the monkey.

3. By shifting the pace of the narration so there is little connection between it and the pace of the plot action. By allowing the story to branch off into tangential scenes and half-scenes that do not belong in

the casual sequence of plot action. The episode in which Mr. Murphy throws a stone at the boy teasing his parrot is wonderfully effective—but quite outside the plot. So are some of the bits about Mrs. Placer among her boarders.

4. By establishing a tone in the opening and concluding scene (the "envelope" around the long flashback) that is at ironic variance with the grim fatalism of the plot.

Now, why were these displacements of focus and emphasis on the plot made? (In finding justifications for the special adjustments made here, we can get some insight into the process of composition. We can never know, of course, how many of the author's choices were rationalized, how many were intuitive. We can make an informed guess as to which could have been dictated by reasoned controls imposed on the material.)

1. The opening of the story provides some engrossing hints about the over-all significance of the action to which we will presently turn. Since the scene of the opening is continuous in time with the scene at the end, it actually represents the resolution of the plot action, though the reader is not in a position to see that clearly until he has finished the story. In a way that provides suspense, the scene is fashioned to hint where the action is tending until such time as the action declares its own goal. See, here is the punctured target, the author says. Now I will take you up the range and re-enact the firing of the shot that struck it.

2. The action of the plot is really a very extensive one. To have kept it all in sharp focus—by developing scenes and groups of scenes—would have meant to build it into a much longer work. It might have been a novel. It would have had to be a novel if the author had not so magnificently solved the problem of compression by showing us, in one episode, the pattern that was essentially repeated in all those imaginable episodes treated sketchily or left to our imagination. Once the encounter between Murphy and Mrs. Placer has taken place, we are made to understand the fatal pattern. Then the task of the rest of the story is merely to establish that this pattern was inevitably repeated on a larger scale. In saying that the transformation of the children into accomplices is the most important phase of the plot, we are not saying that it represents the kind of material that could be given concrete rep-

resentation. The transformation is subtle—the sort of thing which, in reality as in fiction, we grasp better through inference than through observation of concrete acts. Therefore, the author wisely left that process to be inferred once the pattern it must follow was made clear.

3. Given the decision to leave much of the plot to be gathered in by the reader's inferences, it would seem necessary to surround that part of it which is demonstrated concretely with a profusion of fragments suggesting the complexity of appearances beneath which the essential pattern was repeated monotonously. All the departures from the main plot line serve as a kind of compensation for the author's tactic of leaving so much of the plot unstated. She relies on the reader's imagination to fill in the empty stretches. At the same time, the reader has to be stimulated to imagine a turbulence and variety to prevent his conceiving that the plot worked as a subhuman mechanism would. Life does present a kaleidoscope of appearances to our eye, even when our eye has been conditioned to read a simple significance into all those that fall within a given range. The shift of pace is another tactic of compensation for having compressed so extensive an action into a short story.

4. In a somewhat different direction the flip, mocking, less-than-tragic tone of beginning and end help to place the "bleak tragedy" of the flashback in a context that we can accept as representative of whole lifetimes. The grimness has indeed spread through a pair of lives like a stain. We are supposed to believe that everything the sisters have experienced has been to a degree contaminated by the stamp Mrs. Placer put on their character. And yet—could we believe that there were not occasions of better and worse, of laughter as well as despair, in the lives that are the subject of the story? *To a degree* the curse was always present. By indicating that the degree has been variable, the author has actually strengthened the force of her statement, since she has taken these pains to disarm our skepticism. We might indeed be shocked and impressed by a bare, straightforward presentation of the plot. But if it were bare, wouldn't we keep some reservations and tend to protest, "Oh, it couldn't have all been *that* bad"? By foreseeing such reservations, perhaps the author has gained some advantage over them. Has been able to say, "Still, worse than you would like to think . . . ."

Indeed, all the adjustments and subordinations of the plot in this wonderful story seem to me to strengthen it. "What's lightly hid is deepest understood," says a poem of Richard Wilbur's. Here the light camouflage and the significant gaps in the plot help bring it alive and burning into the reader's heart.

Another bit of praise for this deft management would be to point out that it contributes to the lifelikeness of the story. Lifelikeness has no direct connection with plot. But it is a virtue in itself, and a story from which a plot obtrudes awkwardly is not likely to commend itself as a true picture of life as we experience it.

One more thing—at a certain point of understanding what the author has done here, we can feel a purely aesthetic appreciation of her skill. Quite apart from the content of fiction, its movements, subordinations, the establishment and dissolving of formations, and its harmonious progress can give us the kind of satisfaction we get in watching a well-rehearsed group of dancers on a stage. This mechanical control exercised by an author might be called the "choreography" of fiction.

Is it better to talk about a thing for a while before recognizing the need to define it? Or better to define it first and then try to respect the definition in subsequent discussion? I am not sure. I know that in the ordinary course of things we do both, and that in the ordinary course of things we edge—not always directly, but sometimes like a boat tacking into the wind—toward broader and more useful understandings.

I realize I have been talking about plot without yet defining it. And the truth is that I was a bit wary of attempting a definition too soon for fear that the way I defined it might rouse some defensive prejudices that would hinder communication.

Since each of use began to read fiction we have known what plot is. Alas, we seem to know it is different things.

Somehow among readers and critics—and among teachers of fiction writing, too—there have grown up "pro-plot" and "anti-plot" factions. The pro-plot people are bent on condemning fiction which, according to their measure, lacks plot. (It is distressing to find that by *plot* they often mean no more than a particular plot, often closely associated with a standard kind of subject. For instance, in a western story unless the plot involves a conflict between a gunslinging stranger and a corrupt, wealthy landowner, there might appear to be no plot at all.)

The anti-plot people contend that plot is a mechanism that destroys the life in sound fictional material. They are right only in that this *sometimes* happens. Of course it need not. When plot is properly integrated with the over-all unity, it can be first among those elements that give the illusion of life to fiction. For people are actors. Their nature is action.

And plot—plot is no more and no less than a causal sequence of action.

Note that it is not a mere sequence. We have no plot when we say, "Bertha tinted her hair red. That night she dined alone." We have a plot—or rather the small beginnings of one—when we say, "Being too timid to let her friends see that she had dyed her hair, Bertha dined alone that night." The causal connection between dyeing the hair and dining alone is established in the second example, as it is not in the first.

Yet we must note, and be very clear about it, that the causal connection between parts of the whole plot action is very often not stated explicitly. When we outline a plot in isolation from a story, the connections will probably be obvious. When we integrate a plot with other elements, the connections will often be shown indirectly, principally by the altering situation, intent, or emotion of the characters.

In paraphrasing the plot of "In the Zoo," I italicized the words expressing causal connections. However, in the story itself one looks in vain for such drab mechanical linkages. The plot has been, so to speak, dissolved in the fictional medium. But it has not lost its coherence. The links between the parts of the action are all the more impressive for being revealed in the behavior and emotion of the characters instead of being stated by the author.

By supplying and italicizing the word *because* in my paraphrase I meant to demonstrate not only the links of causality, but the continuity from beginning to end of that causal chain.

This continuity is essential to the unity of a plot, but something more is required, a rounding out of the sequence. It is easiest to comprehend plot unity if we look at examples and think of the unity as being rounded out when the questions raised at the beginning of the action are all sufficiently answered by the action that follows. In George P. Elliott's short story, "Sandra," the rather insignificant plot comes to its natural end when the narrator has made a trial of each of the principal choices that follow the purchase of a female slave. In "The Best of Everything" by Richard Yates, there is a resolution of the plot action when Ralph demonstrates the place on his scale of values that will be occupied by the woman he is going to marry. The action of "That Lovely Green Boat" by William Berge, is rounded out when the young people destroy the fragile loveliness that rested momentarily in their keeping.

After we sense the natural "rounding out"—the unity—of some passage of causally related action, we see that its part in the general unity of the story comes from its relation to the needs, desires, and purposeful or capricious choices of characters. The original step in the action of a plot very frequently comes as the response of a character to the situation he must confront. The stimulus provoking the response is what we call *motivation.*

The significance and complexity of motivation may cover a vast range of intensity. If my leg itches, I am moved to scratch it. If Othello becomes suspicious of his wife, he is moved to resolve his suspicions and know the truth. But however important or unimportant the motive, we can hardly think of the action of a plot without acknowledging that it proceeds *through* the passionate decision of characters.

This is true whether the author chooses to use much space in examining the motives of his characters or leaves them to be inferred by the reader. We must never judge the profundity of fiction merely by the author's profundity in examining motives. Their best usage is in serving as the link between character and action. The question of how much motivation the author must supply seems to me best answered by the answer to another question: How much is needed to make the action proceed meaningfully out of the characters?

Criticism—and this means your judgment as you are writing a story as well as your estimate of someone else's work—must draw some fine measurements in determining sufficient motivation for a plot action. We know from personal experience that some things seem to "just happen." These include not only the things that happen to us, but those actions for which we must assume full responsibility before the law and before God. Not all of life, by any means is shaped by those actions we undertake because we have a reason to. Yet, at the other extreme, the picture of an action that unrolls without being checked or furthered by the full choice of one or more characters seems altogether inhuman and therefore not the proper concern of fiction.

There are absolutely no prescriptions for the proper degree of motivation in any particular story. At the misty border where character melts into action and action stimulates changes in character, the author has a particular responsibility for declaring his own view of life. In Thomas Hardy's novels, motives do not count for much against the sweep of an impersonal fate that drives his characters against their will. (In *Jude the Obscure* the chief character quotes Aeschylus: "Things are as they are and will proceed to their destined end." What people may wish or attempt will have little consequence, Hardy seems to say in most of his novels.)

I am afraid it is not so easy to find, in the literature of this century, examples of the opposite extreme. The effectiveness of the personal will is not a theme to which most contemporary writers incline. But it is possible to find, in the novels of Jane Austen, perhaps, or Dickens, or George Eliot, a considerably closer tie between personal motive and the consequence of action.

Plot is a device of expression as well as a means of unifying the subject material of a story. It expresses the author's belief about the nature of human destiny, the importance of will in determining the shape of events.

An author may "make the action come out" this way or that way. Strictly within the possibilities of the material, Jean Stafford in her story, "In the Zoo," might have structured her plot so it would have made an entirely different total statement. Suppose that, instead of causing Murphy to poison the corrupted dog Caesar, the author had told us Murphy stole him back from Mrs. Placer and disappeared into the mountains with him. Evidently this sequence would have suggested to the engrossed girls a way out—a general vision of rebellion and escape —that they could hardly have construed as morbidly as they did the poisoning. Therefore they would have been diverted to a future less bitterly restricted than the one we are to witness.

(Incidentally, I am sure this would have made a poorer story than the one we have. I hasten to apologize for such gross reconstruction of so fine a work of art. But I trust that I have shown how the meaning would at least be *different* if the plot were altered.)

To take a more famous example and distort it even more grossly, let's imagine that the plot of *Madame Bovary* is changed. Instead of winding herself more and more tightly in the moral and practical snares of adultery, Emma Bovary finds the means to thrive and nourish both wit and charm by taking a succession of lovers.

Then what is in its present form a tragedy would become a comedy. If Emma Bovary brought herself to a ripe, autumnal serenity instead of to hysteria and suicide, the spirit of the book would be closer to eighteenth-century optimism and rationalism than to the glooms of nineteenth-century pessimism.

But would it also be closer to the truth about adultery and its consequences? There seems no fixed answer to such a question. One writer in one time might have said yes; another in a different time, no. And the only moral we can make from such speculation is that the shape and outcome of the plot are the prerogative of the author. He will manage them to express what he believes to be the truth he has found on his pilgrimage.

Which does not mean that he may be capricious in his arrangement of the plot. Ordinarily plot must follow lines of probability. But usually in every plot there are a very few strategic points where things might be made to go otherwise than they do. A little luck this way, a little luck that way and the whole course of a life might be altered for better or worse. This principle is as true in fiction as in the life it imitates. As true, but no more true.

Complete caprice in shifting the course of plot action merely destroys the fundamental virtue we expect of a plot, its consistent chain of causality. In making such central shifts in the plot as I have suggested are possible in *Madame Bovary* or "In the Zoo," the author would have found himself under the obligation to "earn" the different outcome of the action by a series of alterations in character, tone, language, and in the sequence of the plot following the point where the crucial change was made. The better the integration of the plot with the other story elements, the more true it is that one change makes others obligatory.

Remember this in revising your own work. Up until the moment you are ready to declare your story finished, the plot ought to be considered tentative or provisional. It's yours to reshape until it expresses your conclusions about the way life goes. But as it is fused with the characters and situations of your invention, they make their own claims on it, too. Those claims must be satisfied in revision.

Often plots are praised for their "inevitability." This means the reader is convinced that if event A took place it is nearly unthinkable that it should not have been followed by B. Once B has happened, then C must follow. Now, of course, any writer is in a position to be skeptical of the inevitability of any plot. He knows that after he has written A into his story, he could follow it with E or J—with K or X. At a certain point of composition when his materials were still fluid in his mind, the arrangement of events could be determined by pure whim.

Yes—at a certain point. The same is true of love. "Love has no conscience," says one of Shakespeare's sonnets. It may, as well as not, begin with a whimsical choice. "But who does not know that conscience comes from love?" The reasons for a whimsical choice in love or in forming a fictional plot begin to develop *after* a choice is made. And you will find that they assert themselves with ever more rigor as the various elements begin to fall into place.

We may agree with E. M. Forster that plot is fiction "in its logical, intellectual aspect." Plot expresses the author's judgment on the way life goes.

Very well. But we are writers, not retired sages. If we have any fixed logical and intellectual judgments about life—life in general—we will find them only remotely valuable in evaluating the particular phase of life about which we have chosen to write. Prejudgments and preconceived plots are apt to be arid or pompous, simply unfair to the material on which they are imposed.

Judgment—and therefore the shape of the plot itself—ought to come from an engagement with experience, in this case the experience of writing. Plots are found as meanings unfold to the writer. A good writer is a sort of midwife to his plots, not a dictator. He helps them emerge —take shape—from character and situation in the way his logic and intellect tell him action *would* emerge in life as he has known it. Judgment should be completed only when the story is fully formed.

It seems to me the best of practices to begin writing a story before you are quite sure what the plot will be.

Of course it is possible to work out a very definite plot before making a real beginning in the language of the story. Perhaps for some writers at some times this may be the most effective approach. The trouble with such a method is that once you begin to add flesh to a predetermined skeleton of a plot, you are almost certain to find that other elements have to be cut and distorted arbitrarily to fit a design which might become nonsensical if it were altered. No matter how experienced the writer, I think he cannot foresee all the nuances of character —their force or weakness, which have so much to do with how they would act — until he begins to develop them within the environment of the story. So to commit them in advance to actions for which they may be imperfectly suited is like the folly of trying to staff a complex enterprise by taking names at random from a telephone book.

All the elements in a story must be, as it were, "consulted" before the writer dares make certain decisions required to give the finished shape to his plot. He makes some initial declarations, arising from his conception. He writes down that his characters have done something. But then he pauses to consider who these characters are and what they might *want* to do next.

Yet, in urging pauses for consultation, I don't mean that characters can be allowed to dictate their own fates. There are writers who say, "I begin by creating characters. When they come to live, they write the story for me." I doubt if this is ever quite the whole truth. If it were, such a method could probably not result in a unified piece of fiction.

Characters make their own demands. So do other elements. But against all these pressures (never ignoring them) the mind of the author goes on urging the demands for continuity and unity of the plot. One requirement is pitted against another, and the story grows the way a vase rises on a potter's wheel, with one hand inside and one outside, both helping to determine the form.

It is not the pressure for a plot, but that pressure plus whatever in the material resists it with its own demands which results in the best plots.

It follows from this that the best plots turn out to be somewhat of a surprise to the author. They have come, of course, from those conceptions that are the roots of all creative work. But as they grew they put out branches and leaves that could hardly have been guessed at until the actual work of composition was done. They represent an achievement of logic and intellect not won in a vacuum but won in a struggle with the recalcitrance of unformed experience.

The happiest mixtures of motive, chance, and unconscious determination probably appear in plots whose outlines were clarified in the process of writing. Why? I don't know exactly, but I'll offer a theory: It may be that the act of writing a story is, for the author, a subtle kind of parallel to the action of his plot. That is, his plot is a disguised account of what happened to him as he wrote. The objective action he describes is a counterpart of the subjective struggle required to shape ideas and get them down on paper. Ernest Hemingway writing about an old man in a boat holding onto a line attached to a great fish he can't see may be writing about Earnest Hemingway composing *The Old Man and the Sea.* So it may be that all the good plots of heroes in action are, in some sense, self-portraits. Not only that, they may be self-portraits of the author committing himself to this very work.

Is this a fanciful theory? I don't mind your thinking so if it has suggested to you the kind of involvement required to make a living plot. A concept begins to unify when the writer sees himself as a kind of supernumerary character, responsible to the fictional situation in the same way as the other characters he will put into it.

I believe that the creation of a plot is merely an extension of this initial sense of personal involvement and responsibility.

When a writer's intuition tells him that what *is* happening to himself as he imaginatively shares the peril of his characters *would* be the next thing to befall them, he is in a position to reveal the deepest truth he knows by shaping the plot according to this intuition.

Dennis Whitcomb

Developing a Short Story from a Premise

The premise of a story is simply a one-line explanation of your story. You might want to start your story by writing out a premise similar to one of these:

1. Overwhelming ambition leads to dishonesty and finally results in discovery and punishment.
2. Love conquers irresponsibility.
3. Bragging leads to humiliation.

But most often, you'll start by getting an idea for a situation that you think is funny or dramatic or hazardous. You might also start by thinking up an interesting character whom you want to write a story around. However you begin, before you begin to write, test the story against a premise. See if your story can be put into a single sentence (as above). You may discover that you are really writing more than one story—or that you are straying from the point of the story. Once you have formed a premise, you know what it is you want the story to say, and you know that every line must further that premise. Anything that does not further the premise is out.

Your premise doesn't have to be a universal truth. It just has to be a statement which you can prove by your story. For example, you could write a story about any one of these premises:

Ambition leads to success.
Ambition leads to failure.
Ambition leads to murder.
Ambition leads to death.

Ambition leads to dishonesty.
Ambition leads to responsibility.

The premise should contain these three things: character, conflict, resolution.

1. You will find that nearly any vice, or any virtue can suggest a good character. For example: revenge, courage, cowardice, jealousy, intelligence, etc.

2. You may express the conflict (the essence of the story) by simply saying "leads to," or, you can be more explicit. For example:

   a. *Overconfidence leads to lack of effort.* That lack of effort causes the opposition to gain ground. Finding itself in danger of losing its goal, overconfidence changes to desperate effort which comes too late to succeed. All this is an elaboration of the simple premise: Overconfidence leads to failure.

   b. *Bragging leads to humiliation.* A soldier happens upon an enemy patrol at rest. Surprising them, he captures five prisoners. He receives a medal for it and is congratulated by his fellow soldiers. As time goes on, he feels that the others are forgetting that he is a hero. He continues to call their attention to the fact that he has won a medal and that it proves his superiority. He even talks back to a superior officer. In reaction to his insubordination, the officer gives him menial tasks. In carrying out the tasks, his fellow soldiers taunt him. In a desperate effort to win back their admiration, the soldier volunteers for a dangerous mission but is turned down because he does not have the necessary qualifications for the mission. He goes on to accomplish it by himself, without authorization. When it's discovered that he has gone, the volunteers go after him, and after a great deal of skillful effort, manage to overcome the enemy force which easily took our main character prisoner. *This entire story was an outgrowth of the premise, bragging leads to humiliation.* An unlimited number of other stories can come from the same premise.

3. The resolution of your premise (as we have demonstrated) can be anything you think you can prove by a story. Examples: success, fail-

ure, triumph, defeat, hope, etc. As you work on your story, you may change your mind about the course you wanted your story to follow. Fine, just discard your premise and form a new one.

Remember, the purpose of a premise is that it insures a central conflict and gives you a path to follow.

Here's a little assignment you might want to give yourself.

1. Demonstrate your understanding of premise by devising four of them (each in one sentence).

2. Take each premise and elaborate upon it. Tell a story in approximately ten or twelve sentences (four separate stories).

3. Take the best of those four premises and develop it into a one-page synopsis of a story.

Remember—the premise must contain *character, conflict, resolution.*

Because nothing is constant (except basic human nature), and all things are subject to change, the entire human race is constantly insecure. A man doesn't know if an accident or sickness may keep him out of work. We never know when we get up whether we'll be alive that night. A child must constantly be reassured that he is still loved by his parents.

This insecurity which all of us are subject to is *necessary.* If we could all be sure of being taken care of without having put out effort, there would be no need to do anything. Life would become static. Insecurity —the fact that we must all put out an effort and sometimes quarrel and fight for the necessities and the desirable things in the world—is what keeps people busy all day long. Consider this: Everything you do, down to the least little thing, is done for yourself. At first it seems unpleasant, doesn't it? Yet, it's true, and really not unpleasant, at all, because out of that self-interest, great good results. When I say everything is done for self, I mean that what you do each day, you do because of what you are. Your actions are governed by your own individual personality. If you refuse to give to a charity, you do it because your sense of insecurity (that is, your greatest concern) makes you feel that you need the money and may have difficulty without it. If, on the other hand, you give money to a charity, you do it, again, out of insecurity. You feel noble for having given the money. You also realize that you may need some kind of help one day, and in giving, you assure yourself that if you needed help, someone would help you. Or, perhaps you don't think of either of those reasons. Perhaps you give because you simply couldn't live with yourself if you didn't help people in need. Either way, you are doing it because your personality dictates that you must.

Since insecurity motivates all action, it also motivates conflict. You want something that someone else wants. Result, conflict. You find it necessary to go out and make a living. That work is conflict in many ways: Your company competes with other companies; you may be competing for a higher position; your union may be competing at a bargaining table with your employer; you may have to force yourself each day to go to work. All these things are conflict, and *conflict is the basis of all stories*. Just look at the different types of stories. They are all based on conflict. The story of decision is a conflict resulting in a decision. The story of accomplishment is conflict resulting in an accomplishment. Without conflict, the story becomes static; nothing happens.

Conflict should move each individual scene—but for the sake of variety, it should be a different kind of conflict in each scene. Think how many conflicts there are: *Physical conflict*—a fight, a baseball game, any sporting event; *a battle of wills*—a debate, a quarrel, a cross-examination; *a battle for self-discipline*—a person on a diet, a drug addict trying to break the habit; *seduction*—a roué trying to lure the sweet young thing to his apartment, the femme fatale trying to coax information from a spy; *a battle with the elements of nature*—survival, medicine, engineering, exploration. Within each of those divisions are many more divisions and millions of scenes possible.

Conflict is the fuel that keeps the characters moving through the story to its conclusion. A strong story requires good motivation, so make sure there is something vital at stake for the characters. Often a character's (or several characters') lives are at stake; sometimes it's money, love, etc. Let's look at what all of us would fight for: love, respect, life (or the life of another), self-justification, wealth, position, power.

All these things are strong motivations. They would make a character struggle to get or keep them. If a character gets involved in a conflict as a whim, his motivation is not strong enough. Make him get into the conflict out of necessity.

Here are some other ways to test your fiction skills:

1. Watch one television show or motion picture and synopsize the

story *on one page,* pointing out the various kinds of conflict. Comment at the end on whether the conflict was strong enough, and why.

2. Watch a television show, a movie or a play and list the foreshadowing conflicts at the beginning of the story. Tell how each grew into a more serious conflict.

3. Make up three different conflicts which you feel would cause *three different stories.* Outline each conflict in a paragraph.

4. Take one of the conflicts you worked out and develop it into a plot outline. Remember, a plot outline must tell us what caused the conflict to start, build to a climax, and finally come to some conclusion so that conditions may return to normal.

John G. Fitzgerald

So Wrong To Tell The Truth

If you can't lie and exaggerate you can't write fiction. I believe it was Shakespeare who said that plotting is nothing but lying. This goes back to the wandering minstrels of old who soon discovered they would starve to death if they didn't lie and exaggerate. That is why a wild animal who killed one little lamb in another province became a man-eating dragon who had swallowed ten men, women and children, by the time the wandering minstrels told it.

Since more than ninety per cent of all short stories published are complication stories, the most important thing for a new writer to learn in writing this type of story is how to plot complications. The dictionary states that a complication is "a situation or a detail of a character entering into and complicating the main thread of a plot." We won't argue with the dictionary, but for our purposes, and to make it easier for you to understand, when I use the word complication think of it as a problem or crisis, or both, facing a character in any work of fiction. This is my definition of a complication story:

> A complication story is the presentation of and solution to a complication in the lives of one or more imaginary persons in a work of fiction, which must be more interesting than those encountered in real life and at the same time believable to the reader.

Almost every day of your life you meet with some minor complication. You burn the toast. You miss the bus and are late for work. You try to phone Alice and the line is busy. Junior won't eat his spinach. A neighbor throws a party and keeps you awake half the night. Your mother-in-law comes to visit you unexpectedly.

But if you used any of these complications in a short story who would want to read it? That is why we say the complication and solution in a complication story must be more interesting than those encountered in real life. To do this, *exaggerate and lie about the complication until you make it more interesting than those encountered in real life.*

Always remember, the more you lie and exaggerate the complication, the more involved it will become; and the more involved the complication, the better your story will be. So, let us take the last minor complication of your mother-in-law coming to visit you and make it a bad enough situation to use as a plot for a short story by lying and exaggerating. We will give you a name, Bill Sheldon, with a wife named Diane, and a twelve-year-old son named Paul.

Minor complication: Bill Sheldon's mother-in-law comes to visit him.

Well you certainly couldn't make a short story out of this because it happens to people every day. But you *can* lie *about the complication.*

Lie No. 1—Bill Sheldon's mother-in-law comes to live with him, his wife Diane and his son Paul, after the death of her husband. This makes the complication worse but is of no interest to the reader. A lot of mothers-in-law live with their married children. So let us tell all the lies we can to make the complication so bad it will be more interesting than real life.

Lie No. 2—Bill's mother-in-law has never liked him and never forgiven him for marrying Diane. She wanted her daughter to marry Harold Carter. (Who is Harold Carter? I don't know, as I am making this up as I go along and the name just popped into my head. Whoever he is, let us use him to make the complication thicker.)

Lie No. 3—Harold Carter is the general manager of the plant where Bill is employed as an expediter in the purchasing department. (This lie makes the complication worse for poor old Bill who has a boss who was his rival suitor for Diane.)

Lie No. 4—Bill's mother-in-law makes his life miserable by constantly harping about how much better off Harold Carter is financially and socially. This is a pretty bad complication. Poor old Bill has a boss who rides him all day and a mother-in-law who makes his life miserable at home.

There are four weaknesses to watch for in plotting complications:

Plotting complications that are too much like those encountered in real life. If we stop with lie No. 4 in our complication plot outline, we would be doing just that. There are a lot of guys who don't like their jobs or their boss in real life. There are a lot of guys with mothers-in-law on their backs in real life.

Plotting complications that are too easily solved. If we have Bill tell Diane that her mother must leave or he will, and she agrees to send her mother to live in an apartment, the complication would be too easily solved. Readers demand that the protagonist must have a very tough time solving his complication and the more difficult it is to solve, the better the reader will like the story.

Plotting complications and then letting some character besides the protagonist solve it. If we have the mother-in-law meet a widower at a church social and fall in love, and one morning, to Bill's delight, tell him she is going to marry the widower, this would certainly solve Bill's complication. But no editor would buy the story. Readers demand that the protagonist must solve his or her own complication.

Plotting complications and then calling upon providence, chance or coincidence to solve it. If we have Bill's sour mother-in-law hit and killed by a truck while shopping one day, it would certainly solve Bill's complication, but no editor would buy the story. This weakness in plotting complications pops up all the time in workshop classes of new writers. They plot a complication, and when they can't find a solution for it, they let providence, chance or coincidence solve it for them.

Fortunately, there is a method which can be employed to avoid making any of the four fatal weaknesses in plotting complications. *In every complication something of importance must be at stake and the solution to the complication must be found within the complication itself.*

Here are three examples from a current magazine:

Complication: A college professor's reputation and career are at stake because a coed who has a crush on him tells lies about him when he rebuffs her advances.
Solution: The professor solves his complication by proving the coed lied.
Complication: A father realizes his son's future is at stake because the boy is running around with a gang of juvenile delinquents.
Solution: The hero-father solves his complication by getting the business men of the town to build a recreation center for teenagers.
Complication: An innocent man's life is at stake because he has been identified as a murderer by three witnesses.

Solution: The hero-criminal attorney solves his complication by discrediting the testimony of the three witnesses during the trial.

To make certain that something of importance is at stake if the complication isn't solved, *make the complication so bad that something of importance must be at stake.*

Let us now go back to Bill Sheldon and see if we can do just this. Bill is a nice easy-going guy and we've got to get him so riled up that he will tell his wife that her mother must leave or he will. Use his son Paul as the foil for doing this. Paul has been listening to his grandma ranting about how much better off Harold Carter is financially and socially than his own father. We are now ready for lie number five in the complication plot outline.

Lie No. 5—Bill becomes aware that his son's attitude towards him has changed since his mother-in-law came to live with them. Paul, who had before been a loving and obedient son, has become disrespectful and at times acts as if he is ashamed of his father. Create a situation to show this where Bill discovers his mother-in-law has poisoned Paul's mind against his father. This is more than even a nice easy-going guy like Bill can take. He issues an ultimatum to Diane that her mother must leave or he will.

We have now made the complication so bad that something of importance is at stake. If the complication isn't solved a marriage will end in divorce and the reader, who is sympathetic towards Bill, would hate to see that happen. But just having something important at stake won't make a salable story unless the solution can be found within the complication itself. For example:

If we let the mother-in-law meet the widower and marry him we are going outside the complication to solve it.

If we allow her to be killed by a truck we are going outside the complication to solve it.

If we move her to live in an apartment by herself, the complication is too easily solved.

Anytime you reach this stage, where you can't find the solution within the complication itself, there is only one way to make your story salable. *Make the complication even worse.* And keep on making it worse and worse until the solution becomes apparent to you.

One of the most frequently used ways to make a complication worse is one I call *discovery and change.*

Discovery and change is letting a character discover something he did not know or did not realize before, which results in his changing his mind. Let us now apply this idea to make Bill's complication even worse.

Lie No. 6—After Bill *discovers* his mother-in-law has poisoned his son's mind against him, he changes his mind about putting up with her for the sake of his wife and issues Diane an ultimatum that her mother must go or he will.

Lie No. 7—Diane reluctantly agrees to move her mother to an apartment. But when she tells her mother this, her mother in a fit of self pity says she won't go to an apartment. If her own daughter won't let her live with her she'll go into a charity home. When Diane *discovers* she can't bring herself to letting her mother go live in a charity home she *changes* her mind and begs Bill to let her mother remain.

Bill is now forced to make a decision which must point out a solution. If he decides to put up with his mother-in-law the rest of her life, the complication will remain unsolved. Bill must, therefore, decide to leave home, give up his job, go to another city and let Diane get a divorce. He figures he's lost the love and respect of his son anyway, and that in time his mother-in-law will brainwash Diane until she will begin regretting she didn't marry Carter. This decision of his must point to the solution to the complication.

The double space denotes a long pause because I can't come up with a solution. I know it must be there because I can't possibly make the complication any worse. Wait a minute. Now it is coming. If it wasn't for Harold Carter there would be no complication. *Somehow Carter must be the agent Bill uses to solve his complication.* What do we know about Carter? That he rides Bill at work. This character trait of Carter must be the key to the solution.

Lie No. 8—The only elation Bill feels is that at long last he will be able to tell Harold Carter what he thinks of him. He has never taken his office troubles home and it suddenly occurs to him that his mother-in-law and Diane probably think Carter is looked upon as a little tin God by his employees. Bill knows that every employee in the plant hates Carter's guts because he is always riding them. He never passes up a chance to bawl out an employee and throw his weight around. This starts Bill thinking that maybe Carter is the same way at home. The only time he ever met Carter's wife she appeared to be a timid woman, afraid to speak. Bill's *discovery* that Carter might be the same type of overbearing person at home as he is in business makes him *change* his mind about quitting his job and leaving home. He sees a last desperate chance to solve his complication by inviting Carter and his family to dinner. He rightly deduces that Carter won't pass up a chance to blow his own horn and show Diane what a mistake she made in not marrying him.

This brings us to the final step in plotting our complication, which writes itself.

Lie No. 9—Carter accepts the invitation and brings his wife, and son who is just a year younger than Paul to dinner. Bill's deductions prove correct. Carter is as overbearing with his wife and son as he is with his employees. His wife is a timid woman, afraid to open her mouth. When questions are put to her Carter answers for her. He is also very domineering with his son, telling the boy to sit up straight in his chair and bawling the boy out for accidently upsetting a dish. After they leave the mother-in-law *changes* her mind about Bill after *discovering* what sort of a family man Carter is. She begs Bill to forgive her. Paul also *changes* his mind about his father after *discovering* how Carter treats his own son. There is love and new found respect in his voice as he tells his father this. The complication is solved and the story ends.

It now becomes simply a matter of fastening the complication plot outline to the plot structure of the formula story, inventing a few minor attempts by Bill to solve his complication only to meet with failure, and we have a plot that will sell.

Now, go back to our definition of a complication story and we find we've created a complication that is more interesting than those encountered in real life, but what about the rest of the definition? Is it believable to the reader?

If you have the slightest doubt you must learn to lie and exaggerate to write fiction, let us consider this complication objectively. In real life it is possible Diane's mother might occasionally mention to her daughter that Diane would have been better off married to Harold Carter, but it is extremely unlikely she would ever mention this to Bill, who is supporting her. It is even more unlikely she would go on harping about it and poison her own grandson's mind against his father. How do you make a reader believe she would do these things? *By exaggerating her dominant character traits.* In backgrounding the circumstances that produced the complication it will be necessary to exaggerate the character trait of an ambitious mother who wants her daughter to marry for money and social position. When her plans fail and Diane marries Bill, it will be necessary to exaggerate the character trait of vindictiveness of this mother and her extreme dislike of Bill in several situations. It will then be believable to the reader that this woman would do the things she does after coming to live with Bill.

In real life it is extremely unlikely that Bill would let his mother-in-law drive him out of his own home and break up his marriage. So it will be necessary to exaggerate Bill's character trait of being a nice easygoing guy who is a plodder knowing his own limitations, a guy who considers himself very lucky to have a good job, even if under a mean boss, a guy who loves his wife and son so dearly he is willing to put up with his mother-in-law's abuse and make the agonizing decision to leave home.

In real life it is extremely unlikely that a man of Harold Carter's stature would accept a dinner invitation just to blow his own horn. Why should he? He is well aware that Diane knows he is Bill's boss and much better off financially and socially than Bill. It will be necessary to exaggerate Carter's character trait of vainess, showing he never got over the blow to his vanity when Diane chose Bill instead of him. It then becomes believeable to the reader that he would accept the dinner invitation to blow his own horn.

And because we've exaggerated these character traits we've prepared the reader to swallow the big hook in the solution.

I am going to end this article by getting you started on a minor complication which you should now be able to make bad enough to use for the plot of a salable short story.

A young housewife enters the kitchen of her home and catches her eight-year-old son stealing cookies from the cookie jar.

Lie No. 1—A young housewife enters the living room of her home and catches her eight-year-old son stealing some money from her purse.

Now you take it from there.

Marilyn Granbeck

Stories Without Plot

As a teacher of creative writing I often am asked the question: "Why do today's magazines publish so many short stories that have no plot or structure?" After hearing the same question dozens of times, I realized that many beginning writers puzzle over the same thing. Is there a way to account for these "non-stories" that are so prevalent today?

Of course there is.

Actually there are two answers to the problem. First, are you sure that the stories you read really do not have the structure you think is missing? Many of them do. It is sometimes hard to decide at first reading.

If you were asked to judge the Miss America Contest, you would see many entrants. As a judge of beauty, you must evaluate the outward appearance of each girl. Some of them appeal to you while others do not. Yet all of them were thought beautiful by someone or they wouldn't be representing their states. Each of them passed a preliminary contest before she got to the main event.

While you are judging, you see the outward appearance of each girl. Her total appeal to you helps you make your choice. You probably don't even think about the girl's skeletal system—the bones inside that make it possible for her to have her good looks and shape. Yet the bones are there.

Published short stories are like beauty contest finalists. Each one that appears in a magazine has passed the preliminaries or it wouldn't be in print. Somewhere, an editor thought it merited the finals of publication. He thought it was good enough to please his readers, and he was willing to pay a writer for it. An editor has to evaluate the story by total appeal, but as a skilled judge, he is aware of the structure beneath the surface because he knows it helps make a good story. In the hands of a skilled writer, the framework of the story is as invisible as the bones of the beauty contestant. Just as the girl's total physical appearance is made possible by her skeletal system, a story is often good because of *its* hidden structure. The experienced writer may disguise the bones so effectively the reader doesn't see them sticking out as separate pieces. The bones of the story can be so well hidden, the reader may think they are not there at all.

"A Sure Thing," by Marlene Fanta Shyer, in the June 1969 issue of *Redbook,* is a good example of a story in which the plot is skillfully constructed without protruding bones. At first reading, the story seems to be nothing more than an incident showing a wife's recognition of the fact that the glow has worn off her marriage. The author depicts the characters easily but precisely as they move through an evening. The limited action seems hardly enough to give the standard elements of plot, yet careful examination reveals they are all there. The reader is caught in the story so completely that he doesn't notice its separate elements.

The narrative problem is shown in the opening paragraphs, summed up by: "After seven years of fidelity, I was not going to feel unsettled over someone like Ruth Anne!" With the problem thus established, the author proceeds to show how her main character reacts to it. First Tess comes in conflict with the theory itself when, despite her "I-have-nothing-to-worry-about" attitude she is increasingly disturbed at seeing her husband with Ruth Anne. At a party Harry cuts in on Ruth Anne's partner and leaves Tess to dance with the other man. Her aplomb wavers. "Of course Harry and Ruth Anne danced off together. I got a glimpse of them a minute later and lost a step." . . . . "I smiled right into John Flood's lapel. But if it was so funny, why was I also getting shakey-mad?"

Tess struggles to recapture the feeling that she has nothing to worry about. She talks herself into being gay until her husband tells her Ruth Anne has invited them home for coffee. Should she refuse or should she go and suffer more? Tess longs for the security of her own house where she is surrounded by familiar things that represent her marriage, but she agrees to go. She encounters another setback when she notices that

Harry and Ruth Anne are not in the room and she is caught in small talk with Ruth's husband. Once again jealousy forces its way to the surface. "Where is Ruth Anne?" I asked. The words came out riveted together." When she finally goes to look for them, she sees them in the garden and hears Harry talking about an incident that happened on the commuter train. Now Tess is forced to face her problem. Why is her husband telling another woman something he never bothered to tell her? This is the crisis.

Tess meets it with the realization that it is she who has stopped listening, not Harry who has stopped talking. She has been too wrapped up in the day-to-day trivia and activity of her life to see that she has been neglecting her husband as an individual. In shock, she returns to the living room where Ruth Anne's husband shows her a card trick. She fails to guess in which pile her card is even though she "thought it was a sure thing." He laughs and tells her that the trick is to shuffle up the cards a little.

Tess realizes that she has been looking at her marriage as a sure thing, and she decides to shuffle up the cards a bit and try to put some of the lost magic back in it. The story ends with her attempt to do this. So, all the short story elements are present: problem, conflict, setbacks, crisis and solution. The author has created a beauty-contest finalist with no bones showing.

But what of the stories that really are unplotted—the stories that despite careful dissection do not reveal the bones of structure a story should have? Many of my students try to pass them off as flukes or credit their publication to "pull" the writer has with an editor. Actually, the answer is much simpler than that. The stories *seem* unplotted because they *are* unplotted, and the unplotted short story is a perfectly acceptable form of fiction, providing the story meets certain other criteria. These "unplotted" stories may be called "planned short stories."

The planned story does not need a plot or all the elements normally in a plotted story. This type of story does not depend on plot; instead its ideas and material are presented in a way designed to create emotional or dramatic effects. The total story is aimed at creating a specific emotion in the reader. The planned short story creates its effect by presenting an incident, a particularly interesting situation or an emotional experience. The author determines the mood or feeling he wants to evoke, and then he deliberately aims every word of his story toward that effect. It may be gaiety, horror, love, sympathy or any of a dozen other feelings, but it is specific and single.

Another story in a recent issue of *Redbook* illustrates planning instead of plotting. In "Puppy Love Is Mainly Flowers" by Robert Meyers, Jr. (April 1969), the title gives a clue to the single emotion the author creates with his story. "When she looked at him, she saw hyacinths touch his head, plumbago kiss his ears." . . . . "When he looked at her, he saw fringed gentian pillowed on her throat, dancing cowbells encircling her neck and soft wisteria in her mane of silkspun hair." From the very beginning of his story, Mr. Meyers points each line toward the emotion of joy of puppy love. He has chosen a universal emotion with which his readers can empathize, and he leads them through a flower-covered emotional experience that leaves them joyous with the memory of their own puppy love. In careful analysis, the story has no narrative problem, but it doesn't need one. It has no conflict, struggle or solution, but it doesn't need them. The author makes sure that the reader *feels* the emotion that the two young people in the story feel. He intends to build this single emotion in his readers, and he succeeds in doing it very well. The reader is left with a smile on his lips and the smell of spring flowers haunting his memory.

The June 1969 issue of *Good Housekeeping* carried a story titled "The Image of the Dream" by Patricia Poston. It is an excellent example of a planned story which creates its effect through the illumination of a character. Keeping in mind that readers like to *feel* more than they like to think, Miss Poston evokes sympathy and empathy by portraying a young wife's fears that her child will be born plain. The human emotion of a mother wanting to spare her daughter the anguish she herself has suffered is deftly shown through Margo's thoughts and dialogue as the birth of the child is imminent. She is sure the baby will be a girl, and she prays that it will be born perfect. As a guilty afterthought she adds a postscript to the prayer. "And then, unbidden, followed more words: And don't let her have red hair. Please."

Miss Poston then takes the reader through the woman's remembered pain of her own childhood of red-headed plainness and freckles.

". . . . . it's not merely the red hair. It's knowing that you're not beautiful and never will be." Women reading the story can put themselves in the place of the main character because many of them suffered the same insecurity as youngsters or one similar enough to produce the same fewings. When the author says "Sometimes Margo half believed a part of her love for Will was pure gratitude that he had looked beyond the plainness, discovered the real Margo hidden inside . . . ," the reader feels the same sense of gratitude. the same need for love and assurance. The reader *wants* Margo to believe that she is beautiful.

Miss Poston tugs at the emotions of her audience deftly and consistently until she reaches the climax of her characterization. After the birth of the baby girl, who does have red hair after all, Will tells Margo the baby is beautiful, just as beautiful as her mother. Margo finally realizes he actually means it—that he believes she is beautiful and is not just saying words to make her happy. She looks at the tiny baby in her arms. *"You're not pretty,"* she thought. *"But you are beautiful. Because I see you through the eyes of love. Like my mother must have seen me. Like Will sees me. That's what makes the difference. . . ."* The reader shares Margo's new awareness and happiness. The total effect of the story has been achieved by painting a word picture of a single character—one that readers can feel strongly about. A good story doesn't need a plot when it is planned as carefully as Miss Poston's.

Planned stories enjoyed great popularity during the nineteen thirties and forties. Perhaps this was because short fiction in general was in its heyday. Then, like long skirts, the planned story went out of fashion. Plotted stories outnumbered planned ones on the pages of magazines. Plotted stories became so popular they took over the markets. During the fifties and most of the sixties, readers and writers began to accept plotted short fiction as the *only* kind. Teachers taught it, writers wrote it, and editors bought it. Some writers and teachers forgot that the planned short story ever existed.

Now the pendulum is swinging back, and the planned fiction is emerging again. Can the trend be explained with any more certainty than the up-again hemlines? Who can say why the pendulum has reversed its swing? Maybe it's because emotion is at a high point in the world today. Digging the emotional scene is *in*. Love-ins, stop the war, ban the bomb, flower children—all have emotional impact. This may account for the appeal of the emotional story—planned fiction as opposed to plotted. Whatever the reason, the planned short story has staged its comeback, and today's writers have to keep pace with editors' and readers' demands.

If you learn the techniques of planned fiction, you can write and sell these stories. But don't make the mistake of believing they are "nothing." They are definitely more than the non-stories you may have first thought them to be. They have something special—emotional impact and appeal. They have a plan, and they succeed in their purpose.

Robert C. Meredith and John D. Fitzgerald

Dramatizing Conflict in the Short Story

Short story writers employ scenes to characterize, to convey information that the reader must know to understand the story, and to produce conflict. For the sake of clarity, we will call those scenes which produce conflict *big scenes* and scenes used for other purposes *small scenes.* We are concerned only with *big scenes.* in this article.

A big scene in a short story is composed of four elements:

1. A meeting between two opposing forces.
2. An exploitation on the part of the writer of the inherent conflict within the meeting.
3. A suggestion as to the result of the meeting.
4. The result of the meeting between two opposing forces must be the primary cause of what happens in the next scene and set up the transition to it.

The sole purpose of the author in bringing two opposing forces together is to produce conflict to hold the reader's interest. The result of the meeting between two opposing forces in every big scene is that somebody or something wins, loses, concedes a point, is forced to make a decision, is made to realize something about themselves or the complication they didn't realize before, or simply withdraws.

Now all this will seem clear to the young writer. The question which will vex him is this: how does one determine what portions of a story to dramatize in big scenes? The question can be answered only if one understands the forms of conflict possible in a short story and can state his conflict as a central issue of the story. When one considers the possible conflicts that can confront an individual, it will readily and somewhat surprisingly be seen that there are only three generic plots in most commercial fiction:

1. Conflict to eliminate an opponent.
2. Conflict to overcome an obstacle.

3. Conflict to avert a disaster.

These generic forms of conflict can be schematized specifically in the following fashion:

Man against man.
Man against men (war).
Man against woman.
Woman against man.
Woman against woman.
Man against nature (God).
Man against disaster.
Man against himself.
Man against his environment.

Let us look at several examples of magazine fiction to illustrate these forms of conflict and to give the new writer clues which will enable him to employ big scenes.

A love story of the eternal triangle. Two men want the same woman—man against man—and the author produces conflict each time the two men meet.

A confession story about a younger sister trying to steal away her older sister's husband—woman against woman—and the author produces conflict each time the two sisters meet.

A young adult slick story about a couple heading for divorce—woman against man—and the author produces conflict each time they meet.

A story about a young city couple buying a farm and facing all kinds of trials—man against nature—and the author produces conflict as the young couple fight natural forces trying to save their crops.

A story about townspeople fighting a fire that threatens to wipe out the entire town—man against disaster—and the author produces conflict as the townspeople fight the blaze trying to save their town.

A mystery story about a man who witnesses a murder. If he comes forward as a witness, it will mean his wife will learn he has been having an affair with another woman—man against himself—and the author produces conflict as the protagonist struggles with his conscience.

Now let us look at some examples of quality stories:

Somerset Maugham's *The Colonel's Lady*: a story about pompous Colonel Peregrine, who faces, as he thinks, social disapproval over his wife's popular book of love poetry—man against man as a social animal—and Maugham produces conflict each time Peregrine faces a representative of his social world.

Maupassant's *The Story of a Farm Girl*: a story about an ignorant peasant girl whose search for love leads her to give birth to an illegitimate child and to face social scorn—woman against her environment—and the author produces conflict each time she faces her small world.

Mark Schorer's *Boy in the Summer Sun*: a story about a young college graduate who in late summer discovers that he faces a new world in which change must be accepted—man against himself—and the author produces conflict each time the protagonist faces his changing world.

Inexperienced writers often get their scenes out of focus by overlooking the fact that the real justification for big scenes lies in an analysis of the elements of conflict inherent in a given situation. To write a one-paragraph summary of his story, as in the above examples, will enable an author to keep his scenes within focus.

Knowing the plot structure of the chronological story will enable a young writer to select the right portions of a story to dramatize in big scenes. Approximately seventy-five percent of all short stories published follow the steps in the plot structures of chronological stories. Let us look at these structures to see what steps specifically call for big scenes.

Beginning:
1. Set the scene.
2. Introduce the principal character or characters with an indication of their approximate ages, and establish the point of view.
3. Suggest in the tone and style of the prose what type of story the reader is reading.
4. Background the circumstances that eventually lead to the complication.
5. Trap the reader into reading the rest of the story with a narrative hook; present a minor problem that later results in the complication, or arouse an interest in the protagonist's welfare.

Middle:
1. Present the complication.
2. Present a series of efforts in which the protagonist attempts to solve his complication only to meet with failure.
3. Present a situation of anticlimax in which it appears the protagonist will finally solve the complication only to meet with such disastrous failure the reader becomes convinced that there is no hope of a satisfactory solution.
4. Step 3 of the middle forces the protagonist to make an agonizing decision that will point to the solution of the complication.

End:
1. The solution to the complication must be satisfactory and believable to the reader.

Our guide in selecting portions of a story to dramatize in big scenes is the following principle: *Dramatize in big scenes only those portions of a story where two opposing forces meet.* We can readily see from the plot structure of the chronological story we will have opposing forces meet in Step 1 of the middle when the protagonist runs head on into his complication; in Step 2 of the middle as he tries to solve his complication only to meet with failure; in Step 3 of the middle as he makes one final attempt to solve his complication only to meet with such failure it leaves the reader convinced the complication is beyond solution; and in Step 4 of the middle as the protagonist makes an agonizing decision that points to the solution. It is also possible the author may see enough conflict to portray Step 5 of the beginning in a big scene. The word length of a story will determine how many big scenes are possible. In a short-short story, an author may well compress Steps 1, 2, 3 and 4 of the middle into a single big scene. A five-thousand-word story or longer will generally have four or five big scenes as described above.

Now while it is true some quality stories faithfully follow the plot structures of the chronological and formula story and the authors employ big scenes as indicated by the plot structures, the great majority of quality stories violate the plot structures of the formula and chronological story. It is this very violation plus good writing that make them quality stories. All commercial stories tend to be optimistic—the reader knows the protagonist will solve the complication.

Quality stories attempt to arrive at conclusions about life which are more profound than in the commercial story. They employ subtlety, intellectuality, and suggestiveness. Quality stories tend to be more concerned with mental events and the underlying issues in character. The result is to prevent the protagonist or other characters from seeing the ultimate significance of the issues in conflict. The reader sees more than the protagonist sees—and hence the big scene in many quality stories tends to suggest more conflict than is ever really dramatized. The point here is that the literary protagonist, blind to the extent of his complication, comes eventually to see it as a part of life; and this arrival at a tragic consciousness of existence usually makes of the big scene less an overt struggle than a growth toward illumination. The only way the quality writer can determine when to use big scenes will be to analyze the pressures in each story toward scenic presentation. To enable the new writer to see how this is done, we will analyze a quality story.

In Flannery O'Connor's story *A Good Man Is Hard To Find,* we are told the very first sentence the grandmother didn't want to go to Florida. Within this statement is comprised the major conflict of the story. The grandmother is a member of an older tradition in America that is represented by her passive son, her son's wife and two children, a boy and girl, both undisciplined and disrespectful. The grandmother doesn't want to go to Florida because she wishes to visit some people in Tennessee and bring her son and his family back into the stream of her own traditions and descent.

The issues which form the heart of the conflict are not directly stated, and hence not directly debated. The story opens, however, with a big scene. The grandmother expostulates with her son, who, preoccupied with the sport pages, does not answer her. She points out that according to the paper there is an escaped criminal loose, called the Misfit, who had been reported headed for Florida. He has been guilty of shocking crimes. She is afraid to take the children to an area where the criminal might attack them. Because her son remains silent the grandmother addresses the mother. The mother pays no attention. At this point the two children begin to argue with the grandmother and virtually call her names.

This big scene employs the four elements we have discussed. There is a meeting between opposing forces but we get the significance of the opposition only indirectly. There is an exploitation on the part of the writer of the inherent conflict within the meeting. The grandmother loses the argument. The family is going to Florida. The result of the meeting sets up the transition to the next scene.

Also important to the scene is the development of characterization. Because the characters tend to stand for symbolic and abstract states (though they are well particularized as individuals), the conflict becomes generalized and applies to what Americans in general are doing with their traditions. This widening of the conflict makes it possible for the author to dramatize scenically a good many situations.

Because this possibility exists, the writer of the quality story may be inclined to think that he has the widest latitude possible to turn anything he wishes into scenes. Yet, this is not true, for the form of his story will prevent it, just as the form of *A Good Man Is Hard To Find* prevents it. This is a tragic quality story. The grandmother faces a complication she struggles against, with some hope of success, only to lose disastrously. The first big scene shows her losing. But both the form of the story, and the struggle itself in its meaning, make her loss unconvincing to the reader. As a consequence, there is pressure in the story for big scenes in which it will appear the grandmother will have some success.

In the big scenes which follow the first one, the grandmother indeed appears to win. She keeps the children preoccupied; she scores off their lack of politeness; she gives a dimension to their lives despite their petulance; she gets the owner of the barbecue place where they stop to agree that "a good man is hard to find"; she persuades the family to turn off the road to see an old plantation; and the children, themselves, force the father to turn off onto an old dirt road, against his inclinations, to satisfy their curiosity.

In all these scenes the grandmother appears to win. And they prepare for the last big scene where the family, after the accident the grandmother inadvertently (but so appropriately in character) causes, they meet the Misfit. The grandmother faces, in this Big scene, the alter ego of her son, the criminal who has escaped from his past and has no place to turn to but to self-indulgent violence. In this Big scene, the characteristic four elements of the Big scene are present. The Misfit, with his cronies, kills off the family though the grandmother tries valiantly to the end to persuade the Misfit he is basically a "good man."

A careful study of the story will reveal that the author has used big scenes following the first one because the character of the grandmother is so strong. The Story is a fine illustration of the adaption of technical means to the ends that lie in the author's vision. The grandmother's struggle to bring her own family to the values of the past is a struggle against the total environment in which she lives. We have a tendency for big scenes to occur when she does not indeed directly confront her son. Only in this fashion could we gain a tragic perspective of the character.

In order to determine what elements of his story are to be put into big scenes, the quality writer must understand the pressures inherent in his conflict. It is as valid for the quality writer as it is for the commercial writer to dramatize the big scene only those portions of a story where two opposing forces meet. But it is essential that the quality writer study each one of his stories in terms of its own significance. Tragic and linear quality stories and offbeat stories violate the plot structures of the formula and chronological story. There is, therefore, no cut-and-dried formula for selection of portions of the story to portray in big scenes. It becomes an individual choice of the author what portions of the story to portray in big scenes. But one fact stands out: a study of quality and off-beat stories indicates the authors invariably use big scenes *when opposing forces meet.*

The old pulp stories placed their protagonists in a physical world. It was conventional here, consequently, for the characters to demonstrate their conflicts in big scenes in terms of physical force and passionate action. The conflict in big scenes in slick stories today is much more restrained, subtle, and sophisticated. In quality stories the conflict in big scenes usually has such overriding symbolic meaning that often enough the participants are not totally aware of their dilemma. Consequently, because of the subtlety of the quality story, the big scenes need not, and usually do not, appear in violent action.

A weakness found in quite a few short stories by new writers is worth mentioning here. It is a mistaken belief that to have a big scene you must have dialogue. It is true the majority of short stories published do employ dialogue accompanied by action in portraying big scenes but many short stories have big scenes in which not a word of dialogue is spoken. The opposing force does not have to be another character. The opposing force can be a physical object, such as the struggle of a company of soldiers to take a hill during a battle with the actuality of the event portrayed in the unspoken thoughts of one of the soldiers. The opposing force can be nature such as a storm, a flood, a typhoon, and so on, that threatens the protagonist. And young writers should remember one of the specific forms of conflict is man against himself. The opposing force in a big scene can be man's conscience with the entire scene portrayed by the protagonist's unspoken thoughts and actions during the scene.

By *Pauline Bloom*

Mistreat Your Characters

One of the most tantalizing editorial comments that any writer ever receives on a rejected script is the phrase "too thin." After you've worked and reworked a story, creating what you think are believable, striking characters and a plot full of action and suspense, it's pretty hard to look at your story coldly and discover just wherein it's "thin."

What an editor usually means by "thin" is lack of conflict in the plot structure. Almost every writer has trouble with conflict, trouble that's all out of proportion to the mental problems the subject presents. And until the problem is solved, it's likely that his stories won't sell, since conflict is the most important single element of successful, commercial fiction writing.

A partial answer to the understanding of why this business of conflict presents such a stumbling block came to me as I watched some of my students struggle with it. They took voluminous notes; they talked intelligently about various aspects of story structure, and they said that they now understood perfectly why their old stories had failed. Then they sat down and wrote new stories with the same failing.

Why? Because, although they had a clear mental picture of what constitutes a good story conflict, they had an emotional resistance to the actual step-by-step development of that same conflict. Building a conflict is an unnatural process. Our day-to-day life consists of looking for the simplest and quickest solution of each problem that arises. We may not always succeed, but that is our aim. Therefore, when the characters we've created are faced with fictional problems, we are as tender with them as we wish Providence to be with us. Out of our deep and abiding affection for our creations, we hurry to smooth things out for them. Just as soon as any difficulties appear, we use all our power as creators to get those difficulties out of the way. And at that point, the story conflict falls flat on its face.

The way to overcome this natural resistance on your part toward building a good, strong story conflict is to understand this resistance and to work out the conflict *consciously* before you begin to do any writing, before you have a chance to identify yourself with your characters.

And herein lies one of the most important differences between the professional and the amateur writer. The amateur dreams while he waits for inspiration to do the work for him. The professional knows that he has to do the work himself and does it. The amateur resists story planning; the professional has made careful story planning a part of his routine.

Don't think that by working from a plan you can produce only "formula" stories which will be the same as "formula" stories produced by other writers. Our skeletons probably look pretty much alike, because each of our bones has evolved to its present form to serve a definite functional purpose. The skeletons of good, sound stories, too, are not uniquely different from one another, because their component parts are there for specific functional purposes. But after we have clothed these skeletons with the flesh and blood and muscles of character, theme, background, emotion, style and the other elements of fiction, our stories will be as varied as our personalities.

The most important contribution which you bring to your story is you yourself, the sum total of all your experiences and of your reactions to those experiences. Experience is not only what happens to you; it's what you do with what has happened to you. You see things not as they are but as *you* are. Walter de la Mare puts it this way:

> It's a very odd thing,
> As odd as can be,
> That whatever Miss T. eats
> Turns into Miss T.

All this wealth of experience, as reprocessed by yourself, is what you bring to your story before you ever begin to plan it. It is the stuff that will determine the theme of your story and all its component parts—

that will make your story different from all other stories even when you start with a basic conflict that has been done many times before. Such fundamental conflicts usually produce the most powerful stories.

As far as the parties to a conflict are concerned, there are three basic combinations possible:

(1) *The conflict of man against nature.* Nature as a menace offers wonderfully dramatic material. Jack London knew how to use the Arctic wastes or a storm at sea to challenge the stamina and resourcefulness of his main character. Jungles, wild animals, fog, hurricanes, floods—pit your protagonist against any of these, and he will have to fight heroically to achieve his objective. Many adventure stories are built around such conflicts.

(2) *The conflict between two sides of a man's character.* The classic example here is, of course, *Dr. Jekyll and Mr. Hyde.* There are many others. Until some years ago an internal psychological struggle of this kind was used mainly for literary or quality stories. But characterization has become more and more important in both the slick and the pulp magazines. Today almost any kind of story may be based on this type of conflict.

(3) *Man against man.* This could be a detective against a murderer in a mystery, a brunette against a blond in a love story, a homesteader against a cattle-rancher in a Western, etc. It is quite possible to use a familiar conflict with a fresh slant to make a highly original story.

In this category also belongs the conflict of one man against more than one man. For example, your main character may set out to defeat a gang of criminals, or saboteurs, or other organized groups which are operating against the common good. Stories of this kind can be highly dramatic if the group attacked rightfully deserves destruction.

A good story is essentially the history of a conflict. It starts with the realization of it, and, as it proceeds, the conflict grows, until a climax, the highest point of interest in a story, is reached. Then the conflict is resolved to end the story.

Between the beginning, the main character's desire to achieve something, and the end, his success or failure, there must be several points in the story where there is a break—where the conflict comes to a peak. This series of peaks must be in an ascending scale, with each one more crucial than the last. The final climax in the action is, of course, the most dramatic. It precipitates the resolution, and brings the story to a satisfying end.

Or, to put it another way: You decide what kind of a story you want to write. You decide what kind of a character your protagonist will be. Then you decide what he wants. It should be something the reader would want very much, too, if he were in the main character's place. Now, your main character takes a step toward the achievement of this important objective. And what do you, the author, do? You beat him down.

The main character tries another tack—he tries even harder—you beat him down even harder. He may make an even more desperate effort. This time you will perhaps relent and let him succeed. Perhaps. It depends on your story.

The thing to bear in mind is that you've got to fight your own resistance to piling up obstacles for your hero. You know now why you'd like to have your character make good at the first try. But if you want to make good yourself as a writer, you must work out various ways to frustrate your main characters.

The number of conflict peaks in a story will depend on the length of the story, and the kind of story it is. For example, a literary story does not need to be so tightly plotted if it is primarily a story of character or atmosphere, especially if the story is not long. A slick story of 3,000 or 4,000 words can get along with two or three conflict peaks, in some very rare cases even one. If it runs to 5,000 or 6,000 words, it would be a stronger story with three conflict peaks than two. On the other hand, a good pulp story of 6,000 words should have at least three conflict peaks, probably four, or even more.

You should know the end of your story before you begin to plan the middle of it, because only that way can you make your story move steadily forward toward a logical end. Only that way will your story have direction and singleness of purpose.

Two conflicting forces might fight each other until one of them achieves a conclusive victory. There must be no compromise, because that would weaken your story. Most stories, written for commercial magazines, have a better chance of publication if the main character succeeds in achieving the most important of his objectives.

Don't think that you are necessarily compromising your integrity by writing stories with "happy endings." If your themes and your conflicts are valid ones, you are making a constructive contribution by an affirmation of the principles in which you believe.

Before you ever remove the cover from your typewriter, however, you should have decided what kind of a story you are going to work on, whether it will be a love story, an adventure story, a marriage problem story, etc. This will, to a certain extent, narrow your choice as to the parties to the conflict. Then ask yourself: Is your story to be man against nature, man against man, or man against himself?

Having answered these questions, you now have a certain kind of a man or woman, living a certain kind of a life, (the character is beginning to take shape) which involves conflicts and problems, as what life doesn't.

Of course, you've read a good many magazines in the field for which you are about to write, and so you have a pretty clear idea of the nature of the conflicts which make the most successful stories in this particular field. So you decide what your main character is up against, what he is trying to achieve and against what odds. Then you put down this nucleus of your story in one sentence.

In a love story, for example, your synopsis might be: "A girl in love with a man tries to win him away from an unscrupulous rival." The fact that this main character has an unscrupulous rival paves the way for a series of conflict peaks before she achieves her objective.

Western: "A cowboy, realizing that the trail boss is taking unnecessary risks with men's safety in order to make more money challenges his authority." A trail boss will not easily surrender his traditional power, particularly where a good deal of money and his own pride are at stake. At the same time, a cowboy with enough character to challenge this constituted authority will fight hard for his principles. So here, too, there are good opportunities for building a strong story, which develops step by step to a logical climax.

Between the opening situation outlined in your story nucleus and the achievement of your main character's goal, will be the conflict peaks mentioned above. After working them out, write a one-page synopsis of your story, indicating each conflict peak and the climax.

Be firm with yourself and don't start the actual writing until you have this one-page synopsis with several acts in it. If you start writing before you know where you're going, there is only a slight chance that your story will accidentally follow the right road. It's not something to count on. Usually, you will get off at a tangent, and after you meander aimlessly for a while, you may be strongly tempted to drop the whole thing and go see a movie instead. Even if you do stick to it and work out a story in hit-or-miss fashion, there will be many, many things wrong with it, and you will not be able to see what they are.

Because words, once they are put down on paper, have a kind of holiness about them, especially to the new writer. "This is a beautiful sentence," he says to himself. "I can't take it out."

Even if he should suspect a flaw here and there—well, what mother ever loved a crippled child less than a perfect one? What usually happens is that he becomes even more protective.

No, the safest way is to plan your story first, and to start writing it only when you know just exactly where you're going.

Planning is a job for the mind, not for the emotions. The firmer you are about planning your story with your mind only, the better your story structure will be.

Certainly the emotions play a vital part in a writer's life. A story must be strongly felt by the writer before it can be strongly felt by the reader. But a writer must understand his emotions and control them so that the magic which they work will exert its spell over the reader and not over him.

Plan your campaign coolly—save your emotions for the heat of actual composition. That way, you can have a sound story and sell it, too.

Louise Boggess

How To Choose the Right Viewpoint for Your Short Story

Imagine that you are an editor. You pick up a manuscript and read:

> The little group cluttered one corner of the airport lounge. Janice wondered why she had been so stupid to come and so completely reveal her true feelings. Paul rubbed at a speck of dust on the camera lens and wished he could get rid of the man who had wrecked his marriage. Lee mentally worded his resignation as press agent for he was finished if that has-been actress didn't show up for this publicity stunt.

A story belongs to the character who dominates the action. In this example, the author has wandered in and out of the minds of three different characters in one paragraph and left only confusion. You, like the editor, probably would stop reading right there. Yet editors daily get stories in which the author has not learned the simple technique of viewpoint.

Viewpoint is the emotional focus from which you develop the action of a story. Objective viewpoint merely reports the facts unemotionally without going into the mind of any character. Since a short story requires strong emotion, it is written in subjective viewpoint.

In the subjective viewpoint, you share the thoughts of one or more characters in a story with the reader. By knowing what a character thinks and feels, the reader identifies emotionally with this person and becomes involved in the action of the story. The character through which you project a story is the *viewpoint* character. The type of subjective viewpoint you select determines the amount of emotion and the degree of dramatic continuity. A large majority of short stories are written in the single major character viewpoint.

1. Single Major Character

If you select the major character as the viewpoint, you do not enter the mind of any other. He alone gives the emotional coloring to the story. Introduce this viewpoint character immediately so as to start the reader identity. Take the story "Bird in Hand" by George R. Clay, which appeared in *Ladies' Home Journal.*

> The way the telephone in his family's apartment started to ring just as he stepped off the elevator was so uncanny that for a moment he stood clutching the newel post, afraid to move. Ever since coming down from New Haven yesterday afternoon, he had had a premonition that something would go wrong—that Leslie would miss her train, or get her weekends mixed up.

While you do not know the viewpoint character's name, you feel his anxiety and want events to go right for him.

Once you introduce the viewpoint character and hook the reader, do not clutter up the story by constantly reestablishing the viewpoint with "he saw," "he heard," or any other such expression. The reader does not need these reminders of the viewpoint. He has stepped inside the viewpoint and identifies any reactions as belonging to the character.

An exception does exist. If you have one or more long paragraphs of only the viewpoint's thoughts in conflict and very little action, you need to remind the reader with an occasional "he thought" or "he decided."

The quoted example above presents the viewpoint in the third person. If you select third person, you must use *he* as the pronoun and not *I* when you express his thoughts or show his action. On occasion, you may want to plant an important fact in the thoughts of the viewpoint character. For this special reason only, you let him think in first person, but you put quotations marks around it and qualify it with a "he thought" or "he reasoned."

Single major character viewpoint adapts easily to first or third person. If you choose first person, the thoughts and actions are expressed with the first person pronoun. Take this example from "Thou Shalt Not Kill" from *Modern Romances.*

> That bright spring Sunday morning, as I sat in church with Dick, I heard very little of my father's sermon. My mind was too filled with the argument that neither of us could win and neither of us could afford to lose.

Whether you use the first person pronoun or the third depends upon the characterization and the author's preference. Usually, the first person gives a picture of a more outgoing individual while third person is more conservative. Some writers prefer first person because they can become the created character easier and write more emotionally as the viewpoint. If your viewpoint is correct, all you need do is change the pronoun. For example, changing the George Clay Story, "Bird in Hand," cited above, to first person:

> The way the telephone in my family's apartment started to ring just as I stepped off the elevator was so uncanny that for a moment I stood clutching the newel post, afraid to move.

If you are a beginning writer, use single major character viewpoint for it offers quick identity for the reader, provides a strong line of continuity, and simplifies character development as well as plot action.

2. *Single Minor Character*

In some stories, the author writes from the viewpoint of a single minor character *about* a major one. Use the narrator or observer viewpoint when the major character is unsympathetic or offers poor reader identity. Sometimes a colorful backgroung in a story projects better to the reader through a minor character. Minor character viewpoint is preferable too if you plan a series of stories with the same character. Introducing new major characters keeps the series going. On occasion, the major character is not in all the scenes of the story, so a minor character viewpoint is necessary, as in "The Cookie Rebellion" by Will Stanton in *Redbook*.

> As so often happens, it was a trivial remark that started the trouble. The family was at the supper table, and for dessert we were having ice cream and cookies.
> "I remember when I was a boy," my father said. "We had a big cookie jar on the shelf next to the bread box. That's where we headed when we got home from school. It didn't matter how many friends we might bring along with us; we knew the cookie jar would always be full."
> "Really?" my mother said.

In this example, neither the mother nor the father are present in all the scenes, but the child narrator appears in all the action. Notice that the author establishes immediately the close relation between the viewpoint and the major characters. Make the observer and the major character of the same sex if at all possible. This doubles the reader identity.

In this type of viewpoint, the narrator becomes involved in the major character's problem, sums up the decisions for action by the major characters, and shares in the character change as expressed in the theme.

A variation of the observer viewpoint is *the implied narrator*. The author assumes the role of observer in the story but never identifies himself with a personal pronoun. He relates the action and furnishes the emotional reactions as the viewpoint. This is not objective viewpoint for the implied narrator provides emotional coloring.

Elizabeth Spencer uses this type of viewpoint in "Those Bufords," published in *McCall's*. Through emotional reactions the narrator emerges as an old timer in the community, possibly with a school connection, and a good memory for the capers of the Bufords.

> There were the windows, high, well above the ground, large, full of sky. There were the child's eyes, settled back mid-distance in the empty room. There was the emptiness, the drowsiness of Miss Jackson's own head, tired from tackling the major problems of little people all day long, from untangling their hair ribbons, their arithmetic, their handwriting, their thoughts. Now there was the silence.
>
> The big, clumsy building was full of silence, stoves cooling off, great boxy rooms growing cool from the floor up, cold settling around her ankles. Miss Jackson sat there two or three afternoons a week, after everybody else had gone, generally with a Buford or because there were Bufords: it was agreed she had the worst grade this year, because there were Bufords in it.

You have the feeling that somebody tells this story but you have no pronoun identifying the narrator. The difficulty in writing this type of viewpoint is to avoid going into any character's mind. With the exception of a few sentences, the author of this story maintained the implied narrator viewpoint.

3. Multiple Viewpoint

Omniscient viewpoint in which you enter the minds of all characters and show their thoughts rarely appears in the short story today. The average short story runs around five thousand words. By the time you make the viewpoint transition from one character to another, you steal too many words from the plot and character development. Hence multiple viewpoint adapts better to novelette or a novel.

Occasionally, a short story appears in various slick magazines written from the viewpoint of two major characters involved in a similar problem. These two characters move toward a joint solution at the moment of revelation and discover each other. In short, you have two story lines which emerge from two different directions and end on a common solution.

"My Child Is Missing" by Gertrude Schweitzer in *Good Housekeeping,* is a good example of dual viewpoint. The first two paragraphs of this story relate the event which brings the two characters together: A little boy is missing, supposedly because his mother has left him unattended. Tony Lewis, a reporter who had lost his child this way, is assigned to interview the mother, "that Carpenter woman." He takes over the viewpoint first, and the reader learns part of his story.

> Tony Lewis drove up in his old car with the press card stuck in the windshield and got out to look around a bit before he went up to her apartment.

Tony keeps the viewpoint until he begins to interview "that Carpenter woman." Here is the first long transition in viewpoint.

> "I'd like you to tell me what happened from the beginning," he said to her. "I won't interrupt or ask questions until you're through, but I'll take notes, if that won't bother you."
> She sat on the edge of her chair, letting her tea get cold, watching the door, never taking her eyes from it. After a minute she began to talk, her voice flat and dead to begin with and then coming to life as she remembered.
> "It began with the bus," she said, "The bus was twenty-five minutes late. I take the 5:10 bus from Stratton Street every evening, after I finish my work at Professor Illingwood's house. He often asks me to work late, but I have to tell him I can't . . . ."
> She began for the hundredth time to relive it all, tracing every step, every detail of that afternoon once again in her mind. . . .

Tony pictures her for the reader, then the Carpenter woman begins to tell her story. The next paragraph is in her viewpoint. She keeps the viewpoint and tells part of her story. The author smoothly transitions viewpoint back and forth between the two major characters until the end of the story.

Dual viewpoint is difficult for beginners because it divides the reader identity, interrupts the continuity, and weakens the suspense. It steals words from characterization and plot. Unless you are an experienced writer like Gertrude Schweitzer and know how to overcome these difficulties, don't try this type of viewpoint.

The best rule to follow is never shift viewpoint unless you gain more than you lose. Master single major character viewpoint before you try the more difficult ones.

Knowing the types of subjective viewpoint is only the first step in mastering the technique of viewpoint. You must now learn how to select the best character in your story for the viewpoint. Some experienced writers take the projected characters in a short story and write several paragraphs from the viewpoint of each. When the words flow easily for a character's viewpoint, that one is selected. But the beginning writer usually has not developed this sensory perception of the experienced writer for the right viewpoint character. There are other ways of selecting the viewpoint.

Since most short stories are written in single major character viewpoint, let's summarize the plot of "The Treasure" by Lawrence Williams in *Good Housekeeping,* so you can see how to give Marcy the six-point test for viewpoint.

Marcy, in filling out a renewal form for a driver's license, feels she needs an extra page to explain that the housewife does a large number of things but not anything specific or very well. Her husband Tim, a housing contractor, asks Marcy to fix dinner for some prospective buyers the next evening. She is elated until he starts bragging on Adella, his decorator, giving her credit for getting the buyers interested. Marcy envies Adella who excels in everything big and who can put decorator down as occupation. She resolves to fix the best dinner possible and play a small role in the sale so her husband will truly appreciate all she does.

The next day one problem after another confronts Marcy. The kids come down with colds and she puts them to bed. The car refuses to start, and she arranges for the service station to fix it. She cleans the house, argues with the plumber over the cost of fixing the washing machine. She goes to the market to get a roast and meets little Tim's teacher who asks about the Sir Galahad costume. Her child has not mentioned it, so she goes to library and sees how to make the costume.

Arriving home, she checks on the kids, puts the roast in the oven, rolls up her hair, goes to work on the costume. She cuts flowers from the garden for the house, fixes the vegetables, feeds the children, and dresses before the guests arrive.

She feels that nobody really paid any attention to the dinner or the conversation, but all seemed eager to discuss business. Adella brings out her prospectus, and Marcy cleans the dishes. When she joins them in the living room, she falls asleep and the guests leave without waking her. This is her dark moment because she feels she has failed her husband.

The next morning Tim pencils in *magician* as occupation on the renewal form and explains that a magician does the impossible and makes it seem easy. Marcy knows he appreciates all she does.

The best way to select your viewpoint character is to know the definite functions he performs in a story. While one or more characters may perform some of these functions, only the viewpoint meets the specifications for all six. Keep the story summary in mind as we check to see if Marcy performs these functions.

1. Emotion

The viewpoint character supplies the brooding hunger or longing for love, popularity, or recognition. The way this character tries to satisfy his longing provides the dominant emotion, such as dramatic, mysterious, romantic, or humorous.

Marcy longs for her husband to appreciate her, a housewife, as much as he does Adella, his decorator. In trying to fix a good dinner and help her husband as much as Adella with the sale of the houses, she must solve one unexpected problem after the other. In showing all that can happen to a housewife, she gives the story a light humorous emotion.

So you select the character who can supply the dominant emotion you, the author, wish to project to the reader.

2. Conflict

The viewpoint furnishes the conflict of the story. This conflict comes from the viewpoint character's traits, her problem and efforts to solve it, the supporting characters, and the setting. So you select the character with the most pressing problem to solve, the trait which provides the most inner conflict and outer struggle with the other characters of the background.

Marcy has the mistaken idea that her husband does not appreciate her. Her problem is to do something which will make him see her in the true light. She agrees to fix a special dinner for his business clients and show Adella, the decorator, that a housewife can do something important. Her husband increases the character conflict by praising Adella. The wife struggles to be more like Adella but the problems coming from running a house keep interfering. Before she can fix the dinner, she must solve other minor problems any housewife faces. So Marcy definitely furnishes the conflict.

3. Suspense

The viewpoint character carries the suspense by being on scene at all times in the story in an effort to solve the problem. The decisions this principal character makes must create new problems. To make decisions which lead to new complications, he must have the least information as to the true situation.

A viewpoint character who knows too much forces the author to cheat the reader by withholding such facts. The reader usually experiences anger or shock by the author not sharing everything the viewpoint character knows. The result is false suspense. Suspense is not a matter of "will the viewpoint character solve the problem" but rather of "how is the correct solution reached?"

Marcy is on scene at all times and does not realize that she plays a major rule in her husband's business. When she tries to plan a special dinner for the business associates, she must solve one small problem after the other. The reader wonders if she will have dinner ready in time. When no one seems interested in the dinner, the reader wonders if Marcy has failed and suffers the same dark moment as the character. But the next morning the license form gives Tim a chance to tell Marcy how much he appreciates her. So Marcy definitely carries the suspense of the story.

4. Reader Identity

The viewpoint must offer the reader the fastest and strongest identity. Hence the reader will identify with the action of the story.

Marcy offers excellent identity for the women who read this magazine. Most women have an Adella in their life. Certainly no mother has ever tried to do something important that everything about the house and family didn't interfere. Too, women can identify with the exhausted feeling of fixing a dinner under pressure. Furthermore, every woman rebels against packaging all she does for the family under the nondescript word, *housewife.* No other character can offer the strong reader identity of Marcy for this market.

5. Author's Message

The viewpoint character, through plot action, must develop the author's message to the reader. This character has the most to win or lose by the outcome of the story and must show a believable change. The change is the bringing of one wrong facet or blind side of a basically good character into the correct focus. You express this change in a theme or universal truth by means of dialogue or thoughts of the viewpoint near the end of the story.

Marcy's happiness depends on the assurance that Tim appreciates all the things she does. When Marcy hears Tim's explanation of a magician, one who does the impossible every day and makes it look easy, she knows that she has been wrong in thinking he didn't know and appreciate all the little things she does each day to keep family affairs running smoothly. So Marcy changes her mistaken idea of her husband and sums up the theme in her thoughts.

> I saw what Tim meant—and what he'd seen all along. A hundred small tricks are at least as important as one big one. And they keep the show on the road.

So Marcy certainly leaves every housewife feeling that she is a magician, the author's message.

6. Ability

The viewpoint character has the ability to solve the problem The author shows Marcy solving one problem after the other and still managing to have the dinner ready on schedule. Certainly she decides which problem to tackle first and never hesitates to take appropriate action. She shows herself as a house cleaner, flower arranger, cook, nurse, seamstress, researcher, a diplomat, or any other occupation associated with housewife.

So give each character in your story this six-point test. The one which best performs all of these functions should be your viewpoint character.

Writing is show business. The reader will see the viewpoint character as you conjure him if you show how the viewpoint acts, talks, and thinks along with how others react to him. Using a document or author's statement to characterize are weak devices and best avoided.

The author projects Marcy as a housewife who spends her time solving little daily emergencies but who longs for her husband to praise her the way he does his assistant, Adella, for a big job.

1. By Action

How the viewpoint character acts reveals her character. Action without conflict reveals little, so put your character under stress. Here the author shows Marcy as a person who can solve daily problems.

> Even after the car was fixed, the kids put to bed, the house more-or-less cleaned, and the plumber and I had spent forty-five minutes of merciless bargaining in the cellar over the washing machine, I *still hadn't had time to give a thought to the all-important dinner.*

2. By Dialogue

Dialogue brings the viewpoint character alive for the reader. Each line of dialogue must characterize or be in character with the projected picture of the character. Marcy meets her son's teacher in the market. The teacher asks how the costume is coming along for the pageant. Marcy knows nothing about the pageant but she is not the type to let the teacher know.

> "Oh, that pageant," I said nervously shucking the store's peas into my shopping bag. I had never heard of it before. "Coming along so-so. Just which part . . . Timmy wasn't too explicit."

Here in dialogue Marcy again shows she can meet the challenge of the unexpected.

3. By Thoughts

The viewpoint character carefully confides his thoughts and reactions to the reader. If he says one thing and does another, he must tell the reader why. Thoughts are the hot line to the reader, so the viewpoint character must share his reactions to other characters or situations, argue the right choice of action, but especially keep the inner conflict mounting.

Tim tells Marcy how Adella has worked up a prospectus on her own time, and he comments on how great she is. Marcy reveals her envy of Adella.

> No, I suppose, we never really give up, not altogether. But I accepted the fact that I was, and would forever be, outclassed. I could do other things, trifling things, totally disparate things, but—in the end—sort of unnoticeable things, expected things.

Again, Marcy downgrades herself in comparison to Adella.

4. By Reaction of Other Characters

The viewpoint character is the star, so you show him through the reactions of other characters. Marcy defines a magician as somebody who does tricks, but Tim corrects her. In doing so he shows Marcy as she really is.

> "They only look like tricks. Marcy, a magician is a person who does the impossible every day and makes it look easy. That's what you do.

So the author gives you the true image of Marcy. Not one time did the author use author's statement or documentary to present any of the characters.

When you have a clear mental picture of your viewpoint character, write several paragraphs using each device and see if each shows a part or the total image of the character you wish to project.

If you select the right type of subjective viewpoint, and choose the character who best performs the six functions of a viewpoint character, and can project the viewpoint character with the four devices, you have learned the technique of viewpoint.

Susan Thaler

How To Use the Flashback in Fiction

Flashback is that indispensable device for giving your characters a kind of depth and dimension they could not otherwise receive. Through the description of an event that happened years ago (or even yesterday, for that matter) to your protagonist, you give the reader a greater understanding of the sort of person he is today—*why* he reacts the way he does in whatever situation you have set up for him.

While the very term *flashback* implies a digression from the present to some other point in time, it can, if skillfully applied, also bring an important sense of *immediacy* to any story. Once you engage the reader in a flashback scene, hopefully he will be so interested, that he is reminded it is flashback only when you gently bring him back to the present action.

Let us suppose that you are writing a father-son story. The boy has just informed his father (the protagonist) that he has dropped out of school to enlist in the service. The father is outraged at what he considers the boy's foolhardiness. They confront each other in a scene which might go something like this:

> "Just what did you think you could prove by this?" Martin (the father) stormed. "Don't you know you're dealing with war—war means death and suffering! Death, you fool! You could *die* out there . . . !"
>
> Jeremy stiffened. "I know that, Dad," he said, jutting out his chin, as if to ward off a blow. "I know what I'm doing."
>
> Such a young face, Martin thought. There was something achingly familiar about it, about that serious determination to grow up in a hurry, to be a man . . . He remembered another time, another war. His own father had seen him to the station. Standing there in the half-light, in all the clamor and confusion going on about them, his father had become suddenly unbearably dear, so much so that Martin had to turn away.
>
> "Now you take care, son," his father kept saying. "You just take good care of yourself . . ."
>
> He wanted to throw himself into his father's arms, to tell him how afraid he

really was—the way he had done when he was a child. But then the conductor
shouted, "Boarrrd!", and Martin straightened, smiling his soldier's smile.

"*You* take care, Pop," he said, for he was no longer a child, after all, and they
shook hands once more before the train pulled away . . .

"Dad?" Jeremy's voice pulled him back, back to this boy who was at once so
young and so old, as he himself had been.

In that random example, several things were accomplished: By recalling an incident similar in his own past to the one taking place, now,
Martin is able to see his son in broader perspective, thereby gaining a
better understanding of Jeremy. More important, the reader is given an
opportunity to view Martin at another period in his life, away from the
role allotted him in the story. (Depth and dimension) The reader sees
that Martin himself has gone through the same experience his son is
about to have, and Martin's reaction—anger, fear, tenderness—is
more understandable.

There is no rule about *when* flashbacks should appear. They can
come about anywhere in the beginning-middle-end sequence of a story
and, in some cases, can launch the action from the first sentence:

Tristeza had been part of our family for nine years, ever since I was seven.

That opening sentence, from "Tristeza, My Friend," published in
The American Girl magazine served as a springboard for a story of
mine that relied a great deal on flashback. Although the heroine, a
teen-ager, was telling the story from the vantage point of the present, a
large portion of it dealt with episodes which had taken place when she
was a little girl growing up. The following paragraph followed the
above-quoted introduction:

That day, when my big sister Cheryl and Donnie from next door let me tag
along with them to the Pound, is one that will never fade from my memory. It was
the second time in a month that Donnie's dog, Jo-Jo, had been picked up by Mr.
Squires, the dog-catcher. "Now, you listen here, young man," Mr. Squires bel-
lowed . . .

The trick is to be able to dip in and out of a character's past without
jarring the continuity or mood you are trying so hard to maintain. Because you want to furnish as much information as possible about your
characters in relatively little space, flashback technique calls for a great

degree of subtlety. And here is where a dextrous handling of tenses comes in: I said *"That* day, when my big sister Cheryl . . ." and ". . . Donnie's dog Jo-Jo *had been* picked up . . ." when I wanted to illustrate that the event being described happened some time ago. But once the reader has been so informed, I want him to forget about it as quickly as possible—to become involved in the action as though it were taking place that very moment. (Immediacy.) So that when Mr. Squires speaks, the dialogue is once again in the present tense: "Now, you listen here, young man . . . if you don't keep your dog off the streets and on a leash where he belongs," etc., and the action proceeds from there.

The length of a flashback can vary from one or two-line flash of memory in the mind of a character to a highly-dramatized incident involving a major action. There is nothing quite like it to create tension in a story. How many of us are familiar with the novel that brings us to the brink of crisis, only to plunk us down, suddenly, in the middle of last year, last month, last week? (J. P. Marquand is famous—or infamous—for this sort of reader-tantalizing!)

But while you have endless room in a novel in which to uncover the past, too many flashbacks in a short story can be frustrating. (How many of us have skipped flashback scenes in order to get to what's happening in the story itself?!). When an author is confined to twenty pages or less, he must be infinitely more selective in choosing the incidents in the past he wants to highlight for the benefit of the present. He must, through a conscious knowledge of just what it is he is trying to express and an instinctive *feel* for the pace of the story, know just when a flashback is called for.

The flashback must, then, *be integral to the action.* It must, if it is to be absorbed neatly into the fabric of the story, bear some degree of *relevancy*—have an emotional tieup—to what is happening in the present.

If you are describing a character who is fighting for his life against a mob's assault, and you want to tell us something more about him (which is why you are using the flashback in the first place!), don't begin by explaining how his mother met his father and they got married and had a son (him!) and when his father went bankrupt they were all forced to move to a part of town on the wrong side of the tracks. Begin immediately with something that would tie in with what's happening to him now—i.e., how he was once attacked by a group of bullies on his way home from school:

> He ran, but his legs would not carry him, the way they failed him that other time. His heart was pounding inside his chest, like then, and he was afraid, like then, but that day there had been no place to run. Butch Hobbs and Tommy Blaine had followed him home from school, running all the way . . .

From there, you can go on to tell as much about his boyhood as you feel is necessary to illustrate whatever point you are making. Once that point is made, however, leave it and resume the telling of the story you sat down to write! While flashbacks provide essential background material, they should never be relied upon to carry a story by themselves, and never be used to "pad" a skimpy plot.

Relating something in retrospect evokes a sense of bittersweet nostalgia in the minds of both character and reader—a sense of something won and lost, never to be reclaimed except in memory. Flashing back to a happier time can offer a sharp poignancy to a short story.

In "The Eight O'Clock of Morning," my heroine is a young wife and mother. In the scene described below, she and her husband are driving to her parents' house after the death of her father. The story is written in first person:

> "Why can't I cry?" I asked Hal as we drove past fields opening up to spring. "I loved him so much, why can't I cry?" I remembered when Mama and Papa bought the house at the Jersey shore. That house. I cannot think of my girlhood without thinking of the summers spent there. Its tiny, screened-in porch and broken flagstone path (which Papa was always going to fix, but never got around to). The little backyard with its stubborn crabgrass tufts, and the hammock where Papa would like to fall asleep on Sunday afternoons.
> "There's a feeling of peace in this house," Papa would say, "which I don't quite get anywhere else. Can't you feel it, Laurie?"
> The house looked deserted now, as we drove up to it on the late afternoon . . .

Not only do you learn a little something about the kind of man Papa was, but the tragic circumstances of the present are heightened by the woman's remembrance of a happy Then.

If you possess a thorough knowledge of the people you are writing about, you should be able to tell what happened to them before the story began without too much trouble.

In a way, you are saying, "Oh, Jack Smith? Why, I've known him all my life. I can tell you hundreds of stories about him . . ." And because you want others to get the same, intimate glimpse into this person's makeup, you will choose the most pertinent (to Jack Smith's present situation) incident you can think of. (Relevancy.) You will let us know just enough so that we can nod our heads and say, "Ah, yes, that's Jack Smith, all right. So *that's* why he did such-and-such . . ."

Flashbacks are, in a sense, the mirrors which an author holds up to the reader, so that the reader gets a front, side and rear view of the character in the story. These mirror peeks, no matter how infrequently they occur, should provide a series of revelations—always titillating with just the correct amount of information and no more, always telling us something we didn't know before.

"And, after all," a teacher of mine once aptly pointed out, "isn't that the essence of the written work?"

Mariana Prieto

What You Should Know about Using the Flashback in Fiction

We have all heard the phrase, "The past is prologue." Certainly this applies to the writing of the flashback.

Sequence can sour. The flashback can keep the story fresh and interesting. But it must be deftly mixed in. Like the pieces in an intricate mosaic, we must fit the flashback in so that it blends with the rest of the story.

I'm sure we all have friends who include in their conversation long explanations about past events. Many times they have no direct bearing on the subject and we are inclined to want to say, "Please go on with it."

This is how a reader feels if the flashback is too long. He wants to flip the page and go on reading the story.

This is why we must be very careful about flashbacks and not let them become *flopbacks* that can cause our story to flop and sag and fall apart.

The short story should *begin* at a high point, a dramatic scene, if possible. If it is necessary for the reader to know how the character got in this situation or what went before, that led up to this situation, then we must introduce a flashback. This device helps clarify the situation. The flashback should carry the reader back and give him relevant information that leads up to where the story opened.

Sometimes a sentence will serve as sufficient flashback, other times a paragraph is needed. Beware, do not let the flashback be so long that it outbalances the rest of your story.

In a short story the span of time should be short. Therefore the flashback technique is important to maintain this brevity of time. The writer can thus give an account of past events that have bearing on the story and bring the reader up to the present situation without transferring from the present. This is where practice, polishing and craftsmanship are important. Try to analyze your material for pace. We live in a fast-paced world and no amount of material, no matter how important, must seem to slow the rhythm and movement of the story line.

In the following passage, the flashback is necessary to the story and in one paragraph gives the life background of the grandfather and acquaints the reader with Carlos' ancestry.

> "Tell me grandfather, about when you were a little boy and learned to fly kites in Spain," Carlos begged.
> So his grandfather told him again about the kites he had made. Then how he and his family had moved to Cuba where he made more kites and later how they had moved again. This time to the United States.

This is the *tell me* technique in order to get into the flashback. Another familiar device used to lead the reader back, is music. A melody can set the character's thoughts back in time and introduce the recounting of that time. A bird song or a shrill noise can set into motion the recall process of a character and smoothly introduce the flashback. In "October Song" by William Sanson (*McCall's*), music is the device used for the leadback, as:

> "Humoresque" cosseted her. Awful tearoom stuff, she thought, but gave in and listened to its soothing tinkle of security. Like the sunny cream walls, like the chintzes, it took her back to the simpler thirties, when the children were babies and they had all lived and laughed together in an ample gabled house in Surrey. Life then had seemed to have a future. Fir trees in the garden, mud-guards glinting on the gravel drive, tradesmen at their entrance, a cook in the kitchen . . .
> Well, now it was a three-roomer in Kensington, the war survived, the children dispersed and bringing up children of their own.

The transition to the present is smoothly accomplished and information about the present setting is given.

Francoise Sagan in her short story, "Help or Something,"

(*Vogue*), gives us another example of clever handling of necessary information. She does it this way:

> That spring we were in Normandy and living in a sumptuous house, all the more sumptuous for our having, after two years of inundations, had the roof repaired. The sudden absence of pans set out strategically under the beams, the absence at night of ice-cold droplets of water on our peaceful, sleeping faces, the absence of a spongy carpet underfoot intoxicated us.

A writer with less craftsmanship might have told these problems in sequence and it would have been dull reading, like the recitation of a tiresome relative. As it is, she opens on the happy note that the roof is repaired, then flashes back to the problems that preceded it, the absence of which accounts for their present happiness.

In my writing classes, I keep telling my students that just because a thing really happened, it isn't necessarily interesting. At least not always if told in the exact sequence of the happening. We must, as writers, select the sequence that will prove most interesting to the other fellow. We must whet his appetitie, gain his attention and then go on from there. This is why it is better to open on a high note, then go back and explain, if explanation is necessary.

Here we have an example from a story published in *Redbook,* the title "Breaking Free" by Ralph McInery. This shows a flashback as presented in a first person story. The narrator gives us the information plus some insight into his own character.

> I nodded. I had never known her husband—he had died when Jane was in her early teens—but I had difficulty imagining Mrs. Reynolds as shattered as my mother now was. Not that my mother's condition could be described as desolate sorrow. My father's fatal attack had taken him in the bed of another woman, one my mother had known about. Whatever check there had been on her drinking had died with my father.

Here is an example of a very short flashback from one of my published adult stories, "The Tinsel Star" in *The Magnificat.*

> As she patted the baby, her eyes caught the gleam of the star in the sapphire ring on her finger. She had accepted that ring as she accepted all Eric's gifts and love, with no intention of return.

This brief passage shows that the character had been selfish in the past as she was now in the present.

Speech, action, dialogue, recall, all can be paths that lead into the smoothly presented flashback. The reader should not be jolted by it, or into it.

No break in the story flow should be occasioned by the flashback and certainly a reader should not have to go back and read it to understand it.

Flashbacks can be presented in segments in the longer story. The entire flashback need not be given all at one time but rather as it contributes to the story progress. Too long a glimpse into the past can cloud the reader's understanding of the present.

Think of newspaper headlines. They give the exciting part of the story to the reader, then after he is hooked, they tell what leads up to the headline. In other words, they resort to flashback technique.

Even the clever conversationalist uses flashbacks to hold his listeners. He opens with, "My house burned down," and the listener listens.

"Why?" the listener asks. "What caused it?"

Just as the reader wants to know what went before, what led up to the present situation or involvement.

Yes, life is full of flashbacks, we can't escape or deny them. But we can by studying the technique of other writers, learn how to introduce them skillfully.

I urge you to become flashback conscious. When you come to a flashback in a story, red pencil it. After you have finished reading the story, put it away and see if you can recall the flashback. Even write it and see if you can remember the introductory sentence that moulded it smoothly into the story.

A flashback, like a guide, should cover only the necessary area, and it can be done. Try a carefully fashioned flashback and see!

Robert C. Meredith and John D. Fitzgerald

Transition

The faults that beginning writers display in writing short stories are to make overly abrupt transitions, or to go to the opposite extreme and make long-winded and self-conscious transitions. There are certain ways to avoid both errors; let us look at them:

1. In writing, it is sometimes effective to indicate a transition merely in terms of the physical appearance of the manuscript. One accomplishes this by leaving a space between the paragraphs twics as great as the customary one.

2. Again, transitions can be indicated by using standard phrases.

In making transitions, it is nearly impossible, nor should the writer necessarily try, to avoid the use of certain standard phrases: "The next day . . . ," "A month passes . . . ," "Winter came to the valley . . ." can be invaluable, when rightly placed.

3. To avoid any abruptness in transition, however, give the reader a clue that the transition is going to take place. The reader's own anticipation of a leap in time will help bridge the gap.

A failure to allow the reader to anticipate a sudden break in the time of a story may result in the story's failure. A reader is too suddenly jarred out of his dream world by a faulty transition he did not anticipate. Let us take an example:

> Jane let Helen off at her apartment and then drove on home.
> The next day when they met for lunch at the Biltmore, Jane noticed that Helen didn't look well.

One moment the reader is with Jane and Helen in the car; the next moment, he is having lunch with them in a hotel dining room. A faulty transition of this sort is sufficient to make many a reader lose interest, and many an editor stop reading. How can one avoid the mistake?

4. Let the reader anticipate a transition through the use of dialogue.

Jane stopped her car in front of the apartment house where Helen lived. "Don't forget our luncheon engagement at the Biltmore tomorrow," she reminded Helen before driving home.

> Jane couldn't help noticing that Helen didn't look well, when they met for lunch the next day. She frowned as the discreet headwaiter showed them through the snowy dining room of the hotel.

Notice this example from Somerset Maugham's *The Colonel's Lady:*

> "I expect it'll be very dull, but they're making rather a point of it. And the day after, the American publisher who's taken my book is giving a cocktail party at Claridge's. I'd like you to come to that if you wouldn't mind."
> "Sounds like a crashing bore, but if you really want me to come I'll come."
> "It would be sweet of you."
> George Peregrine was dazed by the cocktail party . . . .

5. Let the reader anticipate a transition through the use of narration.

Here is an illustration of this method, using our friends Jane and Helen:

> Jane stopped the car in front of the apartment house where Helen lived. After reminding Helen of their luncheon engagement at the Biltmore the following day, she drove on home.

And here is another from the story *Things* by D.H. Lawrence:

> However, New York was not all America. There was the great clean West. So the Melvilles went West, with Peter, but without the things. They tried living the simple life, in the mountains. But doing their own chores became almost a nightmare . . . A millionaire friend came to the rescue, offering them a cottage on the California coast . . . With joy the idealists moved a little farther west . . . .

6. In giving a reader a clue that the transition is going to take place, also let him anticipate the setting of the next scene.

The scene will ordinarily change not only in time but in place. As may be seen in the above examples, the place of the next scene is mentioned; and the writer makes his transition more subtle to a certain degree by giving descriptive details suggestive of the new place to which the action will move:

> "Are we going tomorrow? Are we really going to the circus?" Peter asked with his eyes as big as silver dollars.
> "Yes," his Dad said, reaching down and patting the shiny brown hair with an affectionate hand.
> Lights danced. The trumpets blared. Horses wheeled in the circle. Overhead, in what seemed a vast new sky, aerialists casually clutched at thin lines of steel. Peter sat without making a sound.

If the effort is to capture a mood of excitement in the boy, then such a use of transition will sustain the mood, suggest the boy's own anticipation of the event—perhaps even his dreaming about it during the night—and these suggestions may compensate for any slight abruptness one finds in the transition.

To illustrate faulty transition, here is a representative passage from a student's story:

> Frank Smith ordered his secretary to get him a reservation on the eleven o'clock plane for Washington and to wire Senator Davis he was coming. He wondered what the Senator wanted, as he rode in a taxi from his office to his apartment. After packing an overnight bag, he took a taxi to the airport. Upon arrival at the Washington airport, he took a taxi to the Senate Office Building. The Senator's secretary told him the Senator was waiting for him and to go right in.
> "I appreciate your coming at once," the Senator said as they shook hands.

The student's reason for making such a circumlocutory transition was that he wished to increase suspense. But what suspense can there be in irrelevant detail? The reader is only interested in what Senator Davis wants with Frank Smith, and the sooner the author gets Frank into the Senator's office, the better. The transition may be shortened and made more effective by the use of dialogue:

> Frank Smith pushed down the intercom button on his desk. "Miss Jones, get me a reservation on the eleven o'clock plane for Washington, and wire Senator Davis I'll be in his office by one o'clock."
> "I appreciate your coming at once," Senator Davis said as Frank entered the Senator's office.

We can make the transition even shorter by using narrative:

> Frank Smith asked his secretary to get him a plane reservation for Washington and to wire Senator Davis that he would be there at one o'clock.
> "I appreciate your coming at once," Senator Davis said as Frank entered the Senator's office.

Students frequently are excited about using methods that are now no longer new, but which still remain under the sanction of the experimental rather than the traditional. We have had occasion before to remark upon the technique of stream of consciousness, which was brought to whatever values it may have for the writer by James Joyce and Virginia Woolf. In such a method of procedure, verbal association plays a large part, the innermost recesses of a character's many experiences being crowded together, in frequently fantastic, or at least fanciful, ways, as a substitute for external causal relationships, grammatical syntax, time distinctions, and the other ways in which we usually separate experiences or bring them together logically. The net effect of the stream-of-consciousness technique is to break down all patterns that we normally think of our minds' using and to replace them instead by patterns—if, indeed, one can call them that—that are pre-eminently private and subjective within each individual. One of the chief things to wither under such a technique is the logical nature of the transitions one makes —for logic has nothing to do with the leaps, the skips, the jumps, the sudden shifts in idea, in imagery, in sound, and in rhythm caused by peculiarly private meanings. It is, of course, supernally useless to argue against any new addition to the techniques a writer may use, but we think it wise to voice the warning that the technical advances that a writer makes will depend upon his own growth, rather than upon experimenting with changes that alter the form and structure in the whole field of literature. Hence, as we have indicated before, in discussing the work of great writers, the first steps appear very frequently to be crude, unpolished, largely imitative, and original work emerges through practice in writing— depending upon an author's talent and ability. It certainly will not hurt a beginning writer to attempt lucidity, clarity, and simplicity; he may even find that such an attempt is more difficult than it first appears.

Val Thiessen

Five Suggestions for Writing Transitions

There are five transitional techniques that have been useful to me. All of these depend upon one clear principle. Since the writer skips time, space, and action at will, it is necessary to provide something continuous across the gap.

Suppose, for instance, that in planning a story, we have decided that at the end of the first scene our hero enters his own apartment and discovers the body of his brother, lying there, slain. We also decide that the next scene centers on the questioning of our hero by detectives from Homicide. Obviously, scene one ends with the hero telephoning the police. There was a time when it might have taken me two hundred words to get from the telephone call to the actual interrogation. Now I use one of the five techniques.

First of these is *emotion*. In the following example an emotion is shown at the end of the scene and used again to introduce the new scene. The emotion in the situation described might be shock or grief. The end of the first scene and the beginning of the new one might go like this:

> Moving as if he were in a nightmare, he dialed the police. After he gave the address and facts, he hung up the telephone, his brain dazed and numb.
> The numbness had not worn off when the police lieutenant hurled the first question at him, ten minutes later.

An *object* can be carried across the two scenes as easily as an emotion. In our example one might choose the body itself, the murder weapon, or even a simple, routine object like the telephone. It might go like this:

> "There's been a murder in my apartment," he told the desk sergeant, his hand trembling as he held the telephone receiver against his ear.
> It seemed that he had hardly replaced the receiver in its cradle before the police were there, stabbing questions at him.

Both of these transitions give the feeling of rapid pace, and rush the story along. Though they may seem terribly obvious and crude to you, once they are used in a story this quality vanishes, but the feeling of pace persists.

Weather transitions are not so great for pace, but they do provide a chance for mood work where that fits the story. A weather transition might go like this:

> He dialed the police, and when the sergeant answered he said swiftly, lest his voice should fail, "There's been a murder in my apartment." As he added the details and gave his address, he could hear the monotonous drumming of the rain outside.
> It was still raining when the police stomped into his apartment, leaving great wet spots on his rug and staring at him out of suspicious eyes.

Of particular use in making viewpoint changes is the *name* transition. I do not recommend changing viewpoint, but there are times when shifting is desirable. A transition of name combined with a shift into the viewpoint of the new character might be this:

> The police answered his ring at once, and after a moment's preliminary he was connected with homicide. He said swiftly, "There's been a murder in my apartment, Lieutenant Harrigan. Can you come at once?"
> Lieutenant Harrigan was a thin, hawklike man in a brown suit. He stared at the body now, and then back at the man who had reported it, thinking and wondering, as he always did, just where this one was going to lead him.

Last of my five techniques, and most widely used is *time*. A time transition is simply a brief phrase to let the reader know how much time has passed between scenes. Thus the beginning of scene two, no matter how the telephone call was handled, might go:

> A scant fifteen minutes after his call, the police were ringing the bell at his apartment.

If you have the desire to be fancy, which is not at all necessary, you can find some interesting ways to measure time. Consider the implications in this approach:

> Fifteen chain-smoked cigarettes later, the police were ringing the bell at his apartment.

Be a miser between your scenes, and use these five techniques instead of two or three hundred words of wasted copy. Then take the words saved, and spend them when the time comes, to reveal the heights and the depths of the human heart, when it finds itself caught between passion and fear.

Handle your words as carefully as you handle money, and you'll be a long way toward trading those words for a steady stream of acceptances.

Jack Webb

In the Beginning

In the beginning, heaven and earth were created, and in the beginning you should move them to get off to a good start.

Why?

A good first sentence, first paragraph, first page, each in its turn will do more to sell a story than any other device save one. And that one is to have a story to tell. If you haven't the story, nothing I or the ghost of Bill Shakespeare could say would be of the very least help. Providing you have a yarn, however, let's consider the beginning.

In five seconds you can lose any reader, any editor, on the face of the earth. Or, you can catch him. Catch him, as Sabatini did, with this sentence:

> He was born with the gift of laughter and a sense that the world was mad.

So did Rafael Sabatini begin *Scaramouche.*

So should we all try to begin the next thing we write, and the next, and the next one after that, for once you've engaged a reader's eye and emotions in the first instant, engaged them with pleasure and in high gear, that reader is yours.

The last time the opening sentence of the Sabatini novel was called to my attention, it was quoted by an electronics engineer. He was not a writer, but he was a reader, and after a dozen years, he still could remember the beginning of that one book with the perfect first sentence.

Let's go a step further. Whether you can reach it from your bookcase, or whether you have to go to the library for it, take down the worst novel Mr. Hemingway ever wrote, *To Have And Have Not,* and read the first page. I have another friend, a reader who makes friends of his books, who is prone on his second martini to quote the entire first paragraph of *To Have And Have Not,* with his eyes lit up like a pinball machine.

I can't quote E. Hemingway. Scribners have a habit of charging for that. But you read that first page. Note the clarity of the description, the bit of Havana that is forever yours with scarcely an adjective in it, the terse, clean-cut dialogue that follows with mounting excitement even before the first page is finished, and you'll know what I mean.

In a short story I spend more time on the first paragraph or two than I do on any other part of the business which entails the actual writing. As it is in chess, so it is in fiction, you must command the beginning game before you can handle the middle, or even consider the end.

What is the beginning game? It is a series of carefully considered moves—call them sentences—which will provide the reader with what he wants to find in a story, whether he is thumbing through a magazine from the racks at his local liquor store or browsing among first pages at a table of recent fiction. What the reader wants to find is a sense of adventure with great things to come, a sense of enjoyment that will let him relax in his easy chair (even though paradoxically, he may end up, sitting on the edge of it and biting his nails), and most of all, a sense of movement that will make him turn the page.

The necessary factors in this opening game are not mystical somethings which must emerge from the crystal ball of your subconscious. Once in a while, the combination may come with no conscious effort on your part. Not often. Not unless you have the charm of a Saroyan, the subterranean volcano of a Thomas Wolfe, or the prolificacy and genius of Dickens, say, or Balzac. I'm not so lucky. I have to work hard on the little things I have to sell. I have to know what I want in the beginning and then try to get it.

And, what is it I, the writer, and my target, the reader, must become aware of together in the opening paragraph, the first scene?

A knowledge of time, a knowledge of place, and that feeling of movement.

Look at the first page in your current story. Are they there?

Here's how I did it in a short story for *Manhunt.*

It was a crisp, cold night with enough of a breeze off the ocean to drive the smog inland, so, the city must have looked like a blanket of stars as they slid down

toward the landing strips on the airfield.
 Even for her it must have been a beautiful flight up to a point, a sharp point with four inches of steel behind it.

That is not great writing. I don't pretend it is. But it did help sell the story. It helped because it gave the reader, and the editor who bought the story knowing his readers, atmosphere, violence, and a gentle hint of sex.

I wrote those two short paragraphs, moving determinedly from the general to the particular, a dozen times before they came out "right," before I had cut from them any word, any thought, that could cripple, or lead the reader astray from the story line.

If a story that started like that was the kind of story you wanted to read, you'd know it in an instant, in that fatal twenty seconds when you, the reader at the magazine stand, could turn the page, or the editor who might buy, could say, "This is not for us."

Here's the way I began *The Naked Angel.* I spent two weeks getting this start. If it moves fast and easy, it's because I tried very hard to build with a few handsful of words a complete atmosphere, a complete movement with a beginning, middle and end, in short, a complete scene —a scene which would stand by itself and say: *This is the sort of thing the writer has to give.*

The Church of St. Anne was of white stucco, humble and simple. But the dark green cypresses that grew before it were trim and tall like sentinels, guarding the bells in their shadowy tower and flanking the cross as somber as a sword blade against the gray of predawn.
 Inside, except for the eternal lamp before the Blessed Sacrament and the pale, varigated light sifting through the high stained windows, the church was dark.
 Within the last row of pews, beneath the First Station of the Cross, grotesque in shape with his hands clinging desperately to the back of the pew before him, a man was praying. His words were unclear and peculiarly spaced because of the way in which he was breathing and the taste of blood which was in his mouth.
 ". . . . to confess my sins, to do penance, and to amend my life, Amen." The perfect words, the words he had learned long ago, were hallowing the ugly end of his life as much as any words might in those last moments before he died with three smashed slugs of .45 caliber in the trunk of his body to hasten the Act of Perfect Contrition.

As it appeared in print, this scene was a little less than the first page, the kickoff when you kick high and hope to make the tackle at the instant the ball is caught.

What did it try to do?

A gimmick? You could call it that. It combined the sacred and the profane in the moment both were realized. In a holy moment, it hit you hard in the face with the loud, close echoes of violence.

Take the story itself, take it at the instant it begins. A cheap, little Mexican dope smuggler is dying. He has crawled to the church to die. Logically, chronologically, I could have gone back to when he was shot. I could have taken him through his desperate interlude between the time he was shot and the time he died, taken you along his trail of blood when he went to the parish house and the priest was not there; I could have pulled you along his path of anguish when he crawled from the parish house into the church to die. *I know I could have done these things because I tried them, because I threw the yellow sheets into the wastebasket filled with his final, awful journey.*

Even though I thought they were pretty fine when I wrote them, they did not do the job as well as it could be done. For, by trying, and trying again, I discovered that the point where I must begin the story, the point where the hook held the most bait, was afterwards, in those last terrible moments before the man died. That his hands and the way they grasped the pew before him, his final prayer with the words coming awkward with blood in his mouth, were far more effective than all the banging and crawling I could ever do.

There is, and I'm certain you've heard it, the dreadful chestnut about the teacher of composition who asked her pupils each to bring in an assignment on the beginning of a short story. This beginning was to include elements of deity, royalty, mystery and sex. The next day, one precocious youngster arrived with a single sentence: "My God!" exclaimed the duchess, "Who's pinching my leg?"

So you're blushing for me. But, I'll not apologize. That youngster probably turned into a selling writer. Because while the anecdote is ridiculous, it makes a very important point. Don't waste time. Your potential reader may be intending to waste a large part of his life facing that one-eyed monster in the living room, but when he settles down to read your story, he wants to be entertained at once. Why it's any easier to lay down a magazine or a book than it is to snap the knob on a television set, I don't know, but it is, dear writer, it is! And don't you forget it.

A good beginning will not sell a bad story. The most beautiful scene in literature is worthless if it goes nowhere, but fiction is replete with examples of effective openings. A little time at the library, or among your favorites on the bookshelf, or even at the magazine and paperback racks at your local drugstore—if the druggist is a patient man—will help no end.

Get your story, get the thread of it good and hard. And then, take your time. Hunt, and try, and hunt again until you've found the perfect beginning.

Remember Sabatini.

You can't lay down a story that starts: *He was born with the gift of laughter and a sense that the world was mad.*

Katherine Greer

The Story's Middle

That part of a story between the beginning and the end is sometimes called *the body* and sometimes called *the middle*; and neither term is the right one, nor sufficiently interest-provoking, to my way of thinking.

The word to remember when it comes to the body is *proportion*. That, I believe, is the writer's chief problem, as he goes from the beginning to the end: How many incidents to pile, one upon the other, to prove his point; how much of what he knows to tell, what to suggest and what to leave out, which scenes to play up and how.

The writer's object, as he progresses from page two, to three, and so on, is to bring his reader nearer and nearer his conclusion, and at the same time hold him back, while his story goes on. This is accomplished by making each scene count towards the end, and eliminating irrelevancies. The reader finds out a little more about the main theme or character but never enough to make him satisfied before he has read the story all the way.

In planning the middle of the story, the writer needs to use sharp scissors as he shapes his scenes. He should ask himself before he writes each new scene: "What does it need to accomplish?" And when it is finished: "Has it done that?"

The writer must have the same sharp eye for proportion and tempo as he leads his *characters* through the body of the story. If he introduces a new character—and sometimes he needs to—his reason must be clear not only to himself but to his reader. For example, unless a postman is important to the remainder of the plot, don't let him deliver the important letter; instead, let it be found in the mailbox, after he has passed the house. If, on the other hand, you feel that you need a new character to inject a bit of humor into a too solid middle, find one who will be useful in advancing the plot, as well as funny.

Dialogue must also be a writer's concern throughout the body of the story: swiftly-paced conversation which leads the reader on, yet keeps him in suspense; conversation which never just "passes the time of day," as it so often does in real life, but which at the same time *seems* like "real life" conversation.

With all this in mind the writer selects his ingredients, as I, for example, selected mine in a *Redbook* story called "Be Sure To Stop."

I began with Susan, the young wife of Bill Parker, the overly hospitable husband, vowing—and planning—over a sink full of dirty dishes, that she would get rid of their current week-ending couple and never have another guest as long as she lived.

Before I wrote a word of this beginning, I knew in my mind that Susan was to have a compromise victory; and also that she could have had a complete one, if she hadn't loved Bill too much to hold out for it. But I didn't know exactly how I was going to work it out. I knew that the character of her mother-in-law was going to have a lot to do with it, because she was the character, taken from real life, who had given me the idea for the story. And I knew that her character was the "surprise," which I wished to hold back from my reader, as long as I could. (This, incidentally, was one of the reasons I chose Susan, rather than Bill, to tell the story.)

I decided, also, that this part of the story would be more readable the less time I took with the conversation of the guests. And yet I had to have some of it, since, after all, *they* were the ones who were creating the problem. So I gave them two short scenes; and in one them, I killed two birds with one stone by having their conversation mostly about that person so important to the plot, Susan's mother-in-law.

In the second scene, in the living room, Elva (an older guest from town) drew Susan into the group:

> "I was telling Bill how exactly like his father he's getting to be—a chip off the old block . . . . You didn't know the Judge, did you?"
>
> "No," Susan said . . .
>
> "Susan hasn't even met Mother," Bill put in. "Mother didn't feel up to making the trip from California when we were married . . . ."
>
> "She's coming soon, though," Susan said. "Week after next." She thought: Good heavens, it will take me longer than that to get rested—and I've got to be rested—at my very best to face a mother-in-law!

"Oh, you'll love Betty!" Elva said.

Carl put in, "The way she can devil crabs and turn an ordinary lobster Newburg into ambrosia straight from heaven . . . ."

"And all the time looking like a duchess in a kitchen apron!"

Susan thought: Wait till she gets the shock of her new daughter-in-law in her kitchen apron! She managed dutifully: "She must be wonderful."

"She is," Elva said. "She and Joe always were the most popular couple in town. And the most hospitable. From the time they remodeled this place and moved out here until it was closed after he passed away and she went west, there was continuous open house. I never saw anything like it."

Well, sister, I have! Susan thought. "And you're right about one thing—Bill certainly is a chip off the old block—both blocks!"

The guests from town went soon after that—a quick sentence or two sent them on their way. Another short bit of conversation and the weekend guests were in their bedroom, Bill and Susan in theirs, and I had accomplished my introduction of mother-in-law as an integral part of the story. In their first moment of solitude Susan was about to deliver the ultimatum she had planned but Bill went to sleep; and the only sound, aside from his regular breathing, came from the next room. Their guests, the Trents, were having an argument, Susan thought.

She said aloud, "She knows how to keep him awake! I must be a jellyfish!"

In this scene, I have thought about *proportion*. I could have, for example, gone into more detail about what Susan overheard through the bedroom wall of their guests' argument, or I could have left it out altogether. The reason I mentioned it was that it was a character clue which I needed in the end. It was one of the things which convinced Susan that she didn't want a complete victory—and domination—over Bill. So it didn't really matter why Lucinda Trent was "telling her husband off"; all that mattered was that she was doing it; and the more quickly the reader got the idea, the better. Clues add suspense and pace; long explanations slow down the story.

The next and final scene is the following afternoon—Sunday. In point of time, this story has only two scenes, Saturday night and Sunday afternoon. Not quite the old Greek *unity* idea, but close to it. I believe that the Greeks really had something. It has been my experience that a short story which can take place within a short space of time is much easier to write and more successful as a finished product than one which is spread out over months or years. With a novel it is, of course, different. In that sense a short story is much more like a play. The reader must be held through the whole length of the story or the play.

In place, I have practiced economy too; for television or the stage, this story would require only three sets: the living room, the kitchen and the bedroom.

At the beginning of this scene, the reader knows that nothing has been settled for Susan, that this Sunday afternoon at the Parker farm will be just more of the same. The dispensing of hospitality with food and drink, with cluttering the kitchen sink with plates and glasses later. I knew as a writer, that more of the same can soon become boring. So I planned the scene carefully to avoid it.

Again, I thought about *proportion;* along with it, *tempo.* This time I didn't need to have the guests do much talking; I merely needed to show that they were *there.* Such quick phrases as Bill's greetings: "This is marvelous, Hank!" and "So good of you to take the trouble, Cousin Flora!" And: "About time you were showing up, you old ..." were enough to convince the reader that the Parkers were in for a busy afternoon.

I employed another method to avoid sagging in the middle. I introduced a new character in a short humorous (I hoped!) scene; but not just for the sake of something new and funny. My new character was logical and useful. He was logical because he was the hired man already on the place, therefore he didn't have to *happen to arrive* at the moment he was needed. I wrote:

> Bill slipped out to the barn and drafted Herman, their man-of-all-work, to clear the table and wash the dishes.
> "He'll be all right, honey," he whispered to Susan, when he rejoined the group in the living room. ". . . he must have washed a dish once in a while."
> Could be. Susan tried to keep an open mind. Heaven knew, she'd be thankful to have them out of the way.
> It must have been an hour, and half a dozen guests later, when she went out to the kitchen with a tray of empty glasses.
> Herman was elbow-deep in a greasy, grayish liquid with three of her most prized wedding-present cups floating like capsized rudderless boats on the surface of it, and no telling how many more of them submerged.
> "Thanks, Herman—I'll finish . . ." She hoped she sounded calm and collected. "I know you have a lot to do for the animals."

"Well, reckon I have." He pulled off the soiled towel he had tucked into his jeans. "Guess I'd better tell you, Mis' Parker—had a little accident with the glassware. Those tall ones on pedestals sure are mighty flimsy stuff."

"You broke one of the goblets?"

"Two of 'em. They sorta knocked together. I'm powerful sorry."

"Oh, that's all right." He did sound sorry; and, after all, he hadn't been hired to handle crystal and fine china.

"You've sure got plenty more of 'em, anyway," Herman said, as he parted.

I won't have long at this rate, Susan thought, as she gingerly lifted one of the cups, then another out of their slimy reservoir. I won't have anything . . . she was thinking of the hole Lucinda Trent's cigarette had made on her cushiest armchair.

The hole, the goblets—her whole nervous system . . . yes, the instant they were gone, she'd have a showdown!

The kitchen door opened quietly. She assumed it was Herman returning [*This, then, is the way Herman is useful, as well as logical*] for a postscript of apology. She was busy with the cups, and she didn't turn around until—

"You must be Susan," a voice, pleasantly modulated and cultured, the opposite of Herman's, said, "I might have known—"

"Why—who—you—you're Bill's mother!" Susan gasped.

So here we come swiftly, smoothly, and I hope, surprisingly, into the big scene of the story—the climax, the turning point—whatever you choose to call it. I have surprised the reader (as well as Susan) with the arrival of Susan's mother-in-law, but not too much because I have planted clues about her. They knew she was coming soon; they didn't know the exact date. I made her arrival ahead of time seem natural and logical by having her drop a word or so about "a cancellation of an earlier plane." And I haven't kept anything from the reader, which any of my characters knew.

Nor have I deliberately deceived my readers concerning the character traits of Betty Parker. If you will look back you will notice that I have described her only through the eyes of her friends and her son, and through the conclusions Susan, who has never met her, draws about her. I have also made use, indirectly, of the generally accepted idea that daughters-in-law and mothers-in-law rarely see eye to eye.

This is the scene which, in any number of different forms, had been in my mind ever since the inception of the story. I feel that it is very important that a writer have the general gist of his climactic scene in mind. This is the only way he can hold to a story line without meandering and adding useless scenes. This final scene is the one on which I had pinned my hopes of making "Be Sure To Stop" a top-notch magazine story instead of just run-of-mill marriage problem stuff. It is the scene which I couldn't have left out or played down. In every story there is a scene like that. The trouble is, sometimes the writer himself isn't aware of it. I have found that a beginner, who may have read too much about economy of words in a short story, is as apt to cut his big scene to the bone, or even to omit it altogether, even to tell it later as hearsay, as he is to cut a minor one.

This is where a natural story sense—intuition, hunch, call it what you like—comes to our rescue, the more we write. We get the *feel* of a big scene, just as we get the *hang* of writing it.

I have no idea how many times I rewrote this scene in "Be Sure To Stop" but this is the way it came out:

> After Susan and Betty had exchanged greetings and explanations, Susan said she'd go in and tell Bill; but his mother said:
>
> "I've waited this long, I can wait a little longer. Let me have a good look at you, my dear."
>
> "Oh, I look simply awful," Susan apologized . . . "I've been on the go all day—"
>
> "You must have—from the traffic jam." Mrs. Parker nodded toward the driveway. "Looks like old times."
>
> "Your friends have been very nice to us," Susan said guardedly. "They've all been to call—are calling now, and we have houseguests—"
>
> "Yes, I know." Mrs. Parker was taking off the jacket of her perfectly tailored black suit; turning back the cuffs of her exquisite hand-made blouse. "And there's another car turning into the lane this minute . . . Bill will be out here hunting for you to be at the door with him to tell them how thrilled you are . . Do run along. I'll come in and surprise Bill as soon as I dash these off. It will only take a second."
>
> "Oh re—" Susan was about to protest, when suddenly she was seething again inside . . . .
>
> She turned on her heel and pushed through the swinging door into the dining-room, just in time to hear . . . "my wife's around some place—"
>
> There was a certain husky vibrance in his voice whenever he said "my wife"— or did she imagine it? And how . . . could you love a man and hate him at the same time? . . . How could he be so maddeningly sure of himself and of her? . . . now, she supposed, he'd be even surer—with his mother to back him up! It wasn't fair! Two against one . . . .
>
> Bill was saying: "Make yourself at home—while I see about more liquid refreshment—"
>
> "I'll fix some," Susan said. "You stay here." A million times harder to have her say out, if he had a fresh picture of his mother: Best-Dressed-Woman-in-an-Apron.

Mrs. Parker was lifting a freezing tray out of the refrigerator.

"The ice cubes are running out," she said. "They always did. I never could make Joe understand they wouldn't stretch indefinitely, or that more wouldn't freeze while you waited, any more than you'll be able to make Bill—"

Susan stared at her mother-in-law, while she drew a long breath and let it out again. And, suddenly, in as brief a space of time as that, all the righteous indignation, the self-pity, the rebellion seemed to blow out of her and scatter into nothingness, like scurrying tag-ends of storm clouds in the presence of a glorious silver moon.

She gasped: "Why you're not on Bill's side! Your're his mother—but you're on my side! They said you were like them, that you adored having the place swarming! You didn't."

"Of course, not!"

"You're like me!"

And then the end. All I need for it—including time for the double twist—is half a dozen speeches.

There are other elements which will keep your story from sagging in the middle.

Your trouble may be with your *characters.* If they are the sort neither you nor your readers can care very much about at the beginning, naturally they'll bog down more and more, the more you see of them. I have heard that it is a policy, and a sound one, I think, of some editors never to buy a story, unless they like at least one of the main characters, preferably two of them.

Your trouble may even be as basic as your *idea.* Re-examine it, if you are sagging in the middle of your story. Re-examine whatever it is you have decided to prove—if anything. If it isn't sound, that may be what is at fault. As with the beginning and the end, examine everything you have thought and written. Then, if you believe the other parts are sound, keep working.

By all means, put your story waistline in a good girdle—and by that I mean the actual words and sentences and paragraphs you use to encase it. Your writing style is something about which you need to think in every part of every story.

An original idea, interesting characters, a good writing style, a series of related events, told with a sense of proportion and at the right pace to create suspense and maintain interest to the end—these are only a *few* of the things to strive for in the so-called "body of the story." In writing, as in driving a car, the only time you can relax for an instant is when you come to a full stop; and even then your mind may be going on with what you should have done, or what hazards you may have to face around the next corner!

F. A. Rockwell

How Not to Fizzle the Finale

It hurts an editor more than it does you to have to reject stories that start out with a sparkle but fizzle out exhaustedly. Even if your characters are scintillating and your plot action is good, a poor ending can kill your story.

To avoid this finale-fizzle, many successful writers have been using the write-it-backward method ever since Edgar Allan Poe told authors to write the end first. Adela Rogers St. Johns, for instance, writes the last paragraph and pins it on the curtain in front of her typewriter. She says: "The one sure way to crack up anything is not to know where you're going to land."

So be sure to plan your destination, the best route, and all the necessary detours, as soon as you get an idea for a story, character, or premise. Your story will be easier to write and more surefooted if you use your inspirational impetus to work out an ending that:

1.) *satisfies.* Answers a narrative question honestly, fairly, and never cheats or frustrates (as life often does).

2.) *fits the mood and subject-matter* and inspires a specific emotional reaction from your reader.

3.) *packs a surprise of some kind.* Think of your story as a grab-bag. Your reader must be amazed—usually delighted—with what he pulls out of it. The gee-gaw may be tiny or huge, but it must contain a twist which the reader couldn't foresee.

4.) *is logical.* Even if the solution is a complete surprise, it must be credible and convincing because you've planted subtle signposts along the way.

These are the musts which most commercial story endings have in common. Yet there is a variety within these rules—as within all rules—

and in this case, variety and suspense are achieved by the use of *different* types of endings. You'll find that most modern stories have one of the following kinds of endings: Summation; Ideological; Antennae; Anti-Climax; Reversal; or Gimmick.

In the *summation ending* the protagonist solves the problem with finality and a neat, prim period—as most stories did in the past. The hero lands on the Moon, gets the girl, cleans up local politics, exposes subversion, breaks the sonic barrier, and defeats the enemy, whether outside or within himself. Whether a happy ending with virtue triumphant and vice defeated, or the sad-ending operas and Shakespearean dramas with the characters dead or dying, the end is The End. "That's all folks. There ain't no more."

In Ruth Henning's *Jenny and The Big Bad Wolf,* the "wolf," Paul Pomeroy, says:

> "I guess I'm not much of a genius, either. I didn't even find out I loved you until it was almost too late." He took her into his arms. "Oh Jenny, Jenny darling. Do you think you'll mind being married to an idiot—with ideals?"
> "Mind!" she breathed, her smile breaking out like the sun. "Why, Mr. Pomeroy, darling—that's the very best kind!"
> And that's how little Jenny Moran from Butterfield, Iowa, got the reputation as the best wolf-tamer in Hollywood.

Summation endings are decreasing as the reader's taste turns toward sophistication, variety, and realism. In life, nothing is absolutely final or solved or conquered or ended. Once in a while we flee into fiction to find this security, and editors balance each issue with different endings to keep us guessing.

In the *ideological ending* the author poses a problem, develops it dramatically, but leaves the solution up to the reader. More popular in the intellectual quality market, this type annoys the unimaginative reader who wants the writer to do all the work.

This is the most intriguing and troublesome of all endings and should not be used unless there's a very specific reason. You can be tricky, cute, or cleverly mystifying, a la "lady or the tiger", or you can give the reader a chance to choose between fact and fantasy. Watch for these in Christmas or any *miracle* stories. The devout reader supplies the magic solution which satisfies him; the realist chooses a factual explanation and everybody is happy.

The ideological ending can serve as a rhetorical question, giving you a chance to say what the character should do to solve his problem. Example: *Daddy's Day,* in *Redbook* in which an ex-husband takes his little boy out for the day. When he returns the child to the remarried mother and knows the strain of dividing the boy's love between two fathers, the real Daddy wonders if the child will be better off if he never sees him again.

This type of ending poses questions for the reader to answer. Be sure it pleases him and gives him a chance to be right and happy, not just confused and mad at you for making him do your work!

The *antennae ending* sends feelers into the future, promising more to come after the problem itself is solved. The story action has tangled and untangled threads of interest, the major question has been answered. But we're made to feel the magic promise of new beginnings. One of the most famous antennae endings in literature is Scarlett O'Hara's worry-about-Rhett-tomorrow philosophy at the end of *Gone With The Wind.*

You must know when and why to use this type, and how not to abuse it. Give a brief promising peek into the future, but don't drag the reader there and draw out the story ramblingly.

In many confession stories, the reader has been on such intimate terms with the sins and sufferings of the protagonist, he's not in too much of a hurry to take an abrupt leave. Antennae endings peek into the future when the protagonist has done too terrible a thing to deserve a happy ending, yet we sympathize with his repentance and permit him the "someday hope;" or when the main actor has sinned, suffered, repented, and been forgiven, yet his own transgression will always haunt him.

> He looked up and she was gazing at him curiously. "What's the matter, honey?" she was asking. This was the woman he loved, that he could not help loving, and she was looking at him apparently in innocence and candor. "Aren't you pleased? Aren't you interested?" But beneath the other, smaller voice went on still, inexorably, as he knew it would go on in the years to come: ". . . hate you, hate you, hate you."

The *anti-climax* or *bonus twist* is a double-helping ending that adds an *extra* twist, emotional wallop, or added incidents. Although the story could end before it, the anti-climax improves it.

In "Panic on Strawberry Hill" which was published some years ago in *This Week*, the father worries so about his daughter's safety on her first babysitting job, that he drives to the house to check, is terrified when he sees all blinds up, drapes open, no sign of daughter. Strong arms seize him, and he learns how sensible and mature his daughter is: she has left blinds open as a safety-measure, detected a prowler and called police! End. Daughter can be trusted, has been properly reared, even though husband thought his wife wasn't worrying enough. Anti-climax: He is on his way back to the car when he hears rustling in bushes. Ah! he was right . . . but the "prowler" is his wife, who has also been concerned about their daughter even though she concealed it.

Your anti-climax must solve something, re-emphasize a premise, or turn a new light on characterization. It must be purposeful, never used just because you love your characters so much you can't let go!

Reversal ending presents the exact antithesis of the opening. If the boy and girl are feuding and fighting, they wind up loving; if the villain is winning at first, he is defeated at the end, etc.

All character regeneration and come-to-realize stories have this wind-up, with the protagonist reversing a character-trait, philosophy, mood, or opinion. The main danger is obviousness. If you meet a miserly, misanthropic main character like Scrooge squeezing shillings and hating humanity at Christmas, you know there'll be a reversal ending. The suspense must be achieved in how and why he changes. If the hero in a religious magazine starts out as an agnostic or atheist you know there has to be a reversal end. Since your reader looks for something he doesn't know, you must give him original action, theme, character, or incident.

Today's stories indulge in frequent reversals. At the beginning of William Heuman's story, "Good-By Brooklyn," which was published in the *Saturday Evening Post*, Al, who's never left Brooklyn in his life, refuses to buy a Long Island tract house and become a slave to grass and weeds. He dreads commuting and leaving Brooklyn until he realizes how much his wife and kids want the house. Having decided that a lawnmower will help him lose weight, he calls realtor Benson:

"Put aside one o' them houses you ain't even built," I say. "We'll be out tomorrow to make a down payment."

When I put down the phone I see the bedroom door opening slowly and then
Myrtle is standing there and she's been crying.
"Al," she says. "Dear Al."
So what's a little grass? You know what I mean?

Good characterization, fresh color or a new premise, help keep reversal endings from being too pat, obvious, or anemic.

The *gimmick ending* uses an object, word, idea, or any specific device as a gimmick. This is usually planned and written first. Almost any tidbit of information can be used if it truly affects plot and characters and is built into the story, not just tacked on at the end. In short, the story couldn't *be* without it.

Gimmicks are used in all types of stories, from the pulps to the top slicks.

In "A Woman's Place," the divorcee-narrator envies happily-divorced Martha Tye, who is gay, charming, living graciously without a man. That is, she envies Martha's buoyant happiness until the end:

Martha was saying something about what a pleasure it was to go to bed and not
have to worry about the moods and habit of a husband, when my eyes suddenly
struck a small pillow among the big pillows on her bed. It was a tiny, white linen
baby pillow and across it in stiches of pale-blue thread was *No Tears.*

Whatever your ending, it shouldn't be skimpy, leaving too much for the reader to figure out; and it shouldn't be overloaded with pedantically presented information and description. Nor should it ramble on after solving a major problem; or focus on minor characters. Don't leave the characters' relationships the same as in the beginning, or give away the solution before it happens.

Every story has several possible endings. Select the one that satisfies, fits the mood and subject-matter, springs a surprise, is logical according to characterization, and inspires the reader with a promise. It must tie up all the loose ends and harvest all the dramatic and emotional seeds you've planted in the beginning and cultivated in the middle.

You'll be better able to do this if you use your first fresh inspiration to *plan your ending first.* Then you'll be working like many professionals who write the final scenes before starting a story.

Dennis Whitcomb

The Twist Ending

When I read a story I always seem to begin playing "Guess the Ending" about two-thirds of the way through. If I'm very lucky, I lose. There's a disappointment about winning, and delicious fun in being faked out. Because of my fondness for this sleight-of-hand kind of storytelling, I set out early in my career to study and analyze the work of the masters of deception. In time I learned that there was, indeed, some method to their maskery. Like all hocus-pocus, these illusions take practice; subtlety is practically the name of the game, but there are some basic patterns to turnabout endings.

One of the craftiest bits of literary thimblerigging I have ever encountered is Agatha Christie's immensely entertaining *Witness for the Prosecution*. The entire story, you may recall, was built upon the *supposed* treachery of a wife. That word, "supposed," is an important one. It is the one thing that all types of switch endings have in common. They all lead readers to suppose something that appears most logical; then spring a trap. *Witness for the Prosecution* was filled with unpredictable turns of plot. Miss Christie's story deals with a man accused of the murder of a kindly older woman. The man and his wife go to a lawyer and convince him of the young fellow's innocence. The wife offers to testify that her husband was at home with her at the time the murder was committed. However, at the trial, the entire courtroom is shocked when the wife turns up as the star witness for the *prosecution*. We begin to hate the treacherous wife when she testifies that her husband went out on the night of the murder and returned with blood on his clothes. The prosecution builds an airtight case against the husband. The husband appears completely bewildered that his wife could do such a terrible thing to him. Just when things are looking darkest, though, a mystery woman shows up with a stack of letters written by the wife to a lover. In them, the wife assures the paramour her perjury will get her unwanted husband out of the way. The letters are brought to court and the wife's testimony shattered. Naturally, the husband is acquitted. Now comes the big switch. Alone in the court with the lawyer, the wife tells him that *she* was the mystery woman who came in disguise bringing the love letters. She became the prosecution's witness just so she could discredit herself and get her husband off. The stunned lawyer asks why she didn't trust to justice to find her husband not guilty. "Because," she answers, "he was guilty."

The author neatly takes us in by setting up a false villainess. The reader believes the stories of a wife's treachery and hopes to see her fail in her attempt to railroad a man we are sure is innocent. When she is exposed in court as a liar we see what we think is a satisfying, if somewhat predictable, ending. Suddenly the rug is pulled from under our feet. We learn that the woman we've been hating all this time has actually sacrificed herself out of love for a guilty husband. This is a classic example of one highly effective way of bringing about a surprise finish to a story: Let a character be established as evil or treacherous who is, in reality, carrying off a ruse. At the end show the reader how he has misjudged that character by believing the masquerade.

The reverse of such a hoax will work, too. Instead of setting up a fake villain for us to despise, set up a figure of good as the trusted right hand of the main character who appears to be assisting him all the way through the story. At the end of the tale we see how certain curious inconsistencies suddenly become logical when this man or woman whom the reader has liked is unmasked as a traitor. I used such a device just recently in the story of two San Francisco police officers trying to expose the leader of a powerful Chinese tong. To prove that the man is engaged in illegal business and bribery, the officers try to uncover the gangster's secret files. They have been told by his accountant that these records list every illegal transaction and bribe. Mysteriously, the accountant is murdered before he can lead them to the records. The police assume one of the tong's hatchetmen got to him. They find that the accountant's fiancee knows the whereabouts of the records. The younger of the two police officers is told to guard her from harm. A short time later, evidence comes to light that points to the young policeman as the murderer. The older officer rushes to keep him from killing the fiancee and arrives just in time to save her. Now we learn the truth. The young police officer had accepted a bribe from the gangster and knew that if the records were uncovered, his name and the amount he accepted would be shown, thus, he has done everything he could to keep them from being found. Here again, that word "suppose" has come into play. The switch was possible because the reader supposed both police officers to be honest and sincere in their quest of the files.

If you can get the reader to suppose your main character is striving for a goal and then show he has actually been after something else entirely you have the basis for another bit of flim-flammery. It works like this: The lead character sets out to achieve a purpose and makes his intention clear. His opposition takes measures to stop him. Those who read or watch the story unfold begin to see that the lead character is up against overwhelming odds. We fear he has a slight chance of accomplishing his end. How, we begin to wonder. Can our man ever succeed when the opposition has taken such thorough measures to block him? As the climactic struggle begins we are hoping against hope for our underdog, but he fails. His opposition has just begun to gloat when it realizes it has been deceived. The deception can take any one of at least three different forms:

1. The lead character has caused his opposition to take drastic countermeasures to stop him. Those countermeasures are precisely what our man (or woman) wanted. Example:

> Our hero has been exposed as an officer of the law who has only been posing as a gangster to get evidence on the head man in the rackets. The cop is forced to flee from the gang before he has uncovered sufficient evidence. The gang goes after him and succeeds in catching him. However, the gang leader suddenly finds he has been led into a trap. To catch our man he has gone over an international border into a country where he can legally be extradited. This was the hero's ultimate goal the whole time.

2. The main character's false goal has succeeded in diverting his opposition's attention away from a real goal. Up until the last few paragraphs of the story the true goal has gone unnoticed. Example:

> A young man wants permission to marry a girl. He goes to her father and asks for her hand. The father, a strong, almost ruthless man, turns him down saying

the man who marries his daughter must be more determined than this young man; willing to reach out for what he wants despite all the obstacles. He tells the young fellow that this is the way he has succeeded in building a large chemical plant. The young man says he will prove his determination. The test he proposes is that if he can kidnap the daughter from their heavily guarded home within twenty-four hours, the father must recognize his ability to succeed. The father willingly accepts the challenge. The young man makes his attempt and is caught by bodyguards. The father berates his ineptitude. The young man leaves in anger and resentment. Shortly afterward an anonymous caller tells the father the bitter young man is going to blow up the chemical plant. The father and all the bodyguards race to the plant to stop him, leaving the suitor's path clear to carry out the kidnapping.

3. The lead character has stated his intended goal and the opposition tries to stop him. The reader and the opposition, however, have been diverted by the most *obvious* means of accomplishing the result or, the most obvious *meaning* of the goal. The switch-ending reveals that the goal was not what we understood it to be, nor the obvious meaning. Example:

A rich old man states in his will that his entire fortune will go to the one who is smart enough to find his treasures. The scheming among relatives begins when the old fellow dies and his will is read. They discover clues, they double cross each other and finally discover an old trunk, hidden cleverly within the old mansion. Opening it, the most scheming relative discovers a box of souvenirs and silly mementos. In disgust he starts to throw them out. His housekeeper, knowing what they meant to the old man, asks if she can have them. Hidden in one of them is a note entitling the bearer to the entire estate for having found and recognized his true treasures.

Anytime you find an unconventional use for something, you may have the key to a good ending, provided you can make that unconventional use important in getting out of a tight spot or bringing about a desired end. I remember an old Will Rogers movie called *Steamboat Round the Bend* in which Will captained a steamboat which had to get down river to Baton Rouge with some information that would keep his nephew from being hanged as a murderer. Time was running out and so was his fuel. He broke up everything on board that could be spared to provide wood for the furnace but they were still about a mile away from Baton Rouge. It began to look as if all hope was gone until an old preacher caught a deck hand drinking, snatched his jug of rum and hurled it into the furnace. It exploded up the smokestack and the boat surged forward in the water. Will asked if there was any more rum aboard. Earlier we had seen the deck hand smuggle fifty gallons on board and had thought it was just a bit of comedy. Now, it became their salvation. They heaved the rum into the furnace, got to the nephew and saved his life (at the last possible moment, of course).

Irony in an ending can mean the difference between a sale and a rejection slip. Let's say you've done a yarn about a ruthless young scoundrel who has alienated all his friends and gone through great pains to get the controlling interest in a company. We could show that what he gained was not equal to what he sacrificed, but we could show it even more poignantly with a touch of poetic justice. In the end he achieves his desired end. He gets control of the company, then discovers the firm has been putting up a grand front but is actually floundering in debt.

Another bit of irony reveals after a long hard struggle that it was completely unnecessary. Things would have worked out the exact same way.

The bluff ending, like a bluff in poker, shows us that the main character has succeeded in frightening his opposition into surrender with a completely empty threat.

There are, of course, several other types of surprise finishes to startle the reader, but these, I think, are the most effective. I often go over them to see if I can generate a story idea that will have a built-in twist to it. I'm happy to say they've been very helpful to me because once I have a good ending I can easily find a suitable set of circumstances to lead into it. The plot structure then begins to dictate what kind of characters are needed to carry it out.

Our readers are quite often clever people who have seen and read a tremendous number of stories. They know the cliche paths that so many stories have taken before. I, for one, don't want to become predictable and dull, so I plan my strategy carefully before I match wits with them. Little do they know when they begin reading that things and people may not be what they appear to be. They may try to outguess me, but the element of surprise is on my side.

Charles Turner

Is Slant a Dirty Word?

Every short story writer, whether he admits it or not, slants his material. He directs his story toward a particular market, toward a particular type of reader, or he directs it toward himself and his own integrity. Theme, character, plot, setting, mood—each element of his story, even the sound of the prose, is influenced by his choice of a target.

"Study the markets," some say. "Check what the editors are buying. Set your sights. Why not try to come up with something along the line? After all, it's common sense. Editors have very definite ideas about the fiction they feel their readers enjoy."

Then comes the other side of the argument. *"Don't* aim for a specific magazine. Write the best story you can and give no thought to the marketplace. Write it the way you see it. A truly good story, honest and well turned, will find a market somewhere."

An interesting debate, isn't it? Both views are reasonable though completely opposite. Who could say that one is right and the other is wrong? Not I. In this respect I will offer nothing but my own experience and what has proved profitable for me.

For many years I listened to the voice that said, "Write the best story you can and give no thought to the marketplace." Such advice fell pleasingly on my ears, of course, because it nourished my self-esteem. It spoke of literature as art rather than a mere product. It spoke of personal integrity. Ah, *integrity*—there's a word we all hold dear.

So, through story after story, I marched to the beat of my own drum and enjoyed the perfect freedom of it all. But let me qualify that. I didn't exactly march. I was a slow writer (I still am) and I gave sweat to every phrase. And the perfect freedom wasn't really perfect. It wasn't even freedom, actually. I carefully slanted everything I had toward one goal: my own idea of a superior short story. Somewhere I'd picked up the notion that I must touch something which had never been touched before. I was so determined to be totally creative I cramped myself. Originality walks a narrow path, and I was constantly wary.

Looking back, I see that I resorted to obscurity. Perhaps it was the only way I could feel confident no one would accuse, "This has been done before." If you aren't positive what a story is all about, you can hardly call it run-of-the-mill. Neither can you call it a *good* story, honest and well turned. The hard truth is no matter how I strived to touch something which had never been touched, I touched nothing—nothing of life, at any rate.

When I realized I was thirty-four and unpublished, I decided it was time to stop fooling around. Editors, it seemed, *did* have very definite ideas about the fiction they chose for their readers. It struck me that integrity might be involved on their part also. I don't think I subtracted one shred of me when I gave them that credit.

The year was 1964. The September issue of *Writer's Digest* lay on top of my clutter. I picked it up and read Hayes Jacobs' New York Market Letter. In it he gave a report from Naome Lewis, fiction editor of *Good Housekeeping.* "We really don't get enough good fiction," Mrs. Lewis said. "We try for four stories every month, and it's really hard to find that many. Particularly short-shorts; I don't know why they're so hard to find, but they are." She went on to say that she preferred not to talk about length requirements, that they were flexible there. Mention was made of pay starting at $1,000.

I liked what Mrs. Lewis said about length. I liked short-shorts and I had always felt comfortable writing them. Even when my material called for a standard-length story, I could usually tell all I wanted to tell in ten or twelve pages of manuscript. It was just as though Mrs. Lewis were saying to me personally, "Why don't you try to write something for us?"

Well—? What did she consider a good story? I went to my wife's stack of magazines and found four issues of *Good Housekeeping.* I sat down by the lamp and read all the fiction, *really* read it, dwelling long on each piece, feeling the fabric. I did not discover a pattern or a formula. Each piece held merit of its own. There was, however, a prevailing atmosphere which came across and was fairly definable.

The stories were warm and affirmative. There wasn't a grim one in the lot. Much of the writing was done in a friendly conversational style, polished smooth for the eye. The heroines were recognizable, with problems most women would understand and take to heart. The endings were clearly drawn, meaningful, satisfying, and often they indicated the strengthening of relationships, especially family relationships. The lightest of the stories smacked of more than entertainment value alone.

I began to scrounge around in the attic part of my mind (I suppose every writer has such a place) where ideas and scraps of ideas and what have you—incidents, impressions, bits of stolen talk—are kept. I set out deliberately to put my finger on something for *Good Housekeeping,* a story that could at least feel at home there. I uncovered an old idea which appeared to be usable as a starting point.

> A small-town girl has been working at a secretarial job in the big city for a couple of years. She has acquired what she considers to be a touch of sophistication. Now she is engaged to be married to an uptown young man. What happens when her mother comes up for a visit to meet the young man? Does the girl go overboard in trying to put her mother's best foot forward? Does she feel that her mother's clothes are not suitable? Does she try to remodel her? And does Mama begin to sense that her daughter is ashamed of her? At some point, surely, Mama will turn and say, "He'll just have to like me the way I am or not at all."

I had discarded the idea months before because it had seemed material not suited to my sort of story. And in fact it wasn't. The material was human, believable, and far from the obscure.

Now that I meant business and had a clear objective, I got down to work. Though I endeavored to capture the atmosphere of *Good Housekeeping* fiction, I was not for one word false to the nature of the story or my original concept of it. Nothing was built in or tacked on for the purpose of begging acceptance. I did try for something in the prose, a tone, a certain lilt, and it seemed to click as I went along. I have a feeling the story would have fallen pretty flat if it had been told in a different manner.

The finished manuscript was ten pages. When I mailed it, knowing I had done to the best of my ability the job I set out to do, I felt downright professional.

Instead of a rejection slip there came a letter. The editors liked the story but thought that Milly, the main character, was a bit unsympathetic. Would I consider making a few small changes? I looked at Milly again and I could see what the editors meant. Milly bordered on being a snob, yet this fact was unnecessary to the story. Besides, I knew that Milly wasn't really a snob at all. I took her straight to the typewriter and proceeded to tone her down. Yes, you could say that I was slanting even further.

Revision is never easy. The "few small changes" were simple enough, but labor nonetheless. I plucked sentences here and there and substituted ones of another color. Milly, in the original version, had been afraid that her mother would not compare favorably with *his* mother, who was such an impeccable creature. Only a hint of that could remain. Milly's attempts to stylize Mama had to be motivated by genuine personal interest. Sometimes a single word made all the difference in her general attitude. At the airport, for example, the revised Milly was "embarrassed" rather than "irritated" by the sight of her mother's old scuffed luggage.

"Lady in Blue" appeared in *Good Housekeeping* in September 1965, one year after I read Mrs. Lewis' remarks in Hayes Jacobs' column. In the October '65 *Writer's Digest,* surprisingly, Mr. Jacobs devoted a few lines to my "over-the-transom" sale. He and Mrs. Lewis were both unaware of the part the column had played in prompting my successful effort.

The story also sold to eight foreign magazines. I don't think that's a bad accounting for a piece written with one special market in mind. With Milly I had evidently touched a universal thing.

Since then it's been my good fortune to have a number of winners at *Good Housekeeping.* On the other hand, I must confess I've had a number of losers—and some of them were stories which I had been sure would hit dead center. At times I've aimed at other markets squarely, or so I thought, and missed.

Slanting a story can point it in the right direction, commercially speaking. But first there has to be a story to slant, and it has to be a valid story. Editors know a fake when they see one.

Allan W. Eckert

Checklist for Unsalable Stories

One of the most frequently voiced laments of the unpublished writer is: "Oh, if only I had someone to tell me what's wrong with this story!"

If those words have a familiar ring to you (and chances are they have) then you're missing a bet. You see, ever since you began writing you've had just such a critic available at a moment's notice.

That critic is *you*!

By all means, it's hard work to constructively criticize your own work, but contrary to an impression that seems altogether too prevalent among new writers, it isn't impossible. It's unlikely there's a selling writer anywhere who doesn't regularly tear his unsold brainchildren limb from limb in an attempt to discover why they won't sell. In most cases the cause is quickly spotted and rectified and the manuscript sold. It doesn't always have to happen to someone else, either.

True, you—as a writer, even if unsold—are often too close to your own story to detect its defects, at least while you're writing it or shortly thereafter. But by the time you've put the piece out of mind as much as possible for several weeks or so (during which time it's been bounding from one weary editor to another) you'll be surprised at the startling clarity with which you can detect the errors.

All this, of course, provided you go back and read what you've written. Unfortunately too many would-be writers, after having written the story, never read it carefully again and handle it only long enough to take it from one envelope and dump it into another.

It's treading on tricky ground to set up unbending rules for fiction writing, but let's face it—there *are* certain fundamental rights and wrongs in creative writing and unless you at least know what they are, you're going to have a tough time selling what you write. There are cases where these principles have been ignored by established writers, but these have been cases where the writer knew quite well what he was doing and was skillful enough to put it across anyway. It's the old story of learning to walk before joining a race.

Of the wide variety of wrongs which appear in many rejected stories, 25 stand out as the most frequently committed. Some are so grave that by themselves they can precipitate the peremptory rejection of the story. Others merely indicate an igorance of fundamental writing techniques and lack of clear thinking.

If you have a story that has been kicking around for altogether too long, check it against these 25 errors and you may find that you have been guilty of committing anywhere from one to a dozen or more of them. Using this checklist as a guide will not necessarily guarantee sale of the manuscript, but there is no doubt it will help toward that end.

First, however, a warning: it is all too easy to gloss over your own errors or to justify them in your own mind. As far as it is humanly possible, you must check your manuscript against this list with a cold, analytical eye, being—above all—steadfastly honest with yourself.

1. Have you started in the right place?

Where to begin your story is not always easy to determine. A good way to test whether the lead you've chosen is best is to skip to the second, third or other high points in the piece and mentally formulate the action there as the lead. You'll be surprised at how often you've buried the best lead in the body of the story.

2. Is your beginning too slow?

Have you reached out and irrevocably snagged the reader with your first few lines or at least within the first couple of paragraphs? Retype your first fifty words on a clean sheet of paper and tomorrow glance at them swiftly, as a reader paging through a magazine will do. If the words don't grip you and make you just a wee bit sorry there's not more there, better change it pronto. Probably more potential readers are lost in the first fifty words than at any other points in the narrative.

3. Have you established mood?

By the end of the first page a definite mood should have been created. This mood may change as the story progresses and often it does, but *some* type of mood must be there. It may be happiness or horror, suspense or expectation or any of a dozen others, but it should be there. By the time you finish reading the first page do you feel yourself slipping into the mood? If not, back to the letter-machine, friend!

4. Have you been careful with flashbacks?

Does your story constantly jump backwards? This is tricky writing even for the pro, so be careful. A jarring flashback or an equally abrupt return to the present can lose your reader's interest quickly. I believe one of the most magnificent examples of flashback I've ever encountered occurs in Allen Drury's novel, *Advise and Consent.* The flashback begins on page 148 while U.S. Senator Seabright Cooley walks down a Senate corridor to a meeting. Smoothly it draws the reader back to Cooley's youth and entire career and in one paragraph on page 161 returns to the present so adroitly that one must actually stop and search carefully to find the transition. But in your writing, unless you've really mastered the technique, forget the flashback as much as possible and permit the story to move forward from the start to the finish.

5. Have you written about something you know?

That doesn't mean you have to start chewing hemp or betelnut or rip off your scuba mask at eighty feet under the surface to actually experience it first. But there are reference books which lucidly describe nearly anything you can imagine, so don't be lazy and just make a wild stab at what it's like. You may be able to fool some people, but just a few ill-chosen words can destroy a whole story for many people. Years ago I wrote a story about the Everglades which sounded pretty good and I felt somewhat cocky when a reader asked how long I'd lived in Florida and I modestly explained I'd never been there. My bubble of pride was quickly pricked, however, when a man who had lived there pointed out to me that a central item in the piece—a large sycamore tree—did not grow in Florida. So know of what you write.

6. Have you dated your story?

Unless you were writing a period piece, I'm sure you wouldn't use dialogue (or even worse, straight body copy) incorporating the slang or period terms of a bygone era. Yet, this is a common failing in many modern manuscripts. Also watch how you mention prices, styles and other factors which, as we're often reminded, are "subject to change without notice."

7. Have you included unnecessary action?

If what your characters are seeing or doing or saying is not relevant to the story, you'd better delete it. There are few things more irritating to the reader than being left with a hatful of loose ends that lead nowhere as he sloshes through your masterpiece.

8. Have you been redundant?

Watch out for little traps like "He met her at 8 p.m. that evening" or "She was crying. Tears streamed liberally from her eyes." I have yet to see 8 *a.m.* in the *evening* and unless she's peeling a big onion, those tears streaming from her eyes must mean she's crying. And redundancy does not always occur in the same line or paragraph. Watch for it from one paragraph to the next and page to page. In some cases redundancy may be used as a device for emphasis or mood, but it should always be used with great care.

9. Have you included unnecessary characters?

This might seem like a foolish question, but it is amazing how frequently characters will appear in stories without purpose or need, serving only to confuse the reader. Go back through your story and review every character, *one at a time,* completely through the tale. Before you're finished you may be surprised to find that a character or two you believed could not be done without are really only so much dross.

10. Have you kept your characters in character?

Many a story loses its salability when one or more of the characters, portrayed throughout the story with a distinct personality, suddenly undergoes a complete shift in character traits in order to reach a specific conclusion. Until you become proficient in fiction techniques, steer clear of situations like this which demand an unusually deft touch.

11. Have you overworked a word or phrase?

Even old pros occasionally find themselves using a particular word or phrase to such an extent that a conscious effort must be made to control it. Certainly, many words must be used frequently in a story, but for others, once is sufficient. If you've located a word or phrase in your manuscript that appears too often, read and digest some relevant passages from your thesaurus.

12. Is your dialogue stilted?

If you haven't made it a practice, upon completion of the first draft of your story, to read all dialogue as you have indicated it is to be spoken, make it a point to start doing so now. Mentally formed conversation frequently is a far cry from the way it would have been presented in spoken conversation. When you have read one passage of dialogue aloud (knowing of course what is coming next) attempt to speak it out naturally without reading. You'll frequently find it coming far more naturally than if you keep to the tight limits of your first draft conversation.

13. Are your facts accurate?

Have you described the moon as a planet? (it's a satellite); a Civil War soldier playing a piece on his harmonica that wasn't written until half a century later; an 1820 frontiersman using a revolver when it wasn't invented until 1835? Most people won't know it's a mistake any more than you do, but for those who see it, the story is ruined . . . and editors have amazingly sharp eyes! It only takes a few moments to check facts, so why not make a concerted effort to be right? Don't guess.

14. Have you destroyed your scene or mood?

When hero Bill Jones is stumbling down a treacherous mountain trail, his broken arm creating waves of pain before bloodshot eyes, he's not paying any attention to the aromatic blue lupines growing nearby on the desert floor . . . and neither should you. When Sally, after breathless anticipation, finally sees track star Tom Brown approaching to ask her to dance, she doesn't shove a chunk of bubblegum into her mouth . . . and you shouldn't do it for her. Watch how you bring extraneous matters into your story, particularly during climactic moments.

15. Have you been trite or "cute"?

If her hair is the color of ripe wheat and her eyes like limpid pools and her body like Venus de Milo and she coyly coos "I've never felt like this before," it's a sure bet that the editor *has* and that the feeling is pure nausea. Result: rejection. If you describe an excavation as deep as a well with a hole in the bottom or a fat man in a small chair as being as comfortable as an elephant in a hammock or someone who has just finished a meal as being as full as a mosquito at a nudist convention, you're in trouble. Cuteness and triteness are easy traps to avoid, but they're equally easy to fall into, so be on guard.

16. Has your action been consistent?

If everything you've said, all the way through, has flowed smoothly and naturally then you're in good shape, but if you have unrelated side discussions or descriptions, if your protagonist does not pursue his course in a reasonably acceptable and understandable manner, then you're hurting your chances.

17. Have you said something that means something?

It may be a light romance or a deep mystery or a sharp intrigue, but when you've finished reading it, have you really said anything? Have you put across a message or a moral? In other words, has there been a reason for your story to be read? If it's a story the reader won't remember 10 minutes after he's finished it (if he does), it'll be the one the editor won't remember 10 seconds after he dumps it into his rejection basket.

18. Is your story logical?

Even the wildest science fiction premise, when once established, must follow logical steps. The same holds true for any other story. In most cases, when you depart from logic in a train of events, few readers and even fewer editors can overcome the trauma it creates. In rereading what you've written, always keep the question in mind, "Does this action follow a logical course of events?"

19. Has your protagonist solved his own problems?

Don't depend on earthquakes, lighting, plague, train or auto wrecks or any other type of natural disaster or "act of God" to solve your hero's problem. Nor should it be resolved by any man-made disaster unless the hero has been instrumental in its development. If your protagonist hasn't overcome some obstacle through his own efforts (and not those of someone else), if he hasn't solved his problems in a reasonable, logical way, then your story is left hanging or falls flat.

20. Is it a story or an essay?

It may come as a surprise, but some would-be writers don't know the difference. Each has its place, but don't try to pass one off as the other. A short story is more than a mood or a description. It is a series of events which create a situation necessitating a distinct solution. Remember, each facet of a short story must, of necessity, be a part of the all-encompassing plot. Whereas, an essay is, according to Mr. Webster, "a literary composition, analytical or interpretive in nature, dealing with its subject from a more or less limited or personal standpoint and permitting a considerable freedom of style and method."

21. Is your climax too short?

Have you spent pages and pages building toward a moment of tense action, only to have it occur so quickly that the reader is through it before he realizes what has happened and feels cheated? Remember, the climax is extremely important. Don't make it just another flashing incident that too quickly ties up all loose ends.

22. Have you ended your story too soon or too late?

Ending your story at the very beginning of your climax leaves a reader hanging and irked. Dragging it out far behind the climax leaves him bored and disappointed. When's the right time to quit? As soon as your climax has run its course, end your story quickly . . . but make sure the climax has, in fact, run its course.

23. Have you been too wordy?

Have you used a dozen or more words where you could just have effectively used only a few? Often, the most direct way of stating something is, by the same token, the most effective. Try this some time: go back through your story and imagine you're going to have to telegraph it at 10¢ a word. You'll be astounded at how much verbiage you can eliminate without harming your story line.

24. Have you written just for yourself?

Even if the old high school stadium evokes all kinds of poignant memories in your mind, don't forget that Mr. Reader probably attended a different school, and these memories, unless first given proper foundation, won't mean a thing to him. Certainly a writer should make every attempt to please himself with his writing, but unless what he's writing is his diary, he'd better make it interesting for others as well. It's all too simple a matter for the writer to draw a character from someone he has known in the past and, because he is familiar with that character, neglect to develop him in the writing. Ask yourself, "If all I knew about this person or place is what I see written here, would I be satisfied with what I read?"

25. Have you let your reader think?

Many a story that might otherwise have been good, fails to make the grade because not a single thing has been left to the reader's imagination. Give the reader credit for some ability to visualize and draw conclusions. In writing juvenile material it is often advisable to spell most everything out, but not in the adult short story. However, don't leave a lot of loose ends dangling under the supposition that you're letting the reader think.

The above checklist by no means covers all the errors the writer can make. Nor are those points mentioned to be considered as hard and fast rules which may never be broken. They are merely some of the most common mistakes which plague the novice writer.

Merrill Joan Gerber

Forbidden Subjects—Not What They Used to Be

Pick up any modern magazine today, and you will find in its fiction the problems (or perhaps the pleasures) of adultery, divorce, promiscuity, homo-sexuality and other subjects that some years ago would have been forbidden in print. Today certain matters are treated with the greatest candor, and the more adventurous magazines often present once questionable relationships as possibly desirable (under the right circumstances).

In the course of writing fiction for magazines, I have learned a few surprising facts: there are still definite taboos in fiction, and in areas that one would find it hard to guess at.

Take for example a story I wrote called "Under a Common Roof." It has to do with a neighborhood in which neighbors met most fre-quently—not in one another's homes—but under the common roof of a department store, or a hardware store in the community. They were all there, getting things for "home-improvement" and returning things that had, for a while, improved their homes, but which had eventually broken, and then needed to be taken back for repairs. The heroine despairs:

> So we are going to spend this weekend taking the TV back. A few months ago we spent three of our weekends deciding which TV to buy. We went to all the de-partment stores, and we checked the prices, and we read *Consumer's Report;* then we bought a TV. Then it broke. Like everything else we buy, which breaks, it broke. Like everything else, it is guaranteed. So we spend our days concerned with our purchases. Today we will take the TV back for repair. Next weekend we will go and pick it up. These errands take up time beautifully. They fill up all of our lives, leaving not a moment for thought or boredom.

The story, finally, laments one way of the American way of life, and as such—it turned out—it could not be considered by any magazine that carries advertisements for just such products. Advertisers of television sets and appliances are not going to support any magazines that publish such subversive fiction.

Another story, called "When Will You Get Me?" tells the difficulties of a couple in college who have years to wait until marriage is sensible and possible, but who, in the meantime, have no place to be alone, and no privacy. They spend most of their time sitting on benches, on cold winter nights, and on mosquitoey spring nights, and they argue and cry and kiss, and suffer extreme anguish.

One editor's comment, on seeing this story, was: "People are more resourceful these days." In other words, the modern generation will find a way—motels and apartments are more accessible these days. My story was too moral—and was "too good" to be published.

A third story, called "The Bad Boys," dealt with two brothers who wreaked havoc on a quiet neighborhood by threatening and fighting other children, by damaging property, and by stealing. The story tells about the boys and the family they come from, about the neighbors' refusal to be sympathetic to their problem, and about a single incident that requires prompt action: report the boys to the police and have them put in an institution, or take pity on their problems, and try to help them in a more humane way.

The choice, in this particular story, was the former—there was no way but to turn them in; a child's life had been threatened.

Most of the magazines who saw this story felt they could not buy it, and consequently take a stand on the kind of choice they preferred. They could not endorse any behavior that made a moral judgment. Eventually, the *Saturday Evening Post* bought the story, but went out of business before it saw print. So it is still homeless—because of what amounts to a surprising taboo in fiction-publishing.

Another forbidden subject seems to be alienation in American society. A number of my stories deal with the problems of making friends in suburban communities—people have all these high fences, and everyone has their own barbecue on Sunday afternoons behind these fences, and in general, real communication is difficult.

Magazines don't want to talk about that either. Possibly they feel it is unpatriotic. But what is really unpatriotic is a refusal to present things as they are, instead of as they should be. Magazines have grown up about sex. Now let us hope they will find the maturity to present life honestly; and not only in those ways that are flattering to their readers, and which meet the approval of their advertisers.

Hallie Burnett

The Short Story From a
Purely Personal View

For a number of years I have been writing, teaching and editing the short story, yet panic overtakes me when I am faced with telling how to write one. I think I know; I think there are some (minor) rules to observe in writing a story; but on the great snow-covered plains of literature one cannot be sure if those mounds to the left and to the right are solid rock or simply drifts to be swept away by the next strong wind.

This is to say that the requirements of the short story, while substantially constant, change in manner and technique from season to season, and from generation to generation. Reread stories appearing in American magazines twenty or thirty years ago and see how they not only deal with different attitudes and environments, but are written in a style which now seems florid, over-explicit, or, at best—as in the early and so-called "typical" *New Yorker* stories—pedestrianly realistic. Go back to another generation, when a writer such as O. Henry— whose name identifies one of the annual "best" short-story collection— wrote in a style which now one imitates at risk of appearing ridiculous; and before that, consider a literary masterpiece such as Leo Tolstoi's *The Death of Ivan Ilyitch,* which, unhappily, shows us more about how not to write the short story of today than how one should be written. Yet all these stories have that requirement set forth by Robert Gorham Davis in his *Ten Modern Masters,* [Harcourt, Brace & World] in that a story asks a question: "What is it like to be that kind of a person going through that kind of an experience?" and then answers it. And here is the rock upon which your story may stand.

It is important to begin any article on the short story by speaking of other writers, for if one does not read deeply, it is likely one will not write deeply, or even very successfully, in a commercial sense or any other. Actually the first rule for a beginning writer is simple, painless and even fun: Read before you write—fiction, that is, both short and long. Read to the point of intoxication, if you will, so that your bloodstream is changed by the alcohol of fiction, and then believe in the visions that fill your head.

The sober and important fact about deep and wide reading of other short-story writers is that one begins thinking in fictional terms, and does not lapse into propaganda writing, or merely expository writing, or any other kind that does not contribute to that single, intense and limited effect that is the short story. A parallel here could be the practice of photography, where one's eye becomes so conditioned to the limitation of the lens that all subject matter must be framed in the mind, even before snapping the shutter. The short-story writer must know there are bounds beyond which he cannot go—a limitation which does not apply to the novel writer—and the best way to know this, apart from actually writing a story, is to become familiar with the stories of the good writers and so challenged and excited by what can be accomplished *within* a limited scope, that one does not think of putting his subject matter into any other form. The word length may run from a thousand to eight thousand words, but the effect must have intensity, narrowness, and focus on a single problem and its solution and on a single character—or on a few so linked that the effect is as of one. Too often an editor or a teacher finds the beginning writer has no interest in how other writers have achieved success—if indeed he has read them at all—and patiently must advise: Read Chekhov, Maupassant, Katherine Mansfield, Sherwood Anderson, D.H. Lawrence—there are so many—as well as the good short-story writers of today—Malamud, Roth, Capote, McCullers, Peter Taylor.

The second thing to learn is the necessity of writing as much as you read. Quantity may not make quality, but it is doubtful if quality will become the polished thing it can be without a very great amount of practical work. But there is an intermediate consideration here, too, that of finding out, first, if writing is the thing one really wants to do. Are you a word-oriented person, or do you express yourself, perhaps even more happily, in music, painting, the dance, or even in social conversation? The thing that has sustained many writers through the early discouraging days of learning their craft is, simply, that they find writing more exciting than any other occupation they can think of. Robert Frost said that he wrote poetry because he did not find the same satisfaction in anything else. Writing should be so important to the writer that, even if he has failed in other ways to communicate—or even if he has succeeded—the typewriter is the friend to whom he always returns, not to the stretched canvas, the piano, or the music for the dance. These tastes may also be part of the extra-curricular of a writer, but they are not his release; they are not so deeply loved. There are, in my observation, writers and non-writers; and even though the non-writer may write brilliantly and even sell successfully, he will give it all up when it gets hard or when another and equally interesting form of expression suggests itself.

So, know that you want to write, that you believe from what you have read and observed and thought, that you are ready to try, through characters, event and mood, to work out a story, relating it to the essential drama around you.

How do you know you have a story to tell? Where do you settle first, your wandering and rather anxious imagination.

The prime test of whether you have a story or not is that you find in every contemplated story an *explosion*—muted, perhaps, delayed, sometimes, or completely shattering—but something which explodes and thus changes the status quo. Somewhere, either at the beginning, middle, or end, there is an explosion in which all parts of the whole are expelled from an existing pattern—the lives of the characters are jolted from their rhythm, chaos is produced in their universe, and out of this upheaval, "that kind of person going through that kind of experience," the creative skill of the author must find or imply some sort of solution. Thus the writer, before he begins to write, must anticipate, and comprehend this explosion, and then, without being guided by anything but his own inner logic, create—or suggest—new order from the old.

An explosion can be many things, make use of any subject matter. The breakup of a marriage, the beginning of love, the death of an old man, each can create its own chaos, provide its own solution. Explosion may be used in three ways. One can commence with the explosion—in other words the gun goes off at once, and the universe seems shattered at the point the story begins. It is then up to the author to reassemble the characters, lead on to some final acceptance or solution in their lives, as in Mary McCarthy's *Cruel and Barbarous Treatment* where the marriage breaks up, and the story works out from there.

It may begin with calm and existing order, proceed with rising intensity to an explosion at the center, working back to a new order at the end—which, of course, is never quite the same as the old, such as in *The Man,* by Mel Dinelli, both a story and a play. Or one can withhold ones ammunition to the very end, as in Shirley Jackson's story "The Lottery," when the stoning begins and the full meaning of the preceding pages bursts upon the reader, who is then left to reassemble the parts for himself.

Any story, I think, will fall into one of these three patterns, and the author, by approaching the problem in his own mind before he starts to write, will know the moment in his story when it is most effective to light the fuse, how far back to stand from the subject at the time of the explosion, and whether he is going to set it off at the beginning, the middle, or the end. An author can take his choice, and begin his story accordingly.

Once you start to write your story, the next important thing is to finish it. Writing is as simple, and as difficult as that. An incomplete story is no story at all, while a piece of writing with all the faults in English grammar can be a story if brought to some related end. There is no substitute stage in one's development as a writer for finishing what you have begun. I, myself, can clearly remember the day I became a writer: it was the day I stopped dreaming up ideas without developing them, and forced myself through to the bitter end. Even though that story was never published and has been lost long since, it was an important milestone in my writing. Then, for several months after that I worked as fast as ideas came, and, miraculously, the more I completed, the greater the profusion of stories I thought to tell.

Then came the next stage, when a feeling of uneasiness came over me as I realized I was not yet succeeding, even though I knew then that some day I would. As I went back and reread all I had written, I saw that these stories would have to be rewritten, and maybe even rewritten again. This was the third stage of my becoming a writer; and one that has never ended.

How, though, does a writer get far enough back from his own work so that somehow he becomes no longer the author, but the reader and critic; how does he work to some point where it is as though the story had not been written by himself at all? Here, unfortunately for a writer's personal contacts, begins the notorious bad memory of a writer: at one point, consciously and deliberately, he learns forgetfulness—not memory—and even though he is in danger forever after of being late for dinner and dentist appointments, this brainwashing must take place in order to reach the next stage of self-criticism. For the words an author writes can form a groove in the mind which soon hardens and becomes unerasable. The trick here is to put the story away and practice loss of memory so intensively that—as I found a few months ago—I could pick up my own first novel and read on with curiosity to see what actually happened in the end!

In this most critical stage of judging your own work, what errors do you look for? First, spots in which you have not succeeded in saying what you wanted to say, either because of writing too little, or writing too much. In other words, the balance of its parts is the first thing to worry about; and this properly achieved, will often eliminate any possible moments of lagging, or letdown, in holding the reader's attention. Generally speaking, the beginning takes too long in the novice-writer's work; and frequently the explosion, the big scene, is passed over too quickly, written too sketchily. Savor this big scene, wherever it comes. Make sure it is perfectly realized, clearly visualized, and properly understood; even though your technique is to write subtly and not *tell* all, the logic must be exact enough for those who will read to find the key for themselves.

The second thing to look for is the credibility and sharpness of your character creations. This is a thing a novelist learns, but it is equally important for the short-story writer. In a novel, a reader will want to know some things you have not told; if you cannot say you do know, cannot satisfy his curiosity when he writes to ask what-the-hell—, then you are not close enough to that character to pretend to know how he acts or will act in any given situation. The same thing is obviously true in the theatre. In Lillian Hellman's play, "Toys in the Attic," a foolish sister of the hero stands aside during a scene when the hero's wife telephones the man who will want to kill him; and although the foolish sister has no obvious part in this and answers only when asked a question as though she were not thinking at all, in the end, one knows, because of the author's skill, that the girl's phone call is the very thing the sister has schemed to have happen. In other words, the logic of character development, the consistency of actions and words, must be reconstructed as exactly as in a psychological laboratory.

Next, speak and challenge the things your characters say. Read their words aloud, even to yourself; hear if they speak stiffly, unnaturally, pretentiously—and ask yourself if the rhythm of their speeches suits the kinds of characters you have created. I like to say that dialogue should be thought of in terms of a chromatic and not a whole-tone scale. Use both black and white keys even if your speech is spoken in fifths or even octaves. The power of Hemingway's dialogue is that, even though he skips from C to C he hears all the half-tones that could be spoken between characters and suggests these in the careful selection of their words. Write dialogue as a singer sings, by holding your breath until you reach the end of a thought; and always "sing through your rests," for once you start a story, you must see that your attention does not wander for an instant, and that your reins are never slackened.

This seems to be about all I can say, except that someone else, whose name I wish I knew, has said, "If a story doesn't bore you to write, it won't bore the reader to read." When I begin to feel bored with any part of my writing, I skip to the next point that interests me, intending to come back and fill in—but often I find this unnecessary, and the words I have not written are never missed.

The writer's obligation is to the reader, not out of kindness or weakness, but as the only way to hold his reluctant attention. We must interest him, not by writing what he thinks he wants to read, but, by our own skill and passion, so dominate his interest with what we want to write that he will go where we lead and believe what we want him to know. And the deeper our own involvement, the deeper can be the reader's gain, and our own.

Rust Hills

Slick Fiction and Quality Fiction

We had submitted to us at *Esquire* recently a short story by a very distinguished author. One of his stories, at least, has become a semiclassic; I remember teaching it in freshman English classes. But, like many celebrated authors who may not have *it* anymore, the author has turned to slick fiction, thinking, perhaps, that his skill and his name would carry the fake plot.

It started off well enough, with a neatly characterized sketch: a doting mother trying to console her businessman husband, both worried about the laziness of their college-boy son, who, the father storms, is learning nothing practical and useful in school. In the basement playroom, the scampish young man meanwhile vows to his fiancee he'll make her a million dollars.

Charming to this point, the story turns slick. The boy returns to college, listens listlessly as his English instructor tells of the fortune one could make if he discovered a lost play of Shakespeare's. Suddenly he remembers an old book his mother brought from Italy, rushes back home, steals the book (nothing is made of the ethics of this), annotates it (while lying in the sun on the Riviera), and gets ready to make his million publishing it.

We next see him in a magnificent suite in a magnificent London hotel preparing for tea with the Queen. The father reappears, still suspicious, for he has never heard of Shakespeare; but as his son drives off in his chauffeur-driven Daimler, he looks at him "with a curious awe."

Needless to say, the distinguished author of this undistinguished story is a college professor. In an academic, this story represents the most undisguised sort of daydreaming. Not by any commercial means, but solely by his own academic skills and his scholarship, the hero (and the author with him in his fantasying) is able to make so much money and become so successful that even his old man looks at him "with a curious awe." That last phrase is interesting, because when slick takes over, even the words and phrases turn to cliche.

The story is a harmlessly genial and gentle kind of daydreaming, and one wishes some magazine would publish it, and pay the author a million dollars, and make all his dreams come true.

Leonard Wallace Robinson, who was Managing Editor of *Esquire* when I came here, had a good eye for both slick and quality fiction. More interesting, he was invariably able to tell the difference between them. As I recall his distinction, it was that quality fiction partakes of the nightdream—while slick fiction partakes of the daydream.

In terms of literary history, it seems to me, the distinction between slick and quality goes back to the two writers that Paul Roche calls the twin pillars of the short story: Maupassant and Chekov. I argue with people a lot about short stories and I argued with Paul Roche about this. For he claimed that we were too much under the influence of Chekov and needed more Maupassant. My disagreement is: that the Maupassant method is at the very heart of the more pretentious sort of slick; that his stories are full of beautiful, oversexed women and trick, twisty plot devices; that the stories may occasionally be seamy, but that their plots are such that they are without a truly accurate view of life; but that Chekov sees life as it is and renders it so; and that his accurate vision and uncompromising plotting stand at the head of a literary tradition recently come to a fine flowering in the works of contemporary writers like Bernard Malamud and Saul Bellow; but that this Chekov influence is still not in actual ascendancy, as the majority of magazine fiction is committed to the slick, trick, glamourized methods of Maupassant's fake daydreaming writing.

Too much of the daydream is what's the trouble with most of the fiction we see. Daytime fantasying is at the heart of all the slick, trick, sexy, sadistic, self-pitying, snappy-dialogued, romanticized, glamourized, hard-boiled, or sentimentalized stories that come our way, that we occasionally publish (more or less by accident), and that I read too often in other magazines. The concept of writing as some sort of catharsis, some sort of working out of symbolic terms of a writer's fantasies known or unknown, is a perfectly acceptable concept as long as the writing is successful. But you'll find that the successful writing of this sort stems from the nightdream, not the daydream. When cathartic writing is unsuccessful, it is so unsuccessful that almost anything is better: six years of psychoanalysis for the writer; finger painting; or the cold shower and walk around the block that the YMCA is supposed to advise.

This sort of daydreaming which is at the heart of all slick fiction (both hard-boiled and romantic), is much more forgivable in the young than in the old: In the young writer it may represent a persistence of illusion; in the old it represents an escape from reality. We are much more tolerant of the fantasying slick attitudes in a new, inexperienced writer, than in someone who has the craft to draw a story about how things really are, but hasn't the vision or integrity to do it.

A lot of the undergraduate writing that we see, for instance, will have an over-romantic or false-cynical slickness that we will try to overlook for the promise of a talent and an eye and an ear not yet realized. There was recently, as an example, some very promising work from a very young writer studying at Columbia. *Three Sketches* he called his submission, and one of them, titled "A Momentary Thing," told of a young American sitting at a cafe in Paris approached by an attractive prostitute. The boy has a warm and friendly discussion with her, and the two are obviously very *sympatico;* but at the end he tells her to go on her way, and speaks of her to his friends as "just another whore."

It was a romantic little sketch, and it seemed slick in its youngishness and in its melancholy irony—sentimentalized prositutes are, I suppose, the cliche of cliches. But somehow the story managed not to be slick romantic, but just young romantic, which, as I say, is a very forgivable thing—at least in the young. Forgivable—but not publishable.

As in many of the stories that we get from universities, there was in this sketch a lack of body— a non-attention to standard story values: plot, suspense, characterization in depth, and so forth. Students generally shy away from telling a full-bodied story under the excuse that it is old-fashioned writing. And shying away is actually very sensible of them, because they haven't yet the equipment to handle a full-fledged plot with full-fledged characters—they find their story is likely to bog down into a melodrama, with unconvincing dialogue, unconvincing character shifts, and unsustained tone and mood.

Often they will turn then to some sort of experimental story—full of steam-of-consciousness mixed with newspaper headlines and dirty words. This is useful as an exerise, but the results are seldom worth much. *Esquire* has never, for instance, published an experimental story, even by a celebrated author. It would seem that if a writer has written stories with the control of technique that James Joyce showed in *Dubliners,* that he would then be ready to go on to publish experimental work like *Finnegan's Wake*—not before. Experimentalism in new writers is too often a cover for lack of craft.

Undergraduate writers and beginning writers are much more likely to be successful when they write fragments like these three sketches sent to us from Columbia—because these are, in effect, exercises—and as exercises they are, of course, very useful to a new writer.

Sketches such as these are the first workings out of the amateur writer's "wonderful idea for a short story"—which usually means plot, not idea at all. More is needed: a true something to say. In a mature writer who has found what he has to say, and has said it in many ways and in many stories, this becomes a body of work—with a world of its own: Fitzgerald's world; Hemingway's world; Dickens' world. But it must be found first, with experiments and exercises.

The trouble is that new young writers always want to publish their more or less successful exercises, and they are not savvy enough to know that these are traditionally published in little magazines, not in the big national commercial ones. It is too bad, because publication in the small literary quarterlies, no matter how small, can be a great help. A new writer cannot usually expect to publish first in the large national commercial magazines, and he can't even expect, perhaps, to first publish in some of the more renowned quarterlies like *Kenyon Review, Partisan Review, Sewanee Review,* etc. But publication in the littler of the little—magazines like *Accent* and *Epoch* and *Audience*—and even in any little magazine the writer and his friends might start for themselves, is the natural and traditional road to publishing for pay. Charles Allen published (in *Sewanee Review,* July, 1943) a study showing that of 100 writers important since 1914, eighty-five of them had first appeared in little magazines. And if anyone would take the trouble to read these early contributions, he would see how impossible (and, indeed, how unwarranted) publication of most of these pieces in a large national commericial magazine would have been.

To be worth considering at all, it seems to me, a story must have a point—some point, any point; some intention. But for the story to be good, the point must be inextricably bedded in all the other aspects of the story—in the plot, the characterizations, the mood, the style, the setting, the structure, and so on. If a story has no point, then it is pointless. And if the story does have a point or purpose, but it is not inextricably bedded in all the other aspects, then what one has is at worst a tract, at best some sort of allegory or parable— a "message" story. The point need not then, indeed, *must* not, be demonstrable, capable of being removed, paraphrased.

But if the point of the story *is* inextricably bedded in all the other aspects of a story, then that story says something, tells you something, without being a tract. You get the absolute fusion of form and content that is Art. And further, whatever the theme or point or purpose or intention of the story is, will become a *controlling* intention. The controlling intention will control the selection and presentation of all the other aspects of a short story: the mood the author creates; the style he selects; the structure of the story; the workings-out of the narrative or plot line through the various crises (also determined by the controlling intention); it will control the original delineation and the subsequent development of the characters. In sum: the intention or purpose of a story must be inseparable from all the other aspects, and will at the same time control them.

I always seem to be misunderstood here, and I don't want to be. A key to the quality story is characterization, and let me use the interaction between characterization and theme as an example to qualify what I say about controlling intent. The distinction made between tragedy and melodrama (or between comedy and farce) is that in tragedy plot yields to character, while in melodrama the characterizations will shift according to the devisings of the plot. What is true of drama seems to me equally true of the difference between quality and slick in prose fiction; and what is true of the interaction between characterization and plot seems equally true of the relation of characterization to theme. Characters will not be just chosen to demonstrate the point of the story, they must "somehow live themselves"—and I find I've found a cliche here, myself. The cliche is at the very heart of the slick. In a slick story the conception of the characters will be stereotype—every delineation of them will stem from a stock figure: "a guy who works in a bank"; even simply "a waitress." The situation (and eventually the plot) will partake of the same sort of cliche: "this woman is seated at a bar"; "a young American student is sitting in a Paris cafe"; "this college kid who worries his parents." In quality writing stereotyping can never be a substitute for characterization; in slick, it always is. In good writing the characterization somehow *becomes* the point of the story. The point of the story must be concealed, must in some way be added *into* it, not just worked out. The story's controlling intention must never be thought of as wholly interchangeable with its theme.

How will this work in actual practice? Which will come first? The intention?—the point the author wants to make, and for which he will subsequently find a story to illustrate? Or will the story come first?— the "some incident observed in the subway" which naggles away at the author, until he begins to write about it, seeing only then (but perhaps not really clearly, himself, ever at all) the point of what he is saying, and through the discovered (or, at least, sensed) controlling intention carving and creating all the other aspects further to fit?

It could, of course, be either of these two methods—but it seems to me more likely that the process of creating a successful story is some combination of the two. It seems usual, for instance, that a writer keeps a notebook and in this notebook puts down thoughts and ideas which occur to him and also makes a note of any incident which he has observed or been told of or read of in the newspaper, and which has captured his fancy. It is the marriage of these two elements—the thought and the incident, whether in a notebook or in his own mind alone—that produces the seed that grows (or, more accurately, is *made* to grow through the author's bringing to bear imagination or hard work—depending on which is most necessary) into the final story—which, if it is truly successful, will (as I emphasized at the beginning) appear as if its elements had never been unfused.

And perhaps they never were. I am not a writer, and I have no way of knowing. I used to try, about once every year or so, but I never wrote a story that was even remotely successful. I finally gave it up, under the theory that to try to be a good editor is not much less a thing than being a bad writer, and while it probably isn't much better paid, it is an awful lot happier. A great weight was lifted from me, and I found I could look at life around me with some other interest than just as potential material. No one should ever be encouraged to write. There are too many writers already, and the world is especially full of people who don't want to write, but do want to be writers. What begins as a harmless catharsis will, with encouragement, become a compulsion to publish. We feel it is wrong to encourage bad writers with a soft rejection, no matter how the letter of submission may beg for "just some comment." Writing is hard—almost anything else is easy (again, something Len Robinson used to say). You can do almost anything else if you have a cold or a hangover or a lot of worries—but it is just about impossible to write.

Even if never having written anything successful himself makes it unlikely that a person will be very accurate or positive about how it's done, it shouldn't rule out his chances of recognizing a good piece of writing. I won't develop this, but just state: I think it may improve his chances. And, so far as helping an author to rewrite is concerned, then —if, as I believe, good editing is the ability first to comprehend the work's intentions; and second, to demonstrate to the author ways in which he can more successfully realize them—then, the value of the editor's ability to write is in inverse ratio to the author's ability to edit.

Judging stories, I work on a basis of a mixture of the too academic and the too emotional—and they tend to balance out. The too academic approach is a method (much modified from the lectures of Fred B. Millett, who taught me Freshman English one hundred and eighty years ago at Wesleyan) of asking a series of four questions about the story:

1. What is the author trying to say?
2. How does he say it?
3. How well does he say it?
4. Was it worth saying?

The first two questions are, of course, of interpretation, which must always precede evaluation (the last two). Questions two and three concern form; and questions one and four, content. As I say, this four-point approach to the criticism (interpretation and evaluation) of writing is perhaps too neat and pedantic (question four, for instance, is to all intents and purposes useless, and has as its primary value neatness—although there is this to say: A short story may be defeated right from the start by too limited a conception), but following the method does seem to me to have two advantages: first, by focusing your attention early on the author's purpose (and I'm ignoring what is known in aesthetic theory as The Intentional Fallacy, and I know it and don't think it makes much difference in magazine editing), these questions get you to thinking of the work in its own terms and cut down on snap judgments; and second, by encouraging you to give a run-down to a story you may have been initially enthusiastic about, it gives you a chance to pause, and to see how the effects that made you enthusiastic were created, and why, and if it's a serious story, or merely just a fake one, whose emotion was based in sentimentality, and deliberately evoked.

So much for the too academic approach. The second, the too emotional approach, is responding to what Edmund Wilson may not have had in mind at all with the term "the shock of recognition"—but it's a marvelous term for the experience anyway. The quality of the unsolicited manuscripts we see is so dreadfully low, that when we read a story of any promise at all, we certainly experience some recognition. But when a *really* good story comes in—solicited or unsolicited—when one reads that really good story, it is really a shock!

These are the full-bodied stories that are totally unlike one another and totally unlike any other story. And they are also characterized by a view of life which is neither wishful nor stereotyped.

Fred Shaw

A Writer Never Quits

Recently one of the best of my former students turned down a magazine assignment apparently made to order for her. "Thanks, but no.
I've given it up."

"Buy why?"

"Writing's too hard, too full of heartbreaks. I gave it everything I
had, but obviously it wasn't enough." Most beginners would envy her
—five sales, two of them to national magazines, in less than two years.
But she wasn't impressed.

I tried a new tack. "Name the outstanding novelist of all time."

"Balzac."

Hah, she was in my trap. Balzac's teachers called him a blockhead.
His family tried to starve him into giving up his literary pretensions.
When he proudly brought them his tragedy in verse—the climax of two
years of hard work, they yawned while he read it. A friend, the only
critic he knew, advised him to try anything in the world but writing.
Before he won modest recognition, Balzac wrote for eight more years,
publishing thirty-one volumes of fiction under various pseudonymns.
The big books were yet to come.

"And it's still happening," I said. I picked up an issue of *Writer's
Digest* and read a couple of paragraphs— about John Fitzgerald, who
"after thirty years of trying" won financial independence with *Papa
Married A Mormon*; about Somerset Maugham, who in his first ten
years of writing "never earned more than £100 ($500) a year."

She laughed and shook her head. It was not for her.

Working with college students who want to write professionally is
fun. But it can be depressing too. Too many of my talented students
give up when they've just begun to develop. I don't want to imply that

checks come in with anything like monotonous regularity. Still, in recent years I've seen the by-lines of my students in magazines, including *Western Review, Reader's Digest, The Saturday Evening Post,* and *The New Yorker.* But when a colleague tells me the kids are doing well, I say, "You ought to see the one that got away."

Why do they do it? Why do they give up writing when it once seemed the only thing they wanted to do?

Once I had the good fortune to talk with William Faulkner. "Tell me about your writing course," he said. "Do your students want to write, or do they want to be writers?"

That's part of the answer. Some students and also those who begin this writing business on their own want to write for the wrong reasons. They begin to send out manuscripts before the seat of their pants is shiny, and when editors don't rush to embrace them, they turn to surer things. Or if they write to talk about it, they soon discover that the writing isn't necessary. Their defection from the cause never troubles me.

Yet, when I discount the misfits and the phonies, there still remain many young writers of the sort Faulkner wanted to talk about. They have ability. They want to write. Yet too many of them stop when a teacher is no longer pushing them. Why?

I know some of the reasons and some of the answers. Here they are:

They have to make a living. You too? Me too. The answer is to keep your job and write in off hours. Successful part-time writers are legion. Sarah Jenkins wrote her first novel under hair driers, on bus rides, in 15-minute breaks in her teaching schedule; now after several books she can afford a driver and school bus of her own, if she's hungry for the old writing environment.

No one takes them seriously. One thing we may as well face with good humor: nobody looks like a writer until he hits. The fledgling who has the sympathy and understanding of his family should cherish them. It isn't usual. In the shadowy background beyond Gray's "mute, inglorious Milton" is a woman arguing that if he'd quit writing that drivel, she wouldn't have to blush unseen.

There are worse things than an unsympathetic family. A few years ago, a student of mine sold a story to *McCall's.* Overnight his wife and parents decided they had been overlooking a sure thing. Now every afternoon they shushed the children, cleared out the living room, and left him alone with his typewriter. For two, three hours they tiptoed around the house; but when he finally dragged himself out the door, they came up smiling, jumping at him as if released from springs. "Well now, how'd it go?" Not so good. After a few days the strain was awful. The poor fellow hasn't written anything since.

If an editor would only—Over and over I hear them say, "If anybody would publish my stuff, I'd write every day." Sure, so would anybody else. The real trick is to keep on writing when no one cares if you do or not, to keep on writing in the face of loneliness and fear.

I talk straight to my students. I paint bleak pictures of the mountains of manuscripts an editor works through in a year. I quote a magazine editor who says that every year she gets fewer stories that can be called incompetent. Yes, the competition is getting more severe. I tell them finally that if they can take writing or leave it, the choice is easy; forget it. And if they are shooting for the big money, the odds are better in the Irish Sweepstakes.

If they still want to write, I'm on their side. And if years later they tell me they are not writing and look unhappy in the telling, I try to help them think their way to a solution. In their minds all the difficulties I've discussed have been reduced to one: *the day just isn't long enough.* That's a time-honored excuse. When I've needed one myself, I've loved it like a brother.

The only thing is that it's pure nonsense. Most of us know writers who are busier than we are but still keep turning it out. When Caroline Miller won the Pulitzer prize back in the early thirties, she was married to the principal of a South Georgia high school—hardly the best depression route to leisure and luxury. As I recall, her dedication to *Lamb in His Bosom* read, "To Will D. and Little Will and Nip'n Tuck." Three babies, no money, less time. But she kept on writing. She even wrote at the drugstore table when she went in for a morning coke.

Sometimes I can help the befuddled and bogged-down get started again—but not by arguing they have the time if they'll use it. I tell stories that seem to come closer to their real problems—about Verne Williams, who trained on Sunday newspaper features for his successful attack on Independence Square; about Jane Hawley, who found that teaming up in a two-woman writers' club was one way to fight inertia and despair; about Jean Wardlow, a prize-winning reporter who had the wisdom to drop from a full- to a part-time newspaper job to get time for freelancing. I tell another story about two gifted students who were apparently killed off by big sales they weren't ready for. And I talk about a woman I know, who learned that although no mother of three babies can write a novel, anybody can write a chapter. Last month, somewhat to her surprise and mine, she finished her book.

I encourage them to keep a journal so that writing will become the usual and not the unusual thing. And I quote Somerset Maugham: "Writing is a habit that's easy to get into and hard to break."

There's a final group I like to talk to because I understand them best —those who can't stomach what they write *because their taste outruns their* ability. I know what to say to them because, as Sut Lovingood says, "I've been thar." It's the Balzac story all over again. Beginners who worship at the shrine of Walt Whitman owe it to themselves to read Walt's magazine fiction; reading Sinclair Lewis' *Free Air* is an antidote for excessive admiration of *Babbitt*. There must be a beginning. Have you tried Philip Wylie's pulp fiction lately?

Walter Blair, who wrote a book about Davy you-know-who, introduced me to a little story I like to read to writers who have more confidence in their taste than in their talent. The story, called "The Dandy Frightening the Squatter," appeared in the May 1, 1852, issue of *Carpet-Bag*. It made no anthologies. The language is trite and commonplace, the narrative awkward—but let me quote a few of the most distinguished lines:

> "A tall brawny woodsman stood leaning against a tree . . . gazing at some approaching object, which our readers would easily have discovered to be a steamboat. . . . Now among the many passengers on this boat, both male and female, was a spruce young dandy, with a killing moustache, etc., who seemed bent on making an impression . . . Observing our squatter friend . . ."

Surely there was somewhere an honest critic to tell the author, who signed himself S.L.C., to go and sin no more. If so, the young writer paid him no mind. He continued to write for anyone and everyone who would publish his yarns.

Years later—and some of them long dry years—he published a novel that changed the direction of American literature. He called it *Huckleberry Finn*.

John Howard Griffin

From Boy To Writer in One Night

Like many published authors I often lecture at creative writing classes and conferences, and so I have met many aspiring fellow-writers. And, of course, I have been asked a lot of questions which I try to answer as honestly as possible. One of the most baffling ones is "How much background education do I need to be a writer? It seems to me that the greatest background education and too often the most neglected is experience. By this I do not mean a wild dashing about from place to place, and love affair to love affair; I mean rather an ability to make experience out of everything that happens to you. Experience for the writer is in many ways an attitude of mind; it is an ability to feel adventure in the smallest things in life, a walk in the rain if you like. It is this sense of adventure which many young writers lack, and yet I am sure it can be developed. Perhaps I can explain this best by telling you about something that happened to me, when I was eighteen years old.

I was a student living in a tiny attic room in Tours, France. It was a winter afternoon and I was huddled before a small stove reading an announcement about Kirsten Flagstad's coming Paris performance in *Tristan and Isolde*. It was to be a single gala appearance and a friend had told me that this was something I shouldn't miss. I got out my savings and began to figure. If I went third-class, and bought the cheapest ticket I had just enough to go; but not enough to buy a meal or get a room. Going to Paris would mean a night under a bridge or in a doorway and a day without food. I had never done anything like this. I was far from adventurous then; I was a studious scientist. The whole idea horrified me. But I knew that if I didn't go, I might regret it all my life. I decided to go, and that decision had far-reaching effects. The experience I had that night made me what is known as "adventure-prone" and probably was directly responsible for my becoming a writer.

There are few other vocations that list such a high percentage of adventure-prone people. Almost all writers—from Dante to Hemingway—are capable of tremendous intellectual adventure. They give the impression of living grandly, even when isolated in a lonely room over a work desk. We think of them as people, *to whom things happen.*

An adventure-prone person is not simply someone assaulted by a set of adventurous circumstances. Rather he is someone who can see adventure where the rest of us are blind to it.

It appears to be a matter of conditioning, a technique that can be acquired.

Actual physical adventure has relatively little to do with it. This is proved by the cloistered nuns who sometimes lead most vivid and fascinating lives. On the other hand we have the classic example of the big game hunter in Africa, sitting on his folding chair, swizzling his rum and wondering where in hell all the excitement is.

In an effort to understand what makes an experience high adventure for one person while the same experience merely jades and bores another, let's go back to that night in Paris and see what happened to that 18-year-old boy.

After the opera, which was magnificent, I faced a cold and drizzly night in a strange city with nothing in my pocket except a return ticket to Tours. I was hungry and cold and had no idea where to turn. I began walking and looking for some place to shelter me from the weather.

When I was about to give up, I saw a chestnut vendor folding up his roasting-stand for the night. I went up to him and asked where a man "without a *sou*" could sleep. He told me of a place called the *Cour de Rohan,* a thirteenth century sector across the river from Notre Dame. He explained that the old quarters were for the poor, that the doors were never closed, and that I could probably sleep under the stair-well without being disturbed.

He gave me a sack of hot chestnuts to warm my hands and we walked together to the narrow passageway leading into the *cour.* I gazed down the cobblestoned passage, toward a yellowish, mist-surrounded street lamp at the other end.

"Enter any of the doors," he said, and left. I tried a couple of the doors which were so low I had to stoop to look in. The air inside was fetid. At the third door, I decided they would all smell the same, so I entered and felt for the stairway. I walked around behind it and forced myself to stretch out on the grimy flagstone floor.

For a time I was acutely aware of my discomfort, of the hardness and filth of the floor, of the chill that crept in under my clothes. I was desolate, lonely and somewhat frightened. The opera was forgotten; I was totally absorbed in my misery.

But slowly, another feeling aroused me from my self-preoccupation. It occured to me that all of this was interesting. I began to detach myself from my discomfort, and as I did so, I realized that this was an experience worth having—or rather, one that would someday be worth having *had.* I asked myself how many men had ever slept under the stairway of a thirteenth century house? To sleep in a comfortable bed was fine, but if you looked at it in a certain way, this was fine, too. I would forget the many nights spent in comfort and safety, but I knew that I would never forget this night. Therefore it was worth experiencing, worth giving myself up to.

All things took on new values. The floor became instead of something hard and tormenting, stones that had been laid there centuries before with pride by some craftsman. It became a thing which had known the weight of saints and sinners long dead. It became itself, giving up its secrets to me; because instead of *immersing it in myself, I was immersing myself in it.*

All I had done was change my attitude. I was still miserable, but it had become unimportant. I had ceased to be a person judging everything on the basis of pleasure or comfort. I had gone out of myself to the value of things in themselves and I have never since been able to step back consistently into mere self-interest.

This is the crucial difference between the person whose life is monotonous and the one who is adventure-prone. It is also a crucial point in the richness and originality of a writer's work.

The true writer is an observer of all things, and quite especially of himself. If he sees death close at hand, or the tragic break-up of his own marriage, or suffers any discomfort, he has the strange consolation, although hating the experience, of knowing that even the worst of life is grist for his mill; that all of these things, the seemingly tragic, along with the seemingly pleasant, will teach and develop, and enrich his work.

Most of us live too protected. We do not value our work enough to sacrifice ourselves for it. Life must be a continuing education for the writer. He must learn to abstract constantly from every second of the day. Goethe said: "Talent is formed in solitude, character in the stream of life." Character must exist and yet it must always be in formation in order to render talent fruitful. It will be only half-developed if we live too sheltered and too much involved in the creature comforts. A good way to judge if we are developing into "natural" writers is this. The next time we get caught in the rain, see if we are inclined to curse its discomfort or to study the feel of it on our faces, rolling down from our hair, stippling the backs of our hands.

This is an important discipline for many reasons. It is writing, gaining facility and technique. But far more important, if it is kept honestly, it will give the writer a true knowledge of himself and others. It will show true motives for a wide range of conditional fluctuation. At first, it is humbling to see oneself without illusions; but it is the best way to self-knowledge, wisdom and compassion and incidentally to better writing.

It allows the writer to create from his own truest source. Literary historian Maxwell Geismar once stated: "The real question for the novelist of this period is how to escape from the balm of moderation and the bane of normalcy." All of us are covered by layers of prejudices, false values, vanities, inflated-ego concepts.

When you can do this instead of curse you have an essential ingredient for good writing. You will have had a unique experience because no other person will have identical reactions to the rain.

To develop this ability of detachment I always advise beginning writers to keep a journal with total honesty (and with no thought of another's ever seeing it), their feelings, problems, emotions, reactions, random thoughts, temptations and all of the private dramas and dreams of their days.

Keeping an honest journal allows us to rip this dulling curtain off our thoughts. The act of creation is far more profound than most of us consciously realize. It comes up mysteriously from the very depths of a being, and that "soundbox" which is the spirit must be tempered and balanced as near as possible to the truth to produce the truest work.

Natalie Hagen

To Market, To Market

Marketing your completed story can be as challenging as creating the story itself. Successful marketing depends upon your ability to critically judge your story, and to anticipate the reaction of the specific editor to whom you direct your manuscript. You can, by first studying and selecting the markets, eliminate unnecessary rejections. Editors look for stories which will please, interest, and stimulate their particular circle of readers. It would be a social blunder for a hostess to offer a martini to a fundamentalist preacher or to a child. You can commit this same blunder by sending a story about drinking to a religious or juvenile magazine; or, conversely, by directing a juvenile or religious story to the editor of a swinging men's magazine.

Writer's Market, published annually, lists freelance markets and indicates those which are interested in fiction. If you don't own a copy, ask to see the latest edition at your local library. In this directory, magazines are grouped according to the interest of their readers, with publications buying similar material grouped together. For further guidance of writers, editors specify word-length limits and pay rates for the stories they consider. Choose several publications you believe would be interested in your story. Obtain copies of these magazines either at the newsstand, the library, or by ordering from the publishers. Write your own analysis of each magazine using the following suggested outline:

1. Title. How often is it published? Price per copy? Per year? How long has it been in existence? Name of editor, and editorial address.

2. Who reads this magazine? Is the reader audience comprised of both men and women? If a juvenile or teen publication, what are the approximate upper and lower age limits? Is it for girls only, for boys

only, or for both? If a women's magazine, is it directed toward both single and married women? Toward mothers? What is the estimated range in age of the readers? Is the magazine directed toward a group with common interest such as sports-car enthusiasts; cat-fanciers; residents of a particular region?

3. Advertising gives an excellent indication of the readers' educational and socio-economic levels as well as sex, age groupings, and special interests. Check the full-page and half-page ads in one issue. To whom would they appeal? For example, an around-the-world cruise would appeal to both men and women, affluent, either retired or availing themselves of lengthy vacations. Acne medication would appeal to teenage boys and girls. Cosmetics for aging skin would find its market in the over-35 women's group. Home study courses for high school credit indicate educational level. Clothing ads give a clue to readers' age, sex, and ability to buy.

4. How many stories appear in each issue? Is each story approximately the same length, or does the length vary? What is the estimated word count to the nearest hundred words for each story in one issue? Classify each story as to its type: love, marriage, juvenile, teen, adventure, mystery, science fiction, psychological, satirical, historical, fantasy, other. Compare your list with the types and word lengths for fiction stated by the editor in his *Writer's Market* listing. Does each story fall within the stated limits, or are there exceptions? If the payment for fiction is specified, what would each writer receive for his work?

5. Analyze articles, features, cartoons, photos, art work, even letters to the editor in the same fashion. Would you say this publication is inspirational, informative, sophisticated, cynical, intellectual, controversial, or a combination of these attributes and others?

6. What types of stories would be *un*suitable for this magazine?

If you believe your story is suited to several of the magazines you've analyzed, you're now ready to present your manuscript in a professional manner. The manuscript must be typed, double-spaced, on 8 ½ x 11 white bond typing paper, with one to 1 ½ inch margins. Carbon copies or mechanically reproduced copies are *not* acceptable. Make a carbon copy of your final draft in case your story is lost and you must retype it. The typewriter keys should be cleaned and a new ribbon installed just for this final draft. Pages should be error-free. (Corrections are permissible if not noticeable). On the first page type your name, address, and social security number, double-spaced, in the upper left corner. In the upper right corner type the approximate word count to the nearest fifty words. Center the title in capitals about halfway down the page with your byline beneath (either your own name or pseudonym). The story begins three lines beneath the byline, and continues to within 1 ½ inches from the bottom of the page. At the top of the second page type the title of the story, your last name, and the page number. Space down three lines and continue typing. When the manuscript is finished, fasten the pages together with a paper clip in the upper left corner. No covering letter should be sent with the story. Mail the manuscript flat in a manila envelope, preferably with first-class postage, in case the publication has recently moved. (Sometimes it seems that publications play "musical chairs" moving from one address to another, changing personnel, magazine title, slant and policies faster than the changes can be reported). If you wish, you may insert lightweight cardboard backing for support of pages. The return envelope, properly addressed and stamped, *must* be included with the manuscript. Keep a record of mailing dates and addresses.

When the manuscript comes back from the first editor on your list, mail it to the second. If the story has merit, it will probably pick up comments from editors during its travels. If you exhaust your market list without selling your story, study the markets and your story critically to see how you can revise or rewrite to help it sell.

Keep in mind the fact that rejections are a normal part of the process of selling, and don't let them discourage you. The late Ian Fleming received countless rejection slips before his James Bond series made him one of the most famous writers of this generation. Every successful writer has received rejection slips. This is how he learns . . . to sell what he writes.

Index